T Y P E

THE BEST IN DIGITAL CLASSIC TEXT FONTS

TrPa	Gg	DjRa
Par	GgT	1EaQp
dje	gh	fau
AKrf	5rE2	eagM*a*
Gj	i*g*D4	2ak
T&w.	rD	2kQa

Contents:

Publisher's Remarks	v
Forword	vii
Preface	ix
Garamond	1
Sabon	11
Centaur	21
Bembo	31
Janson	43
Caslon	53
Baskerville	63
Times New Roman	75
Cheltenham	89
Century	99
Bodoni	109
Didot	123
Walbaum	131
News Gothic	143
Futura	153
Gill Sans	171
Helvetica	181
Univers	199

Publisher and Creative Director: B. Martin Pedersen
Editors: Tom Carnase, Baruch Gorkin
Art Directors: B. Martin Pedersen, Tom Carnase, Baruch Gorkin, Alexander Gelman
Photographer: Joanne Dugan

The statement "All the virtues of the perfect wine glass..." used for font
settings in this book is an excerpt from
Printing Should be Invisible by Beatrice Warde

Graphis Press Corp. Zürich (Switzerland)

GRAPHIS PUBLICATIONS

GRAPHIS, THE INTERNATIONAL BI-MONTHLY JOURNAL OF VISUAL COMMUNICATION
GRAPHIS DESIGN, THE INTERNATIONAL ANNUAL OF DESIGN AND ILLUSTRATION
GRAPHIS ADVERTISING, THE INTERNATIONAL ANNUAL OF ADVERTISING
GRAPHIS BROCHURES, A COMPILATION OF BROCHURE DESIGN
GRAPHIS PHOTO, THE INTERNATIONAL ANNUAL OF PHOTOGRAPHY
GRAPHIS ALTERNATIVE PHOTOGRAPHY, THE INTERNATIONAL ANNUAL OF ALTERNATIVE PHOTOGRAPHY
GRAPHIS NUDES, A COLLECTION OF CAREFULLY SELECTED SOPHISTICATED IMAGES
GRAPHIS POSTER, THE INTERNATIONAL ANNUAL OF POSTER ART
GRAPHIS PACKAGING, AN INTERNATIONAL COMPILATION OF PACKAGING DESIGN
GRAPHIS LETTERHEAD, AN INTERNATIONAL COMPILATION OF LETTERHEAD DESIGN
GRAPHIS DIAGRAM, THE GRAPHIC VISUALIZATION OF ABSTRACT, TECHNICAL AND STATISTICAL FACTS AND FUNCTIONS
GRAPHIS LOGO, AN INTERNATIONAL COMPILATION OF LOGOS
GRAPHIS EPHEMERA, AN INTERNATIONAL COLLECTION OF PROMOTIONAL ART
GRAPHIS PUBLICATION, AN INTERNATIONAL SURVEY OF THE BEST IN MAGAZINE DESIGN
GRAPHIS ANNUAL REPORTS, AN INTERNATIONAL COMPILATION OF THE BEST DESIGNED ANNUAL REPORTS
GRAPHIS CORPORATE IDENTITY, AN INTERNATIONAL COMPILATION OF THE BEST IN CORPORATE IDENTITY DESIGN
GRAPHIS TYPOGRAPHY, AN INTERNATIONAL COMPILATION OF THE BEST IN TYPOGRAPHIC DESIGN
ART FOR SURVIVAL: THE ILLUSTRATOR AND THE ENVIRONMENT, A DOCUMENT OF ART IN THE SERVICE OF MAN
THE GRAPHIC DESIGNER'S GREEN BOOK, ENVIRONMENTAL RESOURCES FOR THE DESIGN AND PRINT INDUSTRIES

GRAPHIS PUBLIKATIONEN

GRAPHIS, DIE INTERNATIONALE ZWEIMONATSZEITSCHRIFT DER VISUELLEN KOMMUNIKATION
GRAPHIS DESIGN, DAS INTERNATIONALE JAHRBUCH ÜBER DESIGN UND ILLUSTRATION
GRAPHIS ADVERTISING, DAS INTERNATIONALE JAHRBUCH DER WERBUNG
GRAPHIS BROCHURES, BROSCHÜRENDESIGN IM INTERNATIONAL ÜBERBLICK
GRAPHIS PHOTO, DAS INTERNATIONALE JAHRBUCH DER PHOTOGRAPHIE
GRAPHIS ALTERNATIVE PHOTOGRAPHY, DAS INTERNATIONALE JAHRBUCH ÜBER ALTERNATIVE PHOTOGRAPHIE
GRAPHIS NUDES, EINE SAMMLUNG SORGFÄLTIG AUSGEWÄHLTER AKTPHOTOGRAPHIE
GRAPHIS POSTER, DAS INTERNATIONALE JAHRBUCH DER PLAKATKUNST
GRAPHIS PACKAGING, EIN INTERNATIONALER ÜBERBLICK ÜBER DIE PACKUNGSGESTALTUNG
GRAPHIS LETTERHEAD, EIN INTERNATIONALER ÜBERBLICK ÜBER BRIEFPAPIERGESTALTUNG
GRAPHIS DIAGRAM, DIE GRAPHISCHE DARSTELLUNG ABSTRAKTER TECHNISCHER UND STATISTISCHER DATEN UND FAKTEN
GRAPHIS LOGO, EINE INTERNATIONALE AUSWAHL VON FIRMEN-LOGOS
GRAPHIS EPHEMERA, EINE INTERNATIONALE SAMMLUNG GRAPHISCHER DOKUMENTE DES TÄGLICHEN LEBENS
GRAPHIS MAGAZINDESIGN, EINE INTERNATIONALE ZUSAMMENSTELLUNG DES BESTEN ZEITSCHRIFTEN-DESIGNS
GRAPHIS ANNUAL REPORTS, EIN INTERNATIONALER ÜBERBLICK ÜBER DIE GESTALTUNG VON JAHRESBERICHTEN
GRAPHIS CORPORATE IDENTITY, EINE INTERNATIONALE AUSWAHL DES BESTEN CORPORATE IDENTITY DESIGNS
GRAPHIS TYPOGRAPHY, EINE INTERNATIONALE ZUSAMMENSTELLUNG DES BESTEN TYPOGRAPHIE DESIGN
ART FOR SURVIVAL: THE ILLUSTRATOR AND THE ENVIRONMENT, EIN DOKUMENT ÜBER DIE KUNST IM DIENSTE DES MENSCHEN
THE GRAPHIC DESIGNER'S GREEN BOOK, UMWELTKONZEPTE DER DESIGN- UND DRUCKINDUSTRIE

PUBLICATIONS GRAPHIS

GRAPHIS, LA REVUE BIMESTRIELLE INTERNATIONALE DE LA COMMUNICATION VISUELLE
GRAPHIS DESIGN, LE RÉPERTOIRE INTERNATIONAL DE LA COMMUNICATION VISUELLE
GRAPHIS ADVERTISING, LE RÉPERTOIRE INTERNATIONAL DE LA PUBLICITÉ
GRAPHIS BROCHURES, UNE COMPILATION INTERNATIONALE SUR LE DESIGN DES BROCHURES
GRAPHIS PHOTO, LE RÉPERTOIRE INTERNATIONAL DE LA PHOTOGRAPHIE
GRAPHIS ALTERNATIVE PHOTOGRAPHY, LE RÉPERTOIRE INTERNATIONAL DE LA PHOTOGRAPHIE ALTERNATIVE
GRAPHIS NUDES, UN FLORILÈGE DE LA PHOTOGRAPHIE DE NUS
GRAPHIS POSTER, LE RÉPERTOIRE INTERNATIONAL DE L'AFFICHE
GRAPHIS PACKAGING, LE RÉPERTOIRE INTERNATIONAL DE LA CRÉATION D'EMBALLAGES
GRAPHIS LETTERHEAD, LE RÉPERTOIRE INTERNATIONAL DU DESIGN DE PAPIER À LETTRES
GRAPHIS DIAGRAM, LE RÉPERTOIRE GRAPHIQUE DE FAITS ET DONNÉES ABSTRAITS, TECHNIQUES ET STATISTIQUES
GRAPHIS LOGO, LE RÉPERTOIRE INTERNATIONAL DU LOGO
GRAPHIS EPHEMERA, LE GRAPHISME – UN ÉTAT D'ESPRIT AU QUOTIDIEN
GRAPHIS PUBLICATION, LE RÉPERTOIRE INTERNATIONAL DU DESIGN DE PÉRIODIQUES
GRAPHIS ANNUAL REPORTS, PANORAMA INTERNATIONAL DU MEILLEUR DESIGN DE RAPPORTS ANNUELS D'ENTREPRISES
GRAPHIS CORPORATE IDENTITY, PANORAMA INTERNATIONAL DU MEILLEUR DESIGN D'IDENTITÉ CORPORATE
GRAPHIS TYPOGRAPHY, LE RÉPERTOIRE INTERNATIONAL DU MEILLEUR DESIGN DE TYPOGRAPHIE
ART FOR SURVIVAL: THE ILLUSTRATOR AND THE ENVIRONMENT, L'ART AU SERVICE DE LA SURVIE
THE GRAPHIC DESIGNER'S GREEN BOOK, L'ÉCOLOGIE APPLIQUÉE AU DESIGN ET À L'INDUSTRIE GRAPHIQUE

PUBLICATION NO. 242 (ISBN 3-85709-457-5)
© COPYRIGHT UNDER UNIVERSAL COPYRIGHT CONVENTION
COPYRIGHT © 1995 BY GRAPHIS PRESS CORP., DUFOURSTRASSE 107, 8008 ZURICH, SWITZERLAND
JACKET AND BOOK DESIGN COPYRIGHT © 1995 BY PEDERSEN DESIGN
141 LEXINGTON AVENUE, NEW YORK, N.Y. 10016 USA

NO PART OF THIS BOOK MAY BE REPRODUCED IN ANY FORM WITHOUT WRITTEN
PERMISSION OF THE PUBLISHER

PRINTED IN HONG KONG BY PALACE PRESS INTERNATIONAL

Publisher's Remarks

The classic faces represented in this book were the mainstay of designers before the computer. Typographers in outside service shops at that time, such as the Composing Room and Boro amongst others in New York, took pride in their ability to appropriately set the type requested and then provide inked proofs that best represented the face. With the introduction of the computer, numerous software manufacturers immediately developed interpretations of these faces. Unfortunately, most of the new interpretations were rarely close to the original cuts in quality or kerning, nor did many of these people care.

I've therefore had numerous frustrations over the past few years trying to attain reasonable craft with these faces. I found that there was inconsistency in most manufacturer's total font productions, and though a few came close to mastering one face, they failed to do so on others.

When I called Tom Carnase and Baruch Gorkin, I wasn't surprised to hear that they had similar frustrations, and were seriously considering spending time to research this dilemma for their own quality control. We decided therefore to request fonts from all the major suppliers and selected what we felt were the best representations of the faces. The criteria for this selection are listed in our introduction.

This book therefore can be used as a tool to specify these classic faces, since what you see is what you should get. This of course is history now, and our future books on typography will introduce all the new faces produced on the computer by today's younger generation of typographers. A typeface today—unlike in the past, when each letter had to be drawn by hand and a face would sometimes take years to complete—can be executed by a designer in Fontographer or other software in a fraction of that time. These changes herald an exciting time for all participants in the technological revolution in design. It is also a very challenging time, in which the time-honored verities of these classic faces are all the more crucial.

Foreword

Tom Carnase, a designer who has become known as an original master of letterforms. Principle of Carnase, Inc., a famed New York design organization. In past, vice president and partner of Lubalin, Smith, Carnase, Inc.

Good typography is essential whenever words are used in a visual manner. Unfortunately, many opinions are expressed about good typography, but not enough is produced. When type is set properly no one notices the letters as they cut through white space, because one is too busy reading the text.

The understanding of type and the ability to analyze a message in an original and coherent way is hard work. When the only sense of order is that of faithful copies of the same original, then the creative effort is absent. When a ripped-off fragment of a letter annoys the eye rather than gives pleasure, we should question whether this is progress. When all products are dressed alike to all customers, they become indistinguishable in a chorus of "me-too's."

To the casual eye, the imposing array of designs is proof of the wealth between creative and technological interplay over the last 150 years.

This volume is intended as a practical workbook of type and typography. In essence, it shows careful selections of the best examples of the faces available today—a designer's basic arsenal of faces.

Tom Carnase
New York, 1994

Preface

Baruch Gorkin, graphic designer, creative director of New York based Access Factory Inc.

Digital typography has come of age and a myriad of typefaces is now available on computer. What has been missing is a clear guide as to which of these faces are indeed good enough for even the most discriminating typographer and why. Many of us are all too familiar with the frustration of not having the time to really study the marketplace and determine which foundry has produced the best Bodoni or Caslon. Such an evaluation is further complicated by the fact that, in addition to purely aesthetic considerations, one has to keep in mind all the technical issues peculiar to digital typography and the prepress environment.

Graphis has set out to fill that void. When Martin Pedersen approached Tom Carnase and me with the idea of this book, the coincidence startled us. We were in the midst of planning such a study for our own purposes!

One cannot do justice to such a broad subject as digital text fonts in one book. We therefore agreed to limit the scope of this first publication to the classical text typefaces, those that have already passed the most difficult of tests: the test of time. Our task was to determine which of the digitally available versions of these classics are the best. To make these determinations, we analyzed a great number of typefaces produced by the world's best foundries. This volume is a result of our study.

The book is divided into sections, each devoted to a particular font family and showing the full range of its usage possibilities in text. At the opening of each section a table (fig. 1) lists the foundry that developed the font, the supplier, and our assessments of how the font rates in each of the criteria we established. Before we go on to elaborate upon these criteria, we need to stress that, although the current practice is for a foundry to develop a font and then license it to other foundries for resale, that same font may differ greatly depending upon the supplier. To properly identify a font, one must note *both* the foundry and the supplier. In

Foundry:	
Supplier:	
Letterform authenticity:	
Digital outline:	
Side bearings:	
Kerning:	
Hinting:	
Expert editions:	
Multiple masters:	
Family completeness:	
Formats:	
Platforms:	

fig. 1

making this identification we applied the following system: if the foundry itself acted as a supplier and provided as good a version of the font as other suppliers it licensed this font to, we listed only the foundry itself as the supplier. In all other cases, the best supplier is listed.

We will now elaborate upon these criteria.

Letterform authenticity

This is the number-one criterion. There is no need to further evaluate a typeface if this criterion is not met. Creating an authentic digital version of a given typeface does not depend on faithful copying but on intelligent and sensitive translation and reinterpretation.

The typefaces of old were cut in a way that allowed for "ink spread" and other more subtle effects of the printing process. The metal matrix was not seen as a final letter design, but rather as a step in achieving that design on paper.

Digital fonts, on the other hand, work in such a way that the outline of the letterform reaches the paper it is printed upon virtually without distortion (fig. 2). The best digital renditions of the classical text typefaces take this fact into consideration and their design is therefore modified so that they resemble their metal forbears in printing. Many digital fonts are, however, merely thoughtless copies of the metal matrixes and do not produce authentic results.

To be fair, one must say that some of the more subtle qualities of metal typography are not attainable in the digital environment, and should not be attempted. Part of the allure of metal typesetting is the organic, human feel of that rough edge of the metal letterform and its dimensional "impression." Long before digital typesetting, with the introduction of offset printing, these qualities were lost.

The task of creating truly beautiful digital renditions of the classic text faces is in essence not a new problem. Type

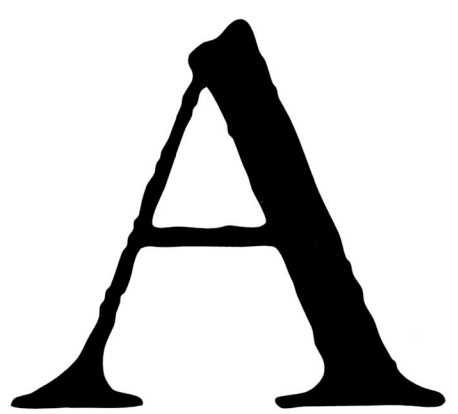

letterpress printed letterform (enlarged to illustrate the rough edge)

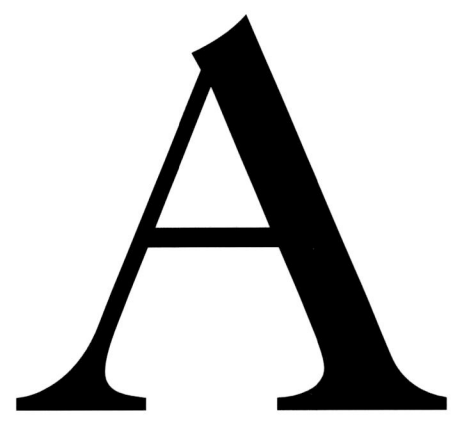

letterform printed from a digital version of the same font

fig. 2

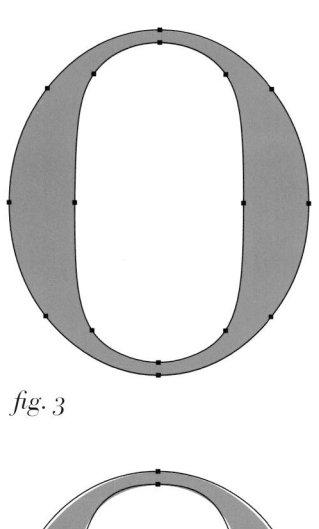
fig. 3

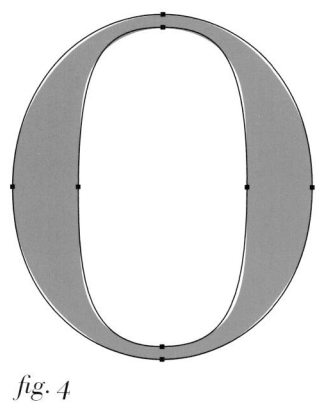
fig. 4

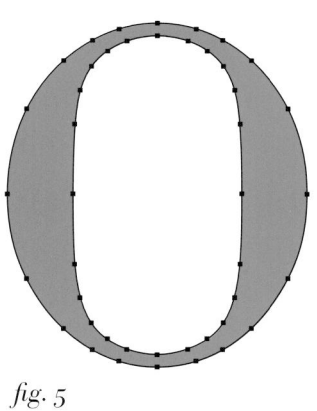
fig. 5

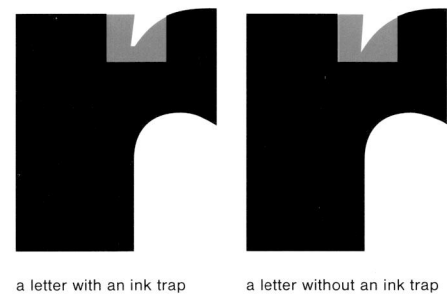
a letter with an ink trap   a letter without an ink trap

fig. 6

designers throughout time have faced similar dilemmas. They had to find a way to "translate" the shapes of the stone-carved letterforms into the visual language of pen-and-ink handwriting. Later, they moved from handwriting to metal type. The best examples of this "translation" work have endured, as the mediocre ones simply "monkeyed" their predecessors.

Digital outline

Letterforms must be well drawn and that fact must be evident in the digital outlines that comprise the font. There are, however, some aspects of font outlines that may be less obvious, but no less deserving of attention.

One of those issues is the "cleanliness" of the actual outline. Barring some instances where the font actually benefits from the uneven, rough outline quality, in most cases the letterforms should be digitized with razor-crisp clarity and precision. To our chagrin, many fonts displayed a marked failing in this area.

Furthermore, each shape has an optimum of coordinate points needed to describe it (fig. 3). Use too few—and loose subtlety (fig. 4), use too many—and create a monster that will take up extra computing time for display and printing (fig. 5). These points must also be properly placed in order for the typeface to later be well *hinted* (see the chapter on *hinting*).

Another important fact to keep in mind is that digitization of the font must be done with current prepress and printing technologies in mind. Many conventions have been carried over from the days of metal typesetting and have not been properly re-evaluated by many foundries.

Let's consider one example: ink traps. While it is debatable whether ink traps are needed in today's fonts (it is our contention they are not needed at all), they certainly should not be done in the same way ink traps where done for metal typesetting (fig. 6). The reason is quite simple: as we discussed earlier, unlike metal type, the outline of the digital let-

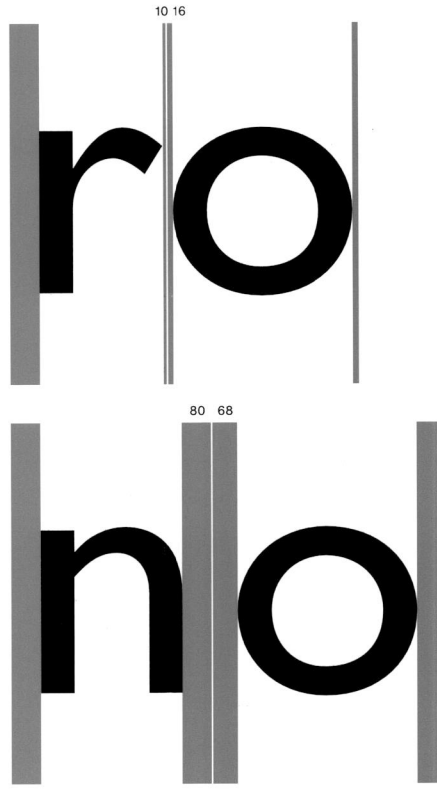

fig. 7

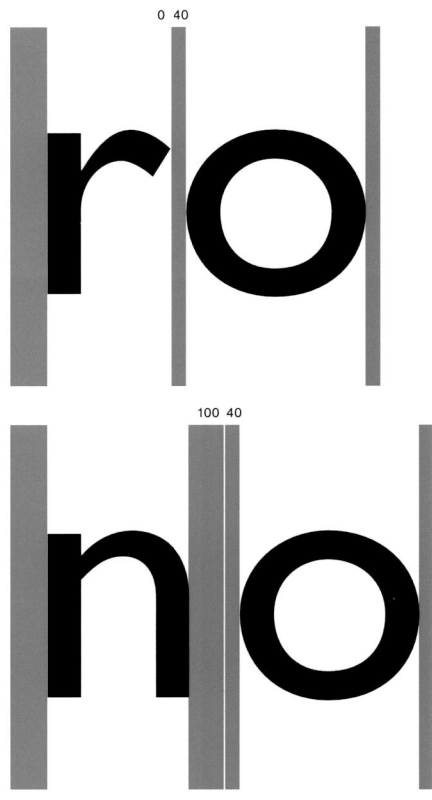

fig. 8

terform reaches the paper without distortion. Therefore the ink "fill in" that these traps were designed to avoid is not likely to occur. The advantage of not having very pronounced ink traps is that the same font can be used at large sizes. This is especially important because an overwhelming majority of typefaces do not have separate outlines for small and large sizes.

Spacing: side-bearings and kerning tables
The next issue of major importance is the spacing of the font. The spacing quality of a typeface consists of two components: side-bearings of the individual characters and a kerning table. The side-bearings of a letterform determine its distance from the letter that precedes it in the text and the letter that follows it. Because good letterspacing is achieved optically and not mathematically, well constructed side-bearings are created by a process of a wrenching visual give-and-take.

To understand this, consider the following: a letter combination "ro" may look best if the *left side-bearing* of the letter "o" equals 16 units of the M-square.(M-square is a term inherited from the days of metal typography and refers to the imaginary boundary of all the letterforms in the font. At the design stage, all type measurements are discussed in terms of M-square units.) However, a letter combination "no" will look best if the *left side-bearing* of the letter "o" equals 68 units (fig. 7). This contradiction is solved by adjusting the side-bearings of all three letters involved until harmony is achieved (fig. 8). Thus constructing side-bearings for the whole font is time consuming.

Even when this work is done exceptionally well, some character combinations will still seem unbalanced and will have to be adjusted further. This is done by programming into the font a "kerning pair" so that every time these particular two characters are set next to each other, their relative position is adjusted in accordance with the kerning number. For example: the best right side-bearing for the

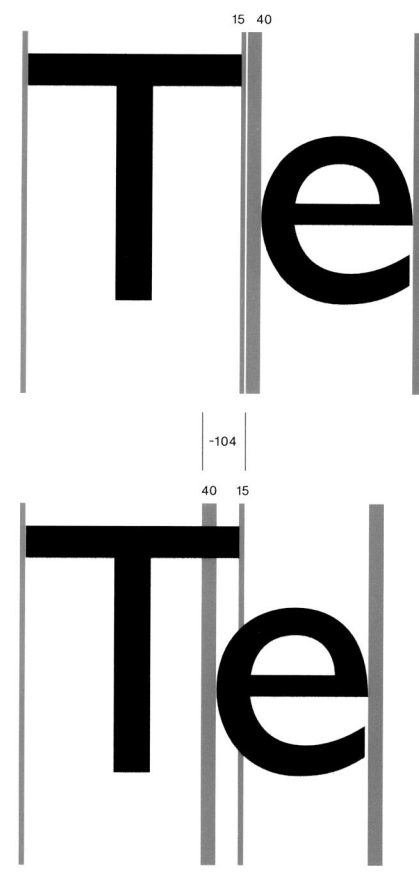

fig. 9

letter "T" in a given font was determined to be 15 units and the best left side-bearing for letter "e" was determined to be 40 units. However, 55 units is just too much space for the "Te" combination. So a kerning pair "Te" is created with a value of -104 units. Thus the position of "T" and "e" relative to all the other characters in the font remains unaffected, but when these letters appear next to each other, the space between them will now be -49 units (fig. 9). A set of such kerning pairs is called a "kerning table."

A font with well constructed side-bearings, set not too tightly, will require a minimal amount of kerning pairs. This is very advantageous on two counts:

a) If a typeface does not have good side-bearings and relies heavily upon a kerning table, its spacing is not easily adjusted. Changing side-bearings is very time consuming and requires creating a new font, while a font that has excellent side-bearings, but lacks a few kerning pairs, can be edited with ease.

b) Fonts with huge kerning tables print out and render on the computer screen very slowly.

Another important note with regard to font spacing is that even a perfectly spaced and kerned font is only raw material for typesetting. Further spacing adjustments must be made in order to obtain pleasing results. Factors such as type size, leading, and line length affect the spacing adjustments. What looks good at one size may not look good at another. If a font sets well at 12 points, chances are, more letterspacing (or "tracking") will be required at smaller point sizes and less at larger ones. At larger sizes, additional kerning adjustments become necessary.

In setting the font showings for this book, we have made such adjustments. So what you actually see is not the raw font set at a given point size, but rather examples of how each particular font should be spaced at those point sizes. Any good design/layout program in use today will provide ample tools to exercise this sort of control.

Hinting

All electronic imaging, be it printed or displayed on a monitor, is done in square *pixels*. The physical size of these pixels varies depending upon the *raster resolution* of the particular device. A computer monitor, for example may have as coarse a resolution as 72 dpi (dots or pixels per linear inch, which usually corresponds to 5,184 pixels per square inch), while a film imagesetter used for color separations will normally be capable of very high resolutions such as 2,540 dpi (6,451,600 pixels per square inch) and higher.

The early digital fonts were stored in pixel form to fit the raster of a particular imaging device. Today, digital fonts are created and stored in *outline* form and are *plotted* to a raster of a particular imaging device in the process of printing (fig. 10). Since these fonts are not tied to a particular device, they are known as *device independent*.

When the outline of a letterform in a font is plotted to the raster of an imaging device, the letterform is converted to a pixel format. The lower the raster resolution of the device (i.e., the larger the pixel), the less accurate this process becomes. At some point (below 600 dpi) the raster becomes too coarse to retain the subtleties of the letterform in text sizes. Thus the resultant letterform becomes distorted.

This distortion alone would not be fatal except for the following problem. The letterforms in a font share many common, but not physically identical, elements. The inconsistencies among these common elements are inherent to the construction of the letterform and are not perceived by the human eye as such.

The plotting process is, however, strictly mathematical: if the outline "covers" most of the particular pixel in the raster—this pixel is "in," if not—it is "out." As a result, in low-resolution devices, one of the abovementioned common elements may get entirely lost in one letter and be exaggerated in another (fig. 11). To alleviate this problem, font manufactur-

letterform outline

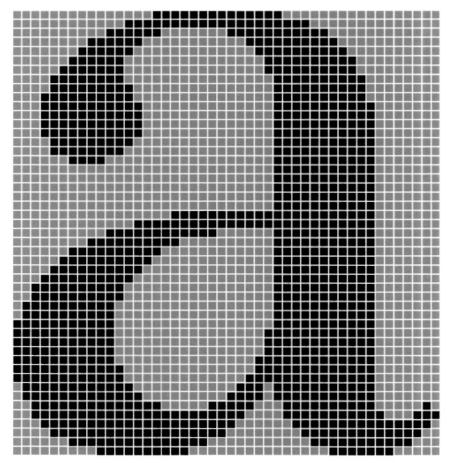

rasterised letterform

fig. 10

xiv

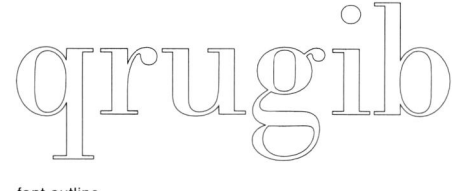

font outline

qrugib

unhinted font set at 12pt and rasterized at 300dpi

qrugib

hinted font set at 12pt and rasterized at 300dpi

fig. 11

ers have developed methods of incorporating into their fonts sets of instructions that control the plotting distortions. These are called *hinting instructions*. Hinting can not miraculously increase the resolution of an imaging device, but the best examples of hinting do maintain the consistency of plotting distortions across the font while retaining legibility and as much of the font's "look" as is possible within a coarse raster (fig. 11).

It should be obvious from this description that hinting is by no means a determining factor in evaluating a font. In those instances, however, where work is outputted to a low-resolution imaging device (e.g., an in-house newsletter that will be printed on a low-resolution printer or an on-screen application), using fonts without very good hinting can result in unacceptable typographic quality.

Expert editions

The availability of such characters as old-style figures, small caps, ligatures and fractions add greatly to the versatility of the font. Many typefaces do include these characters, but the standards in this area leave a lot to be desired.

Because of limitations on the number of characters that can be currently included in one font, these characters are often packaged in separate fonts that are called "expert editions." Using them is extremely arduous. If one wishes to set text with old-style figures, for example, one must manually assign a different font to all the numbers in the text! It makes much more sense for the manufacturer to supply a variation of the entire font with old-style figures instead of lining figures, or small caps instead of lower case letters. Some font vendors are beginning to do just that.

Software companies are also creating more sophisticated operating systems that can support fonts with huge character sets. Some operating systems of this nature are already being released, but it remains to be seen if they will be supported by third-party vendors. At the present time, despite the confusion, expert editions remain a great asset.

For presentation purposes, in this book we show the character range of the font family on one page. In many cases however, multiple fonts must be purchased in order to obtain such a character range.

Family completeness
This category evaluates the sufficiency of the number of weights within a font family. While the basic four weights (regular, italic, bold, bold italic) will do for an old-style font such as Garamond, a san-serif font such as Univers must be available in all weights to be considered complete. In this book, we did not include *all* the weights of every font family, only ones that are likely to be set in text.

Some foundries do not bother to draw the italic versions of their *sans serif* fonts, but simply computer-slant the upright letterforms and package the resulted font under the name "italic" or "oblique." This method is by no means satisfactory as the resulting letterforms appear distorted, their weight distribution unbalanced, and their curve structure deformed (fig. 12). As a matter of good taste, we did not consider such fonts for inclusion in this book.

Multiple masters
Optical illusion plays a crucial role in human perception. This fact was well known to the early printers who realized that in order to make something appear the same in different sizes one must actually make it physically different.

In metal typesetting, the same letterform was cut differently for different point sizes. As a result, it looked visually the same at six points and at 72 points. Such optical scaling was abandoned with the introduction of phototypesetting, in which every point size of a letterform was created by mechanical scaling from a single master.

upright letterforms slanted on computer

letterforms properly drawn on a slant

fig. 12

grey shape: letterforms designed for setting at large sizes
outline: letterforms designed for setting at small sizes

fig. 13

Developed by Adobe Systems, Multiple Masters is a relatively recent technology that allows one typeface to carry "multiple" outlines. Thus such a font may have two "masters": one for the smallest point size and one for the largest (fig. 13). Every size in between is then created by the computer virtually "on the fly"!

Multiple Master fonts may have built into them up to four ways in which the font can be interpolated: by size, by weight, by width, and and by style. Adobe calles these possibilities "axis." Depending on the font need, a Multiple Master font may be a 1-, 2-, 3- or a 4-axis font.

Multiple Master technology offers a great opportunity to reclaim the beauty of old metal typography. However, to date this technology has not been applied to the classical text typefaces.

Two more characteristics related to the practical aspects of using digital fonts need to be addressed: formats for printers, and compatibility across computing platforms. These characteristics, while not intrinsic to the typeface itself, are important in determining what font to use for a particular project.

Formats
The two type formats prevalent today are PostScript Type 1 and TrueType. The main advantage of the TrueType format is that it works on less expensive printers as it does not need a PostScript interpreter built into the printer. In every other way the PostScript Type 1 fonts are more versatile. However, if the foundry supplies an identical font in both formats, it may prove to be quite useful.

Cross-platform compatibility
At a time when cross-platform working environments are becoming commonplace, the number of computer platforms

on which a given font is available becomes an important consideration. To avoid the hassle of converting one's typeface of choice to a different platform format, a font already available on multiple platforms may have to be used instead.

The main purpose of the descriptions given in this preface was to qualify the criteria that governed our font selection process. These explanations should enable the readers to decide which criteria are important to them and thus determine the usefulness of this collection.

Baruch Gorkin
New York, 1994

Garamond

TrPa

Monotype Garamond

Foundry:	*Monotype Typography*
Supplier:	*Monotype Typography*
Letterform authenticity:	*Excellent*
Digital outline:	*Good*
Side bearings:	*Excellent*
Kerning:	*Good*
Hinting:	*Excellent*
Expert editions:	*Yes*
Multiple masters:	*No*
Family completeness:	*Good*
Formats:	*Type 1 / partial TrueType*
Platforms:	*Mac / PC*

In adapting the Garamond family to the digital environment, Monotype made no attempt to "clean up" the letterforms of this beautiful old style face. The resultant typeface, we found, was the only one that retained Garamond's characteristic rough warmth. When a more contemporary rendition of the Garamond is desired, the Sabon family may be used.

Monotype Garamond & Monotype Garamond Expert

72 points

ABCDEFGHIJ
KLMNOPQRST
UVWXYZ&
1234567890$£
ABCDEFGHIJKLMNO
PQRSTUVWXYZ&!?
abcdefghijkl
mnopqrstuvwxyz
1234567890$
fi ff fl ffi ffl ß (!?,.-:;)"

Monotype Garamond Italic, Alternative Italic & Expert Italic

72 points

ABCDEFGHIJKL
MNOPQRSTUV
WXYZ&BDEFHIJ
KLMNPRTUXYZ
1234567890$£
abcdefghijklmnopqrstu
vwxyz1234567890$
fi ff fl ffi ffl ß(!?,.-:;)"

Monotype Garamond

6 / 7

All the virtues of the perfect wine glass are paralleled in typography. There is the long, thin stem that obviates fingerprints on the bowl. Why? Because no cloud must come between your eyes and the fiery heart of the liquid. Are not the margins on book pages similarly meant to obviate the necessity of fingering the type page? Again: the glass is colorless or at the most only faintly tinged in the bowl, because the connoisseur judges wine partly by its color and is impatient of anything that alters it. There are a thousand mannerisms in typography that are as impudent and arbitrary as putting port in tumblers of red or green glass! When a goblet has a base that looks too small for security, it does not matter how cleverly it is weighted; you feel nervous lest it should tip over. There are ways of setting lines of type which may work well enough, and yet keep the reader subconsciously worried by the fear of "doubling" lines, reading three words as one, and so forth. Now the man who first chose glass instead of clay or metal to hold his wine was a "modernist" in the sense in which I am going to use that term. That is, the first thing he asked of this particular object was not "How should it look?" but "What must it do?" and to that extent all good typography is modernist. Wine is so strange and potent a thing that it has been used in the central ritual of religion in one place and time, and attacked by a virago with a

8 / 9

All the virtues of the perfect wine glass are paralleled in typography. There is the long, thin stem that obviates fingerprints on the bowl. Why? Because no cloud must come between your eyes and the fiery heart of the liquid. Are not the margins on book pages similarly meant to obviate the necessity of fingering the type page? Again: the glass is colorless or at the most only faintly tinged in the bowl, because the connoisseur judges wine partly by its color and is impatient of anything that alters it. There are a thousand mannerisms in typography that are as impudent and arbitrary as putting port in tumblers of red or green glass! When a goblet has a base that looks too small for security, it does not matter how cleverly it is weighted; you feel nervous lest it should tip over. There are ways of setting lines of type which may work well

10 / 11

All the virtues of the perfect wine glass are paralleled in typography. There is the long, thin stem that obviates fingerprints on the bowl. Why? Because no cloud must come between your eyes and the fiery heart of the liquid. Are not the margins on book pages similarly meant to obviate the necessity of fingering the type page? Again: the glass is colorless or at the most only faintly tinged in the bowl, because the connoisseur judges wine partly by its color and is impatient of anything that alters it. There are a thousand mannerisms in typography that are

12 / 13

All the virtues of the perfect wine glass are paralleled in typography. There is the long, thin stem that obviates fingerprints on the bowl. Why? Because no cloud must come between your eyes and the fiery heart of the liquid. Are not the margins on book pages similarly meant to obviate the necessity of fingering the type page? Again: the glass is colorless or at the most only faintly tinged in the bowl

14 / 15

All the virtues of the perfect wine glass are paralleled in typography. There is the long, thin stem that obviates fingerprints on the bowl. Why? Because no cloud must come between your eyes and the fiery heart of the liquid. Are not the margins on book pages similarly meant to obviate the necessity of fingering the type page? Again: the glass is colorless or at the most only faintly tinged in the bowl, because the connoisseur judges wine partly by its color and is impatient of anything that alters it. There are a thousand mannerisms in typography that are as impudent and arbitrary as putting port in tumblers of red or green glass! When a goblet has a base

18 / 19

All the virtues of the perfect wine glass are paralleled in typography. There is the long, thin stem that obviates fingerprints on the bowl. Why? Because no cloud must come between your eyes and the fiery heart of the liquid. Are not the margins on book pages similarly meant to obviate the necessity of fingering the type page? Again: the glass is colorless or at the most only faintly tinged in the bowl, because the connois

24 / 24

All the virtues of the perfect wine glass are paralleled in typography. There is the long, thin stem that obviates fingerprints on the bowl. Why? Because no cloud must come between your eyes and the fiery heart of the liquid. Are not th

36 / 36

All the virtues of the perfect wine glass are paralleled in typography. There is the long, thin stem that obviat

Monotype Garamond Italic

6 / 7

All the virtues of the perfect wine glass are paralleled in typography. There is the long, thin stem that obviates fingerprints on the bowl. Why? Because no cloud must come between your eyes and the fiery heart of the liquid. Are not the margins on book pages similarly meant to obviate the necessity of fingering the type page? Again: the glass is colorless or at the most only faintly tinged in the bowl, because the connoisseur judges wine partly by its color and is impatient of anything that alters it. There are a thousand mannerisms in typography that are as impudent and arbitrary as putting port in tumblers of red or green glass! When a goblet has a base that looks too small for security, it does not matter how cleverly it is weighted; you feel nervous lest it should tip over. There are ways of setting lines of type which may work well enough, and yet keep the reader subconsciously worried by the fear of "doubling" lines, reading three words as one, and so forth. Now the man who first chose glass instead of clay or metal to hold his wine was a "modernist" in the sense in which I am going to use that term. That is, the first thing he asked of this particular object was not "How should it look?" but "What must it do?" and to that extent all good typography is modernist. Wine is so strange and potent a thing that it has been used in the central ritual of religion in one place and time, and attacked by a virago with a hatchet in another. There is only one other thing in the world that is capable of stirring and altering men's minds to the same extent, and that is the coherent expression of thought. That is man's chief miracle, unique to man. There is no "explanation" whatever of the fact that I can

8 / 9

All the virtues of the perfect wine glass are paralleled in typography. There is the long, thin stem that obviates fingerprints on the bowl. Why? Because no cloud must come between your eyes and the fiery heart of the liquid. Are not the margins on book pages similarly meant to obviate the necessity of fingering the type page? Again: the glass is colorless or at the most only faintly tinged in the bowl, because the connoisseur judges wine partly by its color and is impatient of anything that alters it. There are a thousand mannerisms in typography that are as impudent and arbitrary as putting port in tumblers of red or green glass! When a goblet has a base that looks too small for security, it does not matter how cleverly it is weighted; you feel nervous lest it should tip over. There are ways of setting lines of type which may work well enough, and yet keep the reader subconsciously worried by the fear of "doubling" lines, reading three words as one, and so forth. Now the man who first chose glass instead of

10 / 11

All the virtues of the perfect wine glass are paralleled in typography. There is the long, thin stem that obviates fingerprints on the bowl. Why? Because no cloud must come between your eyes and the fiery heart of the liquid. Are not the margins on book pages similarly meant to obviate the necessity of fingering the type page? Again: the glass is colorless or at the most only faintly tinged in the bowl, because the connoisseur judges wine partly by its color and is impatient of anything that alters it. There are a thousand mannerisms in typography that are as impudent and arbitrary as putting port in tumblers of red or green glass! When a goblet has a base

12 / 13

All the virtues of the perfect wine glass are paralleled in typography. There is the long, thin stem that obviates fingerprints on the bowl. Why? Because no cloud must come between your eyes and the fiery heart of the liquid. Are not the margins on book pages similarly meant to obviate the necessity of fingering the type page? Again: the glass is colorless or at the most only faintly tinged in the bowl, because the connoisseur judges wine partly by its color and is impatient of

14 / 15

All the virtues of the perfect wine glass are paralleled in typography. There is the long, thin stem that obviates fingerprints on the bowl. Why? Because no cloud must come between your eyes and the fiery heart of the liquid. Are not the margins on book pages similarly meant to obviate the necessity of fingering the type page? Again: the glass is colorless or at the most only faintly tinged in the bowl, because the connoisseur judges wine partly by its color and is impatient of anything that alters it. There are a thousand mannerisms in typography that are as impudent and arbitrary as putting port in tumblers of red or green glass! When a goblet has a base that looks too small for security, it does not matter how cleverly it is weighted; you feel nervous lest it should tip over. There are ways of set

18 / 19

All the virtues of the perfect wine glass are paralleled in typography. There is the long, thin stem that obviates fingerprints on the bowl. Why? Because no cloud must come between your eyes and the fiery heart of the liquid. Are not the margins on book pages similarly meant to obviate the necessity of fingering the type page? Again: the glass is colorless or at the most only faintly tinged in the bowl, because the connoisseur judges wine partly by its color and is impatient of anything that alters it.

24 / 24

All the virtues of the perfect wine glass are paralleled in typography. There is the long, thin stem that obviates fingerprints on the bowl. Why? Because no cloud must come between your eyes and the fiery heart of the liquid. Are not the margins on book pages similarly meant to

36 / 36

All the virtues of the perfect wine glass are paralleled in typography. There is the long, thin stem that obviates fingerprints on t

Monotype Garamond Bold

6 / 7

All the virtues of the perfect wine glass are paralleled in typography. There is the long, thin stem that obviates fingerprints on the bowl. Why? Because no cloud must come between your eyes and the fiery heart of the liquid. Are not the margins on book pages similarly meant to obviate the necessity of fingering the type page? Again: the glass is colorless or at the most only faintly tinged in the bowl, because the connoisseur judges wine partly by its color and is impatient of anything that alters it. There are a thousand mannerisms in typography that are as impudent and arbitrary as putting port in tumblers of red or green glass! When a goblet has a base that looks too small for security, it does not matter how cleverly it is weighted; you feel nervous lest it should tip over. There are ways of setting lines of type which may work well enough, and yet keep the reader subconsciously worried by the fear of "doubling" lines, reading three words as one, and so forth. Now the man who first chose glass instead of clay or metal to hold his wine was a "modernist" in the sense in which I am going to use that term. That is, the first thing he asked of this particular object was not "How should it look?" but "What must it do?" and to that extent all good typography is modernist. Wine is so strange and potent a

8 / 9

All the virtues of the perfect wine glass are paralleled in typography. There is the long, thin stem that obviates fingerprints on the bowl. Why? Because no cloud must come between your eyes and the fiery heart of the liquid. Are not the margins on book pages similarly meant to obviate the necessity of fingering the type page? Again: the glass is colorless or at the most only faintly tinged in the bowl, because the connoisseur judges wine partly by its color and is impatient of anything that alters it. There are a thousand mannerisms in typography that are as impudent and arbitrary as putting port in tumblers of red or green glass! When a goblet has a base that looks too small for security, it does not matter how cleverly it is weighted; you feel nervous lest it sh

10 / 11

All the virtues of the perfect wine glass are paralleled in typography. There is the long, thin stem that obviates fingerprints on the bowl. Why? Because no cloud must come between your eyes and the fiery heart of the liquid. Are not the margins on book pages similarly meant to obviate the necessity of fingering the type page? Again: the glass is colorless or at the most only faintly tinged in the bowl, because the connoisseur judges wine partly by its color and is impatient of anything that alters it. The

12 / 13

All the virtues of the perfect wine glass are paralleled in typography. There is the long, thin stem that obviates fingerprints on the bowl. Why? Because no cloud must come between your eyes and the fiery heart of the liquid. Are not the margins on book pages similarly meant to obviate the necessity of fingering the type page? Again: the glass is colorless or a

14 / 15

All the virtues of the perfect wine glass are paralleled in typography. There is the long, thin stem that obviates fingerprints on the bowl. Why? Because no cloud must come between your eyes and the fiery heart of the liquid. Are not the margins on book pages similarly meant to obviate the necessity of fingering the type page? Again: the glass is colorless or at the most only faintly tinged in the bowl, because the conoisseur judges wine partly by its color and is impatient of anything that alters it. There are a thousand mannerisms in typography that are as impudent and arbitrary as putting port in

18 / 19

All the virtues of the perfect wine glass are paralleled in typography. There is the long, thin stem that obviates fingerprints on the bowl. Why? Because no cloud must come between your eyes and the fiery heart of the liquid. Are not the margins on book pages similarly meant to obviate the necessity of fingering the type page? Again: the glass is colorless or at the most only faintly ti

24 / 24

All the virtues of the perfect wine glass are paralleled in typography. There is the long, thin stem that obviates fingerprints on the bowl. Why? Because no cloud must come between your eyes and the fiery heart of

36 / 36

All the virtues of the perfect wine glass are paralleled in typography. There is the long, thin stem

Monotype Garamond Bold Italic

6 / 7

All the virtues of the perfect wine glass are paralleled in typography. There is the long, thin stem that obviates fingerprints on the bowl. Why? Because no cloud must come between your eyes and the fiery heart of the liquid. Are not the margins on book pages similarly meant to obviate the necessity of fingering the type page? Again: the glass is colorless or at the most only faintly tinged in the bowl, because the connoisseur judges wine partly by its color and is impatient of anything that alters it. There are a thousand mannerisms in typography that are as impudent and arbitrary as putting port in tumblers of red or green glass! When a goblet has a base that looks too small for security, it does not matter how cleverly it is weighted; you feel nervous lest it should tip over. There are ways of setting lines of type which may work well enough, and yet keep the reader subconsciously worried by the fear of "doubling" lines, reading three words as one, and so forth. Now the man who first chose glass instead of clay or metal to hold his wine was a "modernist" in the sense in which I am going to use that term. That is, the first thing he asked of this particular object was not "How should it look?" but "What must it do?" and to that extent all good typography is modernist. Wine is so strange and potent a thing that it has been used in the central ritual of religion in one place and time, and attacked by a

8 / 9

All the virtues of the perfect wine glass are paralleled in typography. There is the long, thin stem that obviates fingerprints on the bowl. Why? Because no cloud must come between your eyes and the fiery heart of the liquid. Are not the margins on book pages similarly meant to obviate the necessity of fingering the type page? Again: the glass is colorless or at the most only faintly tinged in the bowl, because the connoisseur judges wine partly by its color and is impatient of anything that alters it. There are a thousand mannerisms in typography that are as impudent and arbitrary as putting port in tumblers of red or green glass! When a goblet has a base that looks too small for security, it does not matter how cleverly it is weighted; you feel nervous lest it should tip over. There are ways of setting lines of type which may work w

10 / 11

All the virtues of the perfect wine glass are paralleled in typography. There is the long, thin stem that obviates fingerprints on the bowl. Why? Because no cloud must come between your eyes and the fiery heart of the liquid. Are not the margins on book pages similarly meant to obviate the necessity of fingering the type page? Again: the glass is colorless or at the most only faintly tinged in the bowl, because the connoisseur judges wine partly by its color and is impatient of anything that alters it. There are a thousand mannerisms in typogra

12 / 13

All the virtues of the perfect wine glass are paralleled in typography. There is the long, thin stem that obviates fingerprints on the bowl. Why? Because no cloud must come between your eyes and the fiery heart of the liquid. Are not the margins on book pages similarly meant to obviate the necessity of fingering the type page? Again: the glass is colorless or at the most only faintly tinged in th

14 / 15

All the virtues of the perfect wine glass are paralleled in typography. There is the long, thin stem that obviates fingerprints on the bowl. Why? Because no cloud must come between your eyes and the fiery heart of the liquid. Are not the margins on book pages similarly meant to obviate the necessity of fingering the type page? Again: the glass is colorless or at the most only faintly tinged in the bowl, because the connoisseur judges wine partly by its color and is impatient of anything that alters it. There are a thousand mannerisms in typography that are as impudent and arbitrary as putting port in tumblers of red or green glass! When a goble

18 / 19

All the virtues of the perfect wine glass are paralleled in typography. There is the long, thin stem that obviates fingerprints on the bowl. Why? Because no cloud must come between your eyes and the fiery heart of the liquid. Are not the margins on book pages similarly meant to obviate the necessity of fingering the type page? Again: the glass is colorless or at the most only faintly tinged in the bowl, because th

24 / 24

All the virtues of the perfect wine glass are paralleled in typography. There is the long, thin stem that obviates fingerprints on the bowl. Why? Because no cloud must come between your eyes and the fiery heart of the liquid. Are n

36 / 36

All the virtues of the perfect wine glass are paralleled in typography. There is the long, thin stem that ob

Monotype Garamond (Caps) & Garamond Expert (Small Caps)

6/7

All the virtues of the perfect wine glass are paralleled in typography. There is the long, thin stem that obviates fingerprints on the bowl. Why? Because no cloud must come between your eyes and the fiery heart of the liquid. Are not the margins on book pages similarly meant to obviate the necessity of fingering the type page? Again: the glass is colorless or at the most only faintly tinged in the bowl, because the connoisseur judges wine partly by its color and is impatient of anything that alters it. There are a thousand mannerisms in typography that are as impudent and arbitrary as putting port in tumblers of red or green glass! When a goblet has a base that looks too small for security, it does not matter how cleverly it is weighted; you feel nervous lest it should tip over. There are ways of setting lines of type which may work well enough, and yet keep the reader subconsciously worried by the fear of doubling lines, reading three words as one, and so forth. Now the man who first chose glass instead of clay or metal to hold his wine was a modernist in the sense in which I am going to use that term. That is, the first thing he asked of this particular object was not

8/9

All the virtues of the perfect wine glass are paralleled in typography. There is the long, thin stem that obviates fingerprints on the bowl. Why? Because no cloud must come between your eyes and the fiery heart of the liquid. Are not the margins on book pages similarly meant to obviate the necessity of fingering the type page? Again: the glass is colorless or at the most only faintly tinged in the bowl, because the connoisseur judges wine partly by its color and is impatient of anything that alters it. There are a thousand mannerisms in typography that are as impudent and arbitrary as putting port in tumblers of red or green glass! When a goblet has a base that looks too small for security

10/11

All the virtues of the perfect wine glass are paralleled in typography. There is the long, thin stem that obviates fingerprints on the bowl. Why? Because no cloud must come between your eyes and the fiery heart of the liquid. Are not the margins on book pages similarly meant to obviate the necessity of fingering the type page? Again: the glass is colorless or at the most only faintly tinged in the bowl, because the connoisseur judges wine partly by its color an

12/13

All the virtues of the perfect wine glass are paralleled in typography. There is the long, thin stem that obviates fingerprints on the bowl. Why? Because no cloud must come between your eyes and the fiery heart of the liquid. Are not the margins on book pages similarly meant to obviate the necessity of fingering the type page

14/15

All the virtues of the perfect wine glass are paralleled in typography. There is the long, thin stem that obviates fingerprints on the bowl. Why? Because no cloud must come between your eyes and the fiery heart of the liquid. Are not the margins on book pages similarly meant to obviate the necessity of fingering the type page? Again: the glass is colorless or at the most only faintly tinged in the bowl, because the connoisseur judges wine partly by its color and is impatient of anything that alters it. There are a thousand mannerisms in typo

18/19

All the virtues of the perfect wine glass are paralleled in typography. There is the long, thin stem that obviates fingerprints on the bowl. Why? Because no cloud must come between your eyes and the fiery heart of the liquid. Are not the margins on book pages similarly meant to obviate the necessity of fingering the type page? Again: the gla

24/24

All the virtues of the perfect wine glass are paralleled in typography. There is the long, thin stem that obviates fingerprints on the bowl. Why? Because no cloud must come between your eyes and t

36/36

All the virtues of the perfect wine glass are paralleled in typography. There is the long

Sabon

Pan

Linotype Sabon

Foundry:	*Linotype-Hell AG*
Supplier:	*Adobe Systems*
Letterform authenticity:	*Excellent*
Digital outline:	*Good*
Side bearings:	*Excellent*
Kerning:	*Good*
Hinting:	*Excellent*
Expert editions:	*Yes*
Multiple masters:	*No*
Family completeness:	*Good*
Formats:	*Type 1*
Platforms:	*Mac / PC*

This Garamond-based typeface, unlike many others of its kind, is not a sterilized Garamond but a thoughtful contemporary reinterpretation that retains Garamond characteristics without its ruggedness.

Linotype Sabon & Sabon Small Caps

72 points

ABCDEFGHIJ
KLMNOPQRST
UVWXYZ&
1234567890$£
ABCDEFGHIJKLMN
OPQRSTUVWXYZ
abcdefghijklmno
pqrstuvwxyz
1234567890
fiß(!?,.-:;)''

72 points

ABCDEFGHI
JKLMNOPQRS
TUVWXYZ&
1234567890$£
abcdefghijklm
nopqrstuvwxyz
1234567890
fiß(!?,.-:;)"

Linotype Sabon

6 / 8

All the virtues of the perfect wine glass are paralleled in typography. There is the long, thin stem that obviates fingerprints on the bowl. Why? Because no cloud must come between your eyes and the fiery heart of the liquid. Are not the margins on book pages similarly meant to obviate the necessity of fingering the type page? Again: the glass is colorless or at the most only faintly tinged in the bowl, because the connoisseur judges wine partly by its color and is impatient of anything that alters it. There are a thousand mannerisms in typography that are as impudent and arbitrary as putting port in tumblers of red or green glass! When a goblet has a base that looks too small for security, it does not matter how cleverly it is weighted; you feel nervous lest it should tip over. There are ways of setting lines of type which may work well enough, and yet keep the reader subconsciously worried by the fear of "doubling" lines, reading three words as one, and so forth. Now the man who first chose glass instead of clay or metal to hold his wine was a "modernist" in the sense in which I am

8 / 10

All the virtues of the perfect wine glass are paralleled in typography. There is the long, thin stem that obviates fingerprints on the bowl. Why? Because no cloud must come between your eyes and the fiery heart of the liquid. Are not the margins on book pages similarly meant to obviate the necessity of fingering the type page? Again: the glass is colorless or at the most only faintly tinged in the bowl, because the connoisseur judges wine partly by its color and is impatient of anything that alters it. There are a thousand mannerisms in typography that are as impudent and arbitrary as putting port in tumblers of red or green glass! When a goblet

10 / 12

All the virtues of the perfect wine glass are paralleled in typography. There is the long, thin stem that obviates fingerprints on the bowl. Why? Because no cloud must come between your eyes and the fiery heart of the liquid. Are not the margins on book pages similarly meant to obviate the necessity of fingering the type page? Again: the glass is colorless or at the most only faintly tinged in the bowl, because the connoisseur judges wine partly by its color and

12 / 14

All the virtues of the perfect wine glass are paralleled in typography. There is the long, thin stem that obviates fingerprints on the bowl. Why? Because no cloud must come between your eyes and the fiery heart of the liquid. Are not the margins on book pages similarly meant to obviate the necessity of fingering the type pa

14 / 16

All the virtues of the perfect wine glass are paralleled in typography. There is the long, thin stem that obviates fingerprints on the bowl. Why? Because no cloud must come between your eyes and the fiery heart of the liquid. Are not the margins on book pages similarly meant to obviate the necessity of fingering the type page? Again: the glass is colorless or at the most only faintly tinged in the bowl, because the connoisseur judges wine partly by its color and is impatient of anything that alters it. There are a thousand mannerisms

18 / 20

All the virtues of the perfect wine glass are paralleled in typography. There is the long, thin stem that obviates fingerprints on the bowl. Why? Because no cloud must come between your eyes and the fiery heart of the liquid. Are not the margins on book pages similarly meant to obviate the necessity of fingering the type page? Ag

24 / 25

All the virtues of the perfect wine glass are paralleled in typography. There is the long, thin stem that obviates fingerprints on the bowl. Why? Because no cloud must come between your eyes and the fiery heart of t

36 / 37

All the virtues of the perfect wine glass are paralleled in typography. There is the long, thin stem tha

Linotype Sabon Italic

6 / 8

All the virtues of the perfect wine glass are paralleled in typography. There is the long, thin stem that obviates fingerprints on the bowl. Why? Because no cloud must come between your eyes and the fiery heart of the liquid. Are not the margins on book pages similarly meant to obviate the necessity of fingering the type page? Again: the glass is colorless or at the most only faintly tinged in the bowl, because the connoisseur judges wine partly by its color and is impatient of anything that alters it. There are a thousand mannerisms in typography that are as impudent and arbitrary as putting port in tumblers of red or green glass! When a goblet has a base that looks too small for security, it does not matter how cleverly it is weighted; you feel nervous lest it should tip over. There are ways of setting lines of type which may work well enough, and yet keep the reader subconsciously worried by the fear of "doubling" lines, reading three words as one, and so forth. Now the man who first chose glass instead of clay or metal to hold his wine was a "modernist" in the sense in which I am

8 / 10

All the virtues of the perfect wine glass are paralleled in typography. There is the long, thin stem that obviates fingerprints on the bowl. Why? Because no cloud must come between your eyes and the fiery heart of the liquid. Are not the margins on book pages similarly meant to obviate the necessity of fingering the type page? Again: the glass is colorless or at the most only faintly tinged in the bowl, because the connoisseur judges wine partly by its color and is impatient of anything that alters it. There are a thousand mannerisms in typography that are as impudent and arbitrary as putting port in tumblers of red or green glass! When a goblet has a b

10 / 12

All the virtues of the perfect wine glass are paralleled in typography. There is the long, thin stem that obviates fingerprints on the bowl. Why? Because no cloud must come between your eyes and the fiery heart of the liquid. Are not the margins on book pages similarly meant to obviate the necessity of fingering the type page? Again: the glass is colorless or at the most only faintly tinged in the bowl, because the connoisseur judges wine partly by its colo

12 / 14

All the virtues of the perfect wine glass are paralleled in typography. There is the long, thin stem that obviates fingerprints on the bowl. Why? Because no cloud must come between your eyes and the fiery heart of the liquid. Are not the margins on book pages similarly meant to obviate the necessity of fingering the type pag

14 / 16

All the virtues of the perfect wine glass are paralleled in typography. There is the long, thin stem that obviates fingerprints on the bowl. Why? Because no cloud must come between your eyes and the fiery heart of the liquid. Are not the margins on book pages similarly meant to obviate the necessity of fingering the type page? Again: the glass is colorless or at the most only faintly tinged in the bowl, because the connoisseur judges wine partly by its color and is impatient of anything that alters it. There are a thousand mannerisms in

18 / 20

All the virtues of the perfect wine glass are paralleled in typography. There is the long, thin stem that obviates fingerprints on the bowl. Why? Because no cloud must come between your eyes and the fiery heart of the liquid. Are not the margins on book pages similarly meant to obviate the necessity of fingering the type page?

24 / 25

All the virtues of the perfect wine glass are paralleled in typography. There is the long, thin stem that obviates fingerprints on the bowl. Why? Because no cloud must come between your eyes and the fiery heart of

36 / 37

All the virtues of the perfect wine glass are paralleled in typography. There is the long, thin stem th

Linotype Sabon Bold

6 / 8

All the virtues of the perfect wine glass are paralleled in typography. There is the long, thin stem that obviates finger prints on the bowl. Why? Because no cloud must come between your eyes and the fiery heart of the liquid. Are not the margins on book pages similarly meant to obviate the necessity of fingering the type page? Again: the glass is colorless or at the most only faintly tinged in the bowl, because the connoisseur judges wine partly by its color and is impatient of anything that alters it. There are a thousand mannerisms in typography that are as impudent and arbitrary as putting port in tumblers of red or green glass! When a goblet has a base that looks too small for security, it does not matter how cleverly it is weighted; you feel nervous lest it should tip over. There are ways of setting lines of type which may work well enough, and yet keep the reader subconsciously worried by the fear of "doubling" lines, reading three words as one, and so forth. Now the man who first chose glass instead of clay or metal to hold his wine was a "modernist" in the sense in whi

8 / 10

All the virtues of the perfect wine glass are paralleled in typography. There is the long, thin stem that obviates fingerprints on the bowl. Why? Because no cloud must come between your eyes and the fiery heart of the liquid. Are not the margins on book pages similarly meant to obviate the necessity of fingering the type page? Again: the glass is colorless or at the most only faintly tinged in the bowl, because the connoisseur judges wine partly by its color and is impatient of anything that alters it. There are a thousand mannerisms in typography that are as impudent and arbitrary as putting port in tumblers of red or green glass! When a goblet has a base that lo

10 / 12

All the virtues of the perfect wine glass are paralleled in typography. There is the long, thin stem that obviates fingerprints on the bowl. Why? Because no cloud must come between your eyes and the fiery heart of the liquid. Are not the margins on book pages similarly meant to obviate the necessity of fingering the type page? Again: the glass is colorless or at the most only faintly tinged in the bowl, because the connoisseur judges wine partly by its color

12 / 14

All the virtues of the perfect wine glass are paralleled in typography. There is the long, thin stem that obviates fingerprints on the bowl. Why? Because no cloud must come between your eyes and the fiery heart of the liquid. Are not the margins on book pages similarly meant to obviate the necessity of fingering the type page

14 / 16

All the virtues of the perfect wine glass are paralleled in typography. There is the long, thin stem that obviates finger prints on the bowl. Why? Because no cloud must come between your eyes and the fiery heart of the liquid. Are not the margins on book pages similarly meant to obviate the necessity of fingering the type page? Again: the glass is colorless or at the most only faintly tinged in the bowl, because the connoisseur judges wine partly by its color and is impatient of anything that alters it. There are a thousand mannerisms

18 / 20

All the virtues of the perfect wine glass are paralleled in typography. There is the long, thin stem that obviates fingerprints on the bowl. Why? Because no cloud must come between your eyes and the fiery heart of the liquid. Are not the margins on book pages similarly meant to obviate the necessity of fingering the type page?

24 / 25

All the virtues of the perfect wine glass are paralleled in typography. There is the long, thin stem that obviates fingerprints on the bowl. Why? Because no cloud must come between your eyes and the fiery heart of

36 / 37

All the virtues of the perfect wine glass are paralleled in typography. There is the long, thin stem t

Linotype Sabon Bold Italic

6/8

All the virtues of the perfect wine glass are paralleled in typography. There is the long, thin stem that obviates finger prints on the bowl. Why? Because no cloud must come between your eyes and the fiery heart of the liquid. Are not the margins on book pages similarly meant to obviate the necessity of fingering the type page? Again: the glass is col orless or at the most only faintly tinged in the bowl, because the connoisseur judges wine partly by its color and is impa tient of anything that alters it. There are a thousand mann erisms in typography that are as impudent and arbitrary as putting port in tumblers of red or green glass! When a goblet has a base that looks too small for security, it does not mat ter how cleverly it is weighted; you feel nervous lest it should tip over. There are ways of setting lines of type which may work well enough, and yet keep the reader subconsciously worried by the fear of "doubling" lines, reading three words as one, and so forth. Now the man who first chose glass instead of clay or metal to hold his wine was a "modernist"

8/10

All the virtues of the perfect wine glass are par alleled in typography. There is the long, thin st em that obviates fingerprints on the bowl. Wh y? Because no cloud must come between your eyes and the fiery heart of the liquid. Are not t he margins on book pages similarly meant to obviate the necessity of fingering the type pag e? Again: the glass is colorless or at the most o nly faintly tinged in the bowl, because the con noisseur judges wine partly by its color and is impatient of anything that alters it. There are a thousand mannerisms in typography that a re as impudent and arbitrary as putting port in tumblers of red or green glass! When a goble

10/12

All the virtues of the perfect wine gla ss are paralleled in typography. There is the long, thin stem that obviates fin gerprints on the bowl. Why? Because no cloud must come between your ey es and the fiery heart of the liquid. Ar e not the margins on book pages simil arly meant to obviate the necessity of fingering the type page? Again: the gl ass is colorless or at the most only fain tly tinged in the bowl, because the con noisseur judges wine partly by its col

12/14

All the virtues of the perfect win e glass are paralleled in typogra phy. There is the long, thin stem that obviates fingerprints on the bowl. Why? Because no cloud m ust come between your eyes and the fiery heart of the liquid. Are not the margins on book pages similarly meant to obviate the necessity of fingering the type p

14/16

All the virtues of the perfect wine glass are paralleled in typography. There is the long, thin stem that obviates fin gerprints on the bowl. Why? Because no cloud must come between your eyes and the fiery heart of the liquid. Are not the margins on book pages similarly meant to obviate the necessity of fingering the type page? Again: the glass is col orless or at the most only faintly tinged in the bowl, be cause the connoisseur judges wine partly by its color and is impatient of anything that alters it. There are a thou

18/20

All the virtues of the perfect wine glass are pa ralleled in typography. There is the long, thin stem that obviates fingerprints on the bowl. W hy? Because no cloud must come between yo ur eyes and the fiery heart of the liquid. Are not the margins on book pages similarly mea nt to obviate the necessity of fingering the typ

24/25

All the virtues of the perfect wine glass are paralleled in typography. There is the long, thin stem that ob viates fingerprints on the bowl. W hy? Because no cloud must come b etween your eyes and the fiery hea

36/37

All the virtues of the per fect wine glass are paral leled in typography. Th ere is the long, thin stem

LINOTYPE SABON SMALL CAPS

6/8

ALL THE VIRTUES OF THE PERFECT WINE GLASS ARE PARALLELED IN TYPOGRAPHY. THERE IS THE LONG, THIN STEM THAT OBVIATES FINGERPRINTS ON THE BOWL. WHY? BECAUSE NO CLOUD MUST COME BETWEEN YOUR EYES AND THE FIERY HEART OF THE LIQUID. ARE NOT THE MARGINS ON BOOK PAGES SIMILARLY MEANT TO OBVIATE THE NECESSITY OF FINGERING THE TYPE PAGE? AGAIN: THE GLASS IS COLORLESS OR AT THE MOST ONLY FAINTLY TINGED IN THE BOWL, BECAUSE THE CONNOISSEUR JUDGES WINE PARTLY BY ITS COLOR AND IS IMPATIENT OF ANYTHING THAT ALTERS IT. THERE ARE A THOUSAND MANNERISMS IN TYPOGRAPHY THAT ARE AS IMPUDENT AND ARBITRARY AS PUTTING PORT IN TUMBLERS OF RED OR GREEN GLASS! WHEN A GOBLET HAS A BASE THAT LOOKS TOO SMALL FOR SECURITY, IT DOES NOT MATTER HOW CLEVERLY IT IS WEIGHTED; YOU FEEL NERVOUS LEST IT SHOULD TIP OVER. THERE ARE WAYS OF SETTING LINES OF TYPE WHICH MAY WORK WELL ENOUGH, AND YET KEEP THE READER SUBCONSCIOUSLY WORRIED BY THE FEAR OF "DOUBLING" LINES

8/10

ALL THE VIRTUES OF THE PERFECT WINE GLASS ARE PARALLELED IN TYPOGRAPHY. THERE IS THE LONG, THIN STEM THAT OBVIATES FINGERPRINTS ON THE BOWL. WHY? BECAUSE NO CLOUD MUST COME BETWEEN YOUR EYES AND THE FIERY HEART OF THE LIQUID. ARE NOT THE MARGINS ON BOOK PAGES SIMILARLY MEANT TO OBVIATE THE NECESSITY OF FINGERING THE TYPE PAGE? AGAIN: THE GLASS IS COLORLESS OR AT THE MOST ONLY FAINTLY TINGED IN THE BOWL, BECAUSE THE CONNOISSEUR JUDGES WINE PARTLY BY ITS COLOR AND IS IMPATIENT OF ANYTHING THAT ALTERS IT. THERE ARE A THOUSAND MANNERISMS IN TYPOGRAPHY THAT ARE AS IMPUD

10/12

ALL THE VIRTUES OF THE PERFECT WINE GLASS ARE PARALLELED IN TYPOGRAPHY. THERE IS THE LONG, THIN STEM THAT OBVIATES FINGERPRINTS ON THE BOWL. WHY? BECAUSE NO CLOUD MUST COME BETWEEN YOUR EYES AND THE FIERY HEART OF THE LIQUID. ARE NOT THE MARGINS ON BOOK PAGES SIMILARLY MEANT TO OBVIATE THE NECESSITY OF FINGERING THE TYPE PAGE? AGAIN: THE GLASS IS COLORLESS OR AT THE MOST ONLY FAINTLY TIN

12/14

ALL THE VIRTUES OF THE PERFECT WINE GLASS ARE PARALLELED IN TYPOGRAPHY. THERE IS THE LONG, THIN STEM THAT OBVIATES FINGERPRINTS ON THE BOWL. WHY? BECAUSE NO CLOUD MUST COME BETWEEN YOUR EYES AND THE FIERY HEART OF THE LIQUID. ARE NOT THE MARGINS ON BOOK PAGES SIMILARLY MEANT TO

14/16

ALL THE VIRTUES OF THE PERFECT WINE GLASS ARE PARALLELED IN TYPOGRAPHY. THERE IS THE LONG, THIN STEM THAT OBVIATES FINGERPRINTS ON THE BOWL. WHY? BECAUSE NO CLOUD MUST COME BETWEEN YOUR EYES AND THE FIERY HEART OF THE LIQUID. ARE NOT THE MARGINS ON BOOK PAGES SIMILARLY MEANT TO OBVIATE THE NECESSITY OF FINGERING THE TYPE PAGE? AGAIN: THE GLASS IS COLORLESS OR AT THE MOST ONLY FAINTLY TINGED IN THE BOWL, BECAUSE THE CONNOISSEUR JUDGES WINE PARTLY BY ITS COLO

18/20

ALL THE VIRTUES OF THE PERFECT WINE GLASS ARE PARALLELED IN TYPOGRAPHY. THERE IS THE LONG, THIN STEM THAT OBVIATES FINGERPRINTS ON THE BOWL. WHY? BECAUSE NO CLOUD MUST COME BETWEEN YOUR EYES AND THE FIERY HEART OF THE LIQUID. ARE NOT THE MARGINS ON BOOK PAGES SIMILARLY MEANT TO O

24/25

ALL THE VIRTUES OF THE PERFECT WINE GLASS ARE PARALLELED IN TYPOGRAPHY. THERE IS THE LONG, THIN STEM THAT OBVIATES FINGERPRINTS ON THE BOWL. WHY? BECAUSE NO CLOUD MUST COME BETWEEN

36/37

ALL THE VIRTUES OF THE PERFECT WINE GLASS ARE PARALLELED IN TYPOGRAPHY. THERE IS T

Centaur

dje

Monotype Centaur

Foundry:	Monotype Typography
Supplier:	Monotype Typography
Letterform authenticity:	Excellent
Digital outline:	Good
Side bearings:	Excellent
Kerning:	Good
Hinting:	Excellent
Expert editions:	Yes
Multiple masters:	No
Family completeness:	Good
Formats:	Type 1 / partial TrueType
Platforms:	Mac/PC

Monotype Centaur, Centaur Alternative & Centaur Expert

ABCDEFGHIJ
KLMNOPQRQRS
TUVWXYZ&
1234567890$£
ABCDEFGHIJKLMNOP
QRQRSTUVWXYZ &!?
abcdefghijklm
nopqrstuvwxyz
1234567890$
fiffflffifflß(!?,.-:;)"

Monotype Centaur Italic, Alternative Italic & Expert Italic

72 points

ABCDEFGHIJKLM
NOPQQRSTUVWX
YZ&1234567890$£
abcdefghghijklmnopqrstuv
wxyzz1234567890$
ffl ß fi ff fl ffi (!?,.-:;)''

Monotype Centaur

6 / 7

All the virtues of the perfect wine glass are paralleled in typography. There is the long, thin stem that obviates fingerprints on the bowl. Why? Because no cloud must come between your eyes and the fiery heart of the liquid. Are not the margins on book pages similarly meant to obviate the necessity of fingering the type page? Again: the glass is colorless or at the most only faintly tinged in the bowl, because the connoisseur judges wine partly by its color and is impatient of anything that alters it. There are a thousand mannerisms in typography that are as impudent and arbitrary as putting port in tumblers of red or green glass! When a goblet has a base that looks too small for security, it does not matter how cleverly it is weighted; you feel nervous lest it should tip over. There are ways of setting lines of type which may work well enough, and yet keep the reader subconsciously worried by the fear of "doubling" lines, reading three words as one, and so forth. Now the man who first chose glass instead of clay or metal to hold his wine was a "modernist" in the sense in which I am going to use that term. That is, the first thing he asked of this particular object was not "How should it look?" but "What must it do?" and to that extent all good typography is modernist. Wine is so strange and potent a thing that it has been used in the central ritual of religion in one place and time, and attacked by a virago with a hatchet in another. There is only one other thing in the world that is capable of stirring and altering

8 / 9

All the virtues of the perfect wine glass are paralleled in typography. There is the long, thin stem that obviates fingerprints on the bowl. Why? Because no cloud must come between your eyes and the fiery heart of the liquid. Are not the margins on book pages similarly meant to obviate the necessity of fingering the type page? Again: the glass is colorless or at the most only faintly tinged in the bowl, because the connoisseur judges wine partly by its color and is impatient of anything that alters it. There are a thousand mannerisms in typography that are as impudent and arbitrary as putting port in tumblers of red or green glass! When a goblet has a base that looks too small for security, it does not matter how cleverly it is weighted; you feel nervous lest it should tip over. There are ways of setting lines of type which may work well enough, and yet keep the reader subconsciously worried

10 / 11

All the virtues of the perfect wine glass are paralleled in typography. There is the long, thin stem that obviates fingerprints on the bowl. Why? Because no cloud must come between your eyes and the fiery heart of the liquid. Are not the margins on book pages similarly meant to obviate the necessity of fingering the type page? Again: the glass is colorless or at the most only faintly tinged in the bowl, because the connoisseur judges wine partly by its color and is impatient of anything that alters it. There are a thousand mannerisms in typography that are as impudent and arbitrary as

12 / 13

All the virtues of the perfect wine glass are paralleled in typography. There is the long, thin stem that obviates fingerprints on the bowl. Why? Because no cloud must come between your eyes and the fiery heart of the liquid. Are not the margins on book pages similarly meant to obviate the necessity of fingering the type page? Again: the glass is colorless or at the most only faintly tinged in the bowl, because the

14 / 15

All the virtues of the perfect wine glass are paralleled in typography. There is the long, thin stem that obviates fingerprints on the bowl. Why? Because no cloud must come between your eyes and the fiery heart of the liquid. Are not the margins on book pages similarly meant to obviate the necessity of fingering the type page? Again: the glass is colorless or at the most only faintly tinged in the bowl, because the connoisseur judges wine partly by its color and is impatient of anything that alters it. There are a thousand mannerisms in typography that are as impudent and arbitrary as putting port in tumblers of red or green glass! When a goblet has a base that looks too small for security, it does

18 / 19

All the virtues of the perfect wine glass are paralleled in typography. There is the long, thin stem that obviates fingerprints on the bowl. Why? Because no cloud must come between your eyes and the fiery heart of the liquid. Are not the margins on book pages similarly meant to obviate the necessity of fingering the type page? Again: the glass is colorless or at the most only faintly tinged in the bowl, because the connoisseur judges wine partly by

24 / 24

All the virtues of the perfect wine glass are paralleled in typography. There is the long, thin stem that obviates fingerprints on the bowl. Why? Because no cloud must come between your eyes and the fiery heart of the liquid. Are not the margins on book

36 / 36

All the virtues of the perfect wine glass are paralleled in typography. There is the long, thin stem that obviates finge

Monotype Centaur Italic

6 / 7

All the virtues of the perfect wine glass are paralleled in typography. There is the long, thin stem that obviates fingerprints on the bowl. Why? Because no cloud must come between your eyes and the fiery heart of the liquid. Are not the margins on book pages similarly meant to obviate the necessity of fingering the type page? Again: the glass is colorless or at the most only faintly tinged in the bowl, because the connoisseur judges wine partly by its color and is impatient of anything that alters it. There are a thousand mannerisms in typography that are as impudent and arbitrary as putting port in tumblers of red or green glass! When a goblet has a base that looks too small for security, it does not matter how cleverly it is weighted; you feel nervous lest it should tip over. There are ways of setting lines of type which may work well enough, and yet keep the reader subconsciously worried by the fear of "doubling" lines, reading three words as one, and so forth. Now the man who first chose glass instead of clay or metal to hold his wine was a "modernist" in the sense in which I am going to use that term. That is, the first thing he asked of this particular object was not "How should it look?" but "What must it do?" and to that extent all good typography is modernist. Wine is so strange and potent a thing that it has been used in the central ritual of religion in one place and time, and attacked by a virago with a hatchet in another. There is only one other thing in the world that is capable of stirring and altering men's minds to the same extent, and that is the coherent expression of thought. That is man's chief miracle, unique to man. There is no "explanation" whatever of the fact that I can make arbitrary sounds which will lead a total stranger to think my own thought. It is sheer magic that I should be able to hold a one-sided conversation by means

8 / 9

All the virtues of the perfect wine glass are paralleled in typography. There is the long, thin stem that obviates fingerprints on the bowl. Why? Because no cloud must come between your eyes and the fiery heart of the liquid. Are not the margins on book pages similarly meant to obviate the necessity of fingering the type page? Again: the glass is colorless or at the most only faintly tinged in the bowl, because the connoisseur judges wine partly by its color and is impatient of anything that alters it. There are a thousand mannerisms in typography that are as impudent and arbitrary as putting port in tumblers of red or green glass! When a goblet has a base that looks too small for security, it does not matter how cleverly it is weighted; you feel nervous lest it should tip over. There are ways of setting lines of type which may work well enough, and yet keep the reader subconsciously worried by the fear of "doubling" lines, reading three words as one, and so forth. Now the man who first chose glass instead of clay or metal to hold his wine was a "modernist" in the sense in which I am

10 / 11

All the virtues of the perfect wine glass are paralleled in typography. There is the long, thin stem that obviates fingerprints on the bowl. Why? Because no cloud must come between your eyes and the fiery heart of the liquid. Are not the margins on book pages similarly meant to obviate the necessity of fingering the type page? Again: the glass is colorless or at the most only faintly tinged in the bowl, because the connoisseur judges wine partly by its color and is impatient of anything that alters it. There are a thousand mannerisms in typography that are as impudent and arbitrary as putting port in tumblers of red or green glass! When a goblet has a base that looks too small for security, it does not matter how cleverly it is weighted;

12 / 13

All the virtues of the perfect wine glass are paralleled in typography. There is the long, thin stem that obviates fingerprints on the bowl. Why? Because no cloud must come between your eyes and the fiery heart of the liquid. Are not the margins on book pages similarly meant to obviate the necessity of fingering the type page? Again: the glass is colorless or at the most only faintly tinged in the bowl, because the connoisseur judges wine partly by its color and is impatient of anything that alters it. There are a thousand mannerisms

14 / 15

All the virtues of the perfect wine glass are paralleled in typography. There is the long, thin stem that obviates fingerprints on the bowl. Why? Because no cloud must come between your eyes and the fiery heart of the liquid. Are not the margins on book pages similarly meant to obviate the necessity of fingering the type page? Again: the glass is colorless or at the most only faintly tinged in the bowl, because the connoisseur judges wine partly by its color and is impatient of anything that alters it. There are a thousand mannerisms in typography that are as impudent and arbitrary as putting port in tumblers of red or green glass! When a goblet has a base that looks too small for security, it does not matter how cleverly it is weighted; you feel nervous lest it should tip over. There are ways of setting lines of type which may work well enough, and yet keep the reader subconsciously wor

18 / 19

All the virtues of the perfect wine glass are paralleled in typography. Th ere is the long, thin stem that obviates fingerprints on the bowl. Why? Because no cloud must come between your eyes and the fiery heart of the liquid. Are not the margins on book pages similarly meant to obvi ate the necessity of fingering the type page? Again: the glass is colorless or at the most only faintly tinged in the bowl, because the connoisseur judges wine partly by its color and is impatient of anything that alters it. There are a thousand mannerisms in typography that are as impu

24 / 24

All the virtues of the perfect wine glass are paralleled in typography. There is the long, thin stem that obvia tes fingerprints on the bowl. Why? Because no cloud must come between your eyes and the fiery heart of the liquid. Are not the margins on book pages simi larly meant to obviate the necessity of fingering the

36 / 36

All the virtues of the perfect wine gla ss are paralleled in typography. There is the long, thin stem that obviates fi ngerprints on the bowl. Why? Beca

Monotype Centaur Bold

6 / 7

All the virtues of the perfect wine glass are paralleled in typography. There is the long, thin stem that obviates fingerprints on the bowl. Why? Because no cloud must come between your eyes and the fiery heart of the liquid. Are not the margins on book pages similarly meant to obviate the necessity of fingering the type page? Again: the glass is colorless or at the most only faintly tinged in the bowl, because the connoisseur judges wine partly by its color and is impatient of anything that alters it. There are a thousand mannerisms in typography that are as impudent and arbitrary as putting port in tumblers of red or green glass! When a goblet has a base that looks too small for security, it does not matter how cleverly it is weighted; you feel nervous lest it should tip over. There are ways of setting lines of type which may work well enough, and yet keep the reader subconsciously worried by the fear of "doubling" lines, reading three words as one, and so forth. Now the man who first chose glass instead of clay or metal to hold his wine was a "modernist" in the sense in which I am going to use that term. That is, the first thing he asked of this particular object was not "How should it look?" but "What must it do?" and to that extent all good typography is modernist. Wine is so strange and potent a thing that it has been used in the central ritual of religion in one place and time, and attacked by a virago with a hatchet in another. There is only

8 / 9

All the virtues of the perfect wine glass are paralleled in typography. There is the long, thin stem that obviates fingerprints on the bowl. Why? Because no cloud must come between your eyes and the fiery heart of the liquid. Are not the margins on book pages similarly meant to obviate the necessity of fingering the type page? Again: the glass is colorless or at the most only faintly tinged in the bowl, because the connoisseur judges wine partly by its color and is impatient of anything that alters it. There are a thousand mannerisms in typography that are as impudent and arbitrary as putting port in tumblers of red or green glass! When a goblet has a base that looks too small for security, it does not matter how cleverly it is weighted; you feel nervous lest it should tip over. There are ways of setting lines of type which may work well enough, and yet

10 / 11

All the virtues of the perfect wine glass are paralleled in typography. There is the long, thin stem that obviates fingerprints on the bowl. Why? Because no cloud must come between your eyes and the fiery heart of the liquid. Are not the margins on book pages similarly meant to obviate the necessity of fingering the type page? Again: the glass is colorless or at the most only faintly tinged in the bowl, because the connoisseur judges wine partly by its color and is impatient of anything that alters it. There are a thousand mannerisms in typography that are as impu

12 / 13

All the virtues of the perfect wine glass are paralleled in typography. There is the long, thin stem that obviates fingerprints on the bowl. Why? Because no cloud must come between your eyes and the fiery heart of the liquid. Are not the margins on book pages similarly meant to obviate the necessity of fingering the type page? Again: the glass is colorless or at the most only y faintly tinged in the bowl, because

14 / 15

All the virtues of the perfect wine glass are paralleled in typography. There is the long, thin stem that obviates fingerprints on the bowl. Why? Because no cloud must come between your eyes and the fiery heart of the liquid. Are not the margins on book pages similarly meant to obviate the necessity of fingering the type page? Again: the glass is colorless or at the most only faintly tinged in the bowl, because the connoisseur judges wine partly by its color and is impatient of anything that alters it. There are a thousand mannerisms in typography that are as impudent and arbitrary as putting port in tumblers of red or green glass! When a goblet has a base that looks too small

18 / 19

All the virtues of the perfect wine glass are paralleled in typography. There is the long, thin stem that obviates fingerprints on the bowl. Why? Because no cloud must come between your eyes and the fiery heart of the liquid. Are not the margins on book pages similarly meant to obviate the necessity of fingering the type page? Again: the glass is colorless or at the most only faintly tinged in the bowl, because the connoisseur

24 / 24

All the virtues of the perfect wine glass are paralleled in typography. There is the long, thin stem that obviates fingerprints on the bowl. Why? Because no cloud must come between your eyes and the fiery heart of the liquid. Are not the margi

36 / 36

All the virtues of the perfect wine glass are paralleled in typography. There is the long, thin stem that obviat

Monotype Centaur Bold Italic

6 / 7

All the virtues of the perfect wine glass are paralleled in typography. There is the long, thin stem that obviates fingerprints on the bowl. Why? Because no cloud must come between your eyes and the fiery heart of the liquid. Are not the margins on book pages similarly meant to obviate the necessity of fingering the type page? Again: the glass is colorless or at the most only faintly tinged in the bowl, because the connoisseur judges wine partly by its color and is impatient of anything that alters it. There are a thousand mannerisms in typography that are as impudent and arbitrary as putting port in tumblers of red or green glass! When a goblet has a base that looks too small for security, it does not matter how cleverly it is weighted; you feel nervous lest it should tip over. There are ways of setting lines of type which may work well enough, and yet keep the reader subconsciously worried by the fear of "doubling" lines, reading three words as one, and so forth. Now the man who first chose glass instead of clay or metal to hold his wine was a "modernist" in the sense in which I am going to use that term. That is, the first thing be asked of this particular object was not "How should it look?" but "What must it do?" and to that extent all good typography is modernist. Wine is so strange and potent a thing that it has been used in the central ritual of religion in one place and time, and attacked by a virago with a hatchet in another. There is only one other thing in the world that is capable of stirring and altering men's minds to the same extent, and that is the coherent expression of thought. That is man's chief miracle, unique to man. There is no "explanation" whatever of the fact that I can make arbitrary

8 / 9

All the virtues of the perfect wine glass are paralleled in typography. There is the long, thin stem that obviates fingerprints on the bowl. Why? Because no cloud must come between your eyes and the fiery heart of the liquid. Are not the margins on book pages similarly meant to obviate the necessity of fingering the type page? Again: the glass is colorless or at the most only faintly tinged in the bowl, because the connoisseur judges wine partly by its color and is impatient of anything that alters it. There are a thousand mannerisms in typography that are as impudent and arbitrary as putting port in tumblers of red or green glass! When a goblet has a base that looks too small for security, it does not matter how cleverly it is weighted; you feel nervous lest it should tip over. There are ways of setting lines of type which may work well enough, and yet keep the reader subconsciously worried by the fear of "doubling" lines, reading three words as one, and so forth. Now the man who first chose glass instead of clay or metal to

10 / 11

All the virtues of the perfect wine glass are paralleled in typography. There is the long, thin stem that obviates fingerprints on the bowl. Why? Because no cloud must come between your eyes and the fiery heart of the liquid. Are not the margins on book pages similarly meant to obviate the necessity of fingering the type page? Again: the glass is colorless or at the most only faintly tinged in the bowl, because the connoisseur judges wine partly by its color and is impatient of anything that alters it. There are a thousand mannerisms in typography that are as impudent and arbitrary as putting port in tumblers of red or green glass! When a goblet has a base that looks too small for secu

12 / 13

All the virtues of the perfect wine glass are paralleled in typography. There is the long, thin stem that obviates fingerprints on the bowl. Why? Because no cloud must come between your eyes and the fiery heart of the liquid. Are not the margins on book pages similarly meant to obviate the necessity of fingering the type page? Again: the glass is colorless or at the most only faintly tinged in the bowl, because the connoisseur judges wine partly by its color and is impatient of anything that

14 / 15

All the virtues of the perfect wine glass are paralleled in typography. There is the long, thin stem that obviates fingerprints on the bowl. Why? Because no cloud must come between your eyes and the fiery heart of the liquid. Are not the margins on book pages similarly meant to obviate the necessity of fingering the type page? Again: the glass is colorless or at the most only faintly tinged in the bowl, because the connoisseur judges wine partly by its color and is impatient of anything that alters it. There are a thousand mannerisms in typography that are as impudent and arbitrary as putting port in tumblers of red or green glass! When a goblet has a base that looks too small for security, it does not matter how cleverly it is weighted; you feel nervous lest it should tip over. There are ways of setting lines of type

18 / 19

All the virtues of the perfect wine glass are paralleled in typography. There is the long, thin stem that obviates fingerprints on the bowl. Why? Because no cloud must come between your eyes and the fiery heart of the liquid. Are not the margins on book pages similarly meant to obviate the necessity of fingering the type page? Again: the glass is colorless or at the most only faintly tinged in the bowl, because the connoisseur judges wine partly by its color and is impatient of anything that alters it. There are a thousan

24 / 24

All the virtues of the perfect wine glass are paralleled in typography. There is the long, thin stem that obviates fingerprints on the bowl. Why? Because no cloud must come between your eyes and the fiery heart of the liquid. Are not the margins on book pages similarly meant to obviate the necess

36 / 36

All the virtues of the perfect wine glass are paralleled in typography. There is the long, thin stem that obviates fingerprints on the bo

Monotype Centaur (Caps) & Centaur Expert (Small Caps)

6/7

All the virtues of the perfect wine glass are paralleled in typography. There is the long, thin stem that obviates fingerprints on the bowl. Why? Because no cloud must come between your eyes and the fiery heart of the liquid. Are not the margins on book pages similarly meant to obviate the necessity of fingering the type page? Again: the glass is colorless or at the most only faintly tinged in the bowl, because the connoisseur judges wine partly by its color and is impatient of anything that alters it. There are a thousand mannerisms in typography that are as impudent and arbitrary as putting port in tumblers of red or green glass! When a goblet has a base that looks too small for security, it does not matter how cleverly it is weighted; you feel nervous lest it should tip over. There are ways of setting lines of type which may work well enough, and yet keep the reader subconsciously worried by the fear of doubling lines, reading three words as one, and so forth. Now the man who first chose glass instead of clay or metal to hold his wine was a modernist in the sense in which I am going to use that term. That is, the first thing he asked of this particular object was not How should it look? but What must it do? and to that extent all good typography is modernist. Wine is so strange and potent a

8/9

All the virtues of the perfect wine glass are paralleled in typography. There is the long, thin stem that obviates fingerprints on the bowl. Why? Because no cloud must come between your eyes and the fiery heart of the liquid. Are not the margins on book pages similarly meant to obviate the necessity of fingering the type page? Again: the glass is colorless or at the most only faintly tinged in the bowl, because the connoisseur judges wine partly by its color and is impatient of anything that alters it. There are a thousand mannerisms in typography that are as impudent and arbitrary as putting port in tumblers of red or green glass! When a goblet has a base that looks too small for security, it does not matter how cleverly it is weighted; you feel nervous

10/11

All the virtues of the perfect wine glass are paralleled in typography. There is the long, thin stem that obviates fingerprints on the bowl. Why? Because no cloud must come between your eyes and the fiery heart of the liquid. Are not the margins on book pages similarly meant to obviate the necessity of fingering the type page? Again: the glass is colorless or at the most only faintly tinged in the bowl, because the connoisseur judges wine partly by its color and is impatient of anything that alters it

12/13

All the virtues of the perfect wine glass are paralleled in typography. There is the long, thin stem that obviates fingerprints on the bowl. Why? Because no cloud must come between your eyes and the fiery heart of the liquid. Are not the margins on book pages similarly meant to obviate the necessity of fingering the type page? Again: the glass is colorless or at the m

14/15

All the virtues of the perfect wine glass are paralleled in typography. There is the long, thin stem that obviates fingerprints on the bowl. Why? Because no cloud must come between your eyes and the fiery heart of the liquid. Are not the margins on book pages similarly meant to obviate the necessity of fingering the type page? Again: the glass is colorless or at the most only faintly tinged in the bowl, because the connoisseur judges wine partly by its color and is impatient of anything that alters it. There are a thousand mannerisms in typography that are as impudent and arbitrary as putting port in

18/19

All the virtues of the perfect wine glass are paralleled in typography. There is the long, thin stem that obviates fingerprints on the bowl. Why? Because no cloud must come between your eyes and the fiery heart of the liquid. Are not the margins on book pages similarly meant to obviate the necessity of fingering the type page? Again: the glass is colorless or at the most only

24/24

All the virtues of the perfect wine glass are paralleled in typography. There is the long, thin stem that obviates fingerprints on the bowl. Why? Because no cloud must come between your eyes and the fiery heart

36/36

All the virtues of the perfect wine glass are paralleled in typography. There is the long, thin stem

Bembo

AKrf

Monotype Bembo

Foundry:	Monotype Typography
Supplier:	Monotype Typography
Letterform authenticity:	Excellent
Digital outline:	Good
Side bearings:	Good
Kerning:	Fair
Hinting:	Excellent
Expert editions:	Yes
Multiple masters:	No
Family completeness:	Excellent
Formats:	Type 1 / partial TrueType
Platforms:	Mac / PC

Monotype Bembo, Bembo Alternative & Bembo Expert

72 points

ABCDEFGHIJ
KLMNOPQRRS
TUVWXYZ&
1234567890$£
ABCDEFGHIJKLMNO
PQRSTUVWXYZ&!?
abcdefghijklm
nopqrstuvwxyz
1234567890$
fi ff fl ffi ffl ß (!?,.-:;)''

72 points

ABCDEFGHIJ
KLMNOPQRRS
TUVWXYZ&
1234567890$£
abcdefghijklmno
pqrstuvwxyz
1234567890$
fi ff fl ffi ffl ß (!?,.-:;)"

Monotype Bembo Italic, Alternative Italic & Expert Italic

Monotype Bembo

6 / 7

All the virtues of the perfect wine glass are paralleled in typography. There is the long, thin stem that obviates fingerprints on the bowl. Why? Because no cloud must come between your eyes and the fiery heart of the liquid. Are not the margins on book pages similarly meant to obviate the necessity of fingering the type page? Again: the glass is colorless or at the most only faintly tinged in the bowl, because the connoisseur judges wine partly by its color and is impatient of anything that alters it. There are a thousand mannerisms in typography that are as impudent and arbitrary as putting port in tumblers of red or green glass! When a goblet has a base that looks too small for security, it does not matter how cleverly it is weighted; you feel nervous lest it should tip over. There are ways of setting lines of type which may work well enough, and yet keep the reader subconsciously worried by the fear of "doubling" lines, reading three words as one, and so forth. Now the man who first chose glass instead of clay or metal to hold his wine was a "modernist" in the sense in which I am going to use that term. That is, the first thing he asked of this particular object was not "How should it look?" but "What must it do?" and to that extent all good typography is modernist. Wine is so strange and potent a thing that it has been used in the central ritual of religion in one place and time, and attack

8 / 9

All the virtues of the perfect wine glass are paralleled in typography. There is the long, thin stem that obviates fingerprints on the bowl. Why? Because no cloud must come between your eyes and the fiery heart of the liquid. Are not the margins on book pages similarly meant to obviate the necessity of fingering the type page? Again: the glass is colorless or at the most only faintly tinged in the bowl, because the connoisseur judges wine partly by its color and is impatient of anything that alters it. There are a thousand mannerisms in typography that are as impudent and arbitrary as putting port in tumblers of red or green glass! When a goblet has a base that looks too small for security, it does not matter how cleverly it is weighted; you feel nervous lest it should tip over. There are ways of setting lines of type which

10 / 11

All the virtues of the perfect wine glass are paralleled in typography. There is the long, thin stem that obviates fingerprints on the bowl. Why? Because no cloud must come between your eyes and the fiery heart of the liquid. Are not the margins on book pages similarly meant to obviate the necessity of fingering the type page? Again: the glass is colorless or at the most only faintly tinged in the bowl, because the connoisseur judges wine partly by its color and is impatient of anything that alters it. There are a thousand mannerisms in ty

12 / 13

All the virtues of the perfect wine glass are paralleled in typography. There is the long, thin stem that obviates fingerprints on the bowl. Why? Because no cloud must come between your eyes and the fiery heart of the liquid. Are not the margins on book pages similarly meant to obviate the necessity of fingering the type page? Again: the glass is colorless or at the most only faintly ting

14 / 15

All the virtues of the perfect wine glass are paralleled in typography. There is the long, thin stem that obviates fingerprints on the bowl. Why? Because no cloud must come between your eyes and the fiery heart of the liquid. Are not the margins on book pages similarly meant to obviate the necessity of fingering the type page? Again: the glass is colorless or at the most only faintly tinged in the bowl, because the connoisseur judges wine partly by its color and is impatient of anything that alters it. There are a thousand mannerisms in typography that are as impudent and arbitrary as putting port in tumblers of red or green glass! When a go

18 / 19

All the virtues of the perfect wine glass are paralleled in typography. There is the long, thin stem that obviates fingerprints on the bowl. Why? Because no cloud must come between your eyes and the fiery heart of the liquid. Are not the margins on book pages similarly meant to obviate the necessity of fingering the type page? Again: the glass is colorless or at the most only faintly tinged in the bowl, beca

24 / 24

All the virtues of the perfect wine glass are paralleled in typography. There is the long, thin stem that obviates fingerprints on the bowl. Why? Because no cloud must come between your eyes and the fiery heart of the liquid. Ar

36 / 36

All the virtues of the perfect wine glass are paralleled in typography. There is the long, thin stem that o

Monotype Bembo Italic

6 / 7

All the virtues of the perfect wine glass are paralleled in typography. There is the long, thin stem that obviates fingerprints on the bowl. Why? Because no cloud must come between your eyes and the fiery heart of the liquid. Are not the margins on book pages similarly meant to obviate the necessity of fingering the type page? Again: the glass is colorless or at the most only faintly tinged in the bowl, because the connoisseur judges wine partly by its color and is impatient of anything that alters it. There are a thousand mannerisms in typography that are as impudent and arbitrary as putting port in tumblers of red or green glass! When a goblet has a base that looks too small for security, it does not matter how cleverly it is weighted; you feel nervous lest it should tip over. There are ways of setting lines of type which may work well enough, and yet keep the reader subconsciously worried by the fear of "doubling" lines, reading three words as one, and so forth. Now the man who first chose glass instead of clay or metal to hold his wine was a "modernist" in the sense in which I am going to use that term. That is, the first thing he asked of this particular object was not "How should it look?" but "What must it do?" and to that extent all good typography is modernist. Wine is so strange and potent a thing that it has been used in the central ritual of religion in one place and time, and attacked by a virago with a hatchet in another. There is only one other thing in the world that is capable of stirring and altering men's minds to the same extent, and that is the coherent

8 / 9

All the virtues of the perfect wine glass are paralleled in typography. There is the long, thin stem that obviates fingerprints on the bowl. Why? Because no cloud must come between your eyes and the fiery heart of the liquid. Are not the margins on book pages similarly meant to obviate the necessity of fingering the type page? Again: the glass is colorless or at the most only faintly tinged in the bowl, because the connoisseur judges wine partly by its color and is impatient of anything that alters it. There are a thousand mannerisms in typography that are as impudent and arbitrary as putting port in tumblers of red or green glass! When a goblet has a base that looks too small for security, it does not matter how cleverly it is weighted; you feel nervous lest it should tip over. There are ways of setting lines of type which may work well enough, and yet keep the reader subconsciously worried by the fear of "doubling" li

10 / 11

All the virtues of the perfect wine glass are paralleled in typography. There is the long, thin stem that obviates fingerprints on the bowl. Why? Because no cloud must come between your eyes and the fiery heart of the liquid. Are not the margins on book pages similarly meant to obviate the necessity of fingering the type page? Again: the glass is colorless or at the most only faintly tinged in the bowl, because the connoisseur judges wine partly by its color and is impatient of anything that alters it. There are a thousand mannerisms in typography that are as impudent and arbitrary as putting port in tumblers of

12 / 13

All the virtues of the perfect wine glass are paralleled in typography. There is the long, thin stem that obviates fingerprints on the bowl. Why? Because no cloud must come between your eyes and the fiery heart of the liquid. Are not the margins on book pages similarly meant to obviate the necessity of fingering the type page? Again: the glass is colorless or at the most only faintly tinged in the bowl, because the connoisseur judges wine par

14 / 15

All the virtues of the perfect wine glass are paralleled in typography. There is the long, thin stem that obviates fingerprints on the bowl. Why? Because no cloud must come between your eyes and the fiery heart of the liquid. Are not the margins on book pages similarly meant to obviate the necessity of fingering the type page? Again: the glass is colorless or at the most only faintly tinged in the bowl, because the connoisseur judges wine partly by its color and is impatient of anything that alters it. There are a thousand mannerisms in typography that are as impudent and arbitrary as putting port in tumblers of red or green glass! When a goblet has a base that looks too small for security, it does not matter how cleverly it is weighted;

18 / 19

All the virtues of the perfect wine glass are paralleled in typography. There is the long, thin stem that obviates fingerprints on the bowl. Why? Because no cloud must come between your eyes and the fiery heart of the liquid. Are not the margins on book pages similarly meant to obviate the necessity of fingering the type page? Again: the glass is colorless or at the most only faintly tinged in the bowl, because the connoisseur judges wine partly by its color and is

24 / 24

All the virtues of the perfect wine glass are paralleled in typography. There is the long, thin stem that obviates fingerprints on the bowl. Why? Because no cloud must come between your eyes and the fiery heart of the liquid. Are not the thousand manneris

36 / 36

All the virtues of the perfect wine glass are paralleled in typography. There is the long, thin stem that obviates fingerprint

Monotype Bembo Semi Bold

6 / 7

All the virtues of the perfect wine glass are paralleled in typography. There is the long, thin stem that obviates fingerprints on the bowl. Why? Because no cloud must come between your eyes and the fiery heart of the liquid. Are not the margins on book pages similarly meant to obviate the necessity of fingering the type page? Again: the glass is colorless or at the most only faintly tinged in the bowl, because the connoisseur judges wine partly by its color and is impatient of anything that alters it. There are a thousand mannerisms in typography that are as impudent and arbitrary as putting port in tumblers of red or green glass! When a goblet has a base that looks too small for security, it does not matter how cleverly it is weighted; you feel nervous lest it should tip over. There are ways of setting lines of type which may work well enough, and yet keep the reader subconsciously worried by the fear of "doubling" lines, reading three words as one, and so forth. Now the man who first chose glass instead of clay or metal to hold his wine was a "modernist" in the sense in which I am going to use that term. That is, the first thing he asked of this particular object was not "How should it look?" but "What must it do?" and to that extent all good typography is modernist. Wine is so strange and

8 / 9

All the virtues of the perfect wine glass are paralleled in typography. There is the long, thin stem that obviates fingerprints on the bowl. Why? Because no cloud must come between your eyes and the fiery heart of the liquid. Are not the margins on book pages similarly meant to obviate the necessity of fingering the type page? Again: the glass is colorless or at the most only faintly tinged in the bowl, because the connoisseur judges wine partly by its color and is impatient of anything that alters it. There are a thousand mannerisms in typography that are as impudent and arbitrary as putting port in tumblers of red or green glass! When a goblet has a base that looks too small for security, it does not matter how cleverly it is weighted; you feel nervous les

10 / 11

All the virtues of the perfect wine glass are paralleled in typography. There is the long, thin stem that obviates finger prints on the bowl. Why? Because no cloud must come between your eyes and the fiery heart of the liquid. Are not the margins on book pages similarly meant to obviate the necessity of fingering the type page? Again: the glass is colorless or at the most only faintly tinged in the bowl, because the connoisseur judges wine partly by its color and is impatient of anything that alters it. T

12 / 13

All the virtues of the perfect wine glass are paralleled in typography. There is the long, thin stem that obviates fingerprints on the bowl. Why? Because no cloud must come between your eyes and the fiery heart of the liquid. Are not the margins on book pages similarly meant to obviate the necessity of fingering the type page? Again: the glass is colorless or at

14 / 15

All the virtues of the perfect wine glass are paralleled in typography. There is the long, thin stem that obviates fingerprints on the bowl. Why? Because no cloud must come between your eyes and the fiery heart of the liquid. Are not the margins on book pages similarly meant to obviate the necessity of fingering the type page? Again: the glass is colorless or at the most only faintly tinged in the bowl, because the connoisseur judges wine partly by its color and is impatient of anything that alters it. There are a thousand mannerisms in typography that are as impudent and arbitrary as putting port in tum

18 / 19

All the virtues of the perfect wine glass are paralleled in typography. There is the long, thin stem that obviates fingerprints on the bowl. Why? Because no cloud must come between your eyes and the fiery heart of the liquid. Are not the margins on book pages similarly meant to obviate the necessity of fingering the type page? Again: the glass is colorless or at the most o

24 / 24

All the virtues of the perfect wine glass are paralleled in typography. There is the long, thin stem that obviates fingerprints on the bowl. Why? Because no cloud must come between your eyes and the fiery heart of the l

36 / 36

All the virtues of the perfect wine glass are paralleled in typography. There is the long, thin st

Monotype Bembo Semi Bold Italic

6 / 7

All the virtues of the perfect wine glass are paralleled in typography. There is the long, thin stem that obviates fingerprints on the bowl. Why? Because no cloud must come between your eyes and the fiery heart of the liquid. Are not the margins on book pages similarly meant to obviate the necessity of fingering the type page? Again: the glass is colorless or at the most only faintly tinged in the bowl, because the connoisseur judges wine partly by its color and is impatient of anything that alters it. There are a thousand mannerisms in typography that are as impudent and arbitrary as putting port in tumblers of red or green glass! When a goblet has a base that looks too small for security, it does not matter how cleverly it is weighted; you feel nervous lest it should tip over. There are ways of setting lines of type which may work well enough, and yet keep the reader subconsciously worried by the fear of "doubling" lines, reading three words as one, and so forth. Now the man who first chose glass instead of clay or metal to hold his wine was a "modernist" in the sense in which I am going to use that term. That is, the first thing he asked of this particular object was not "How should it look?" but "What must it do?" and to that extent all good typography is modernist. Wine is so strange and potent a thing that it has been used in the central ritual of religion in one place and time, and attacked by a virago with a hatchet in another. There is only one other thin

8 / 9

All the virtues of the perfect wine glass are paralleled in typography. There is the long, thin stem that obviates fingerprints on the bowl. Why? Because no cloud must come between your eyes and the fiery heart of the liquid. Are not the margins on book pages similarly meant to obviate the necessity of fingering the type page? Again: the glass is colorless or at the most only faintly tinged in the bowl, because the connoisseur judges wine partly by its color and is impatient of anything that alters it. There are a thousand mannerisms in typography that are as impudent and arbitrary as putting port in tumblers of red or green glass! When a goblet has a base that looks too small for security, it does not matter how cleverly it is weighted; you feel nervous lest it should tip over. There are ways of setting lines of type which may work well enough, and

10 / 11

All the virtues of the perfect wine glass are paralleled in typography. There is the long, thin stem that obviates fingerprints on the bowl. Why? Because no cloud must come between your eyes and the fiery heart of the liquid. Are not the margins on book pages similarly meant to obviate the necessity of fingering the type page? Again: the glass is colorless or at the most only faintly tinged in the bowl, because the connoisseur judges wine partly by its color and is impatient of anything that alters it. There are a thousand mannerisms in typography that are as impudent and

12 / 13

All the virtues of the perfect wine glass are paralleled in typography. There is the long, thin stem that obviates fingerprints on the bowl. Why? Because no cloud must come between your eyes and the fiery heart of the liquid. Are not the margins on book pages similarly meant to obviate the necessity of fingering the type page? Again: the glass is colorless or at the most only faintly tinged in the bowl, because the co

14 / 15

All the virtues of the perfect wine glass are paralleled in typography. There is the long, thin stem that obviates fingerprints on the bowl. Why? Because no cloud must come between your eyes and the fiery heart of the liquid. Are not the margins on book pages similarly meant to obviate the necessity of fingering the type page? Again: the glass is colorless or at the most only faintly tinged in the bowl, because the connoisseur judges wine partly by its color and is impatient of anything that alters it. There are a thousand mannerisms in typography that are as impudent and arbitrary as putting port in tumblers of red or green glass! When a goblet has a base that looks too small for

18 / 19

All the virtues of the perfect wine glass are paralleled in typography. There is the long, thin stem that obviates fingerprints on the bowl. Why? Because no cloud must come between your eyes and the fiery heart of the liquid. Are not the margins on book pages similarly meant to obviate the necessity of fingering the type page? Again: the glass is colorless or at the most only faintly tinged in the bowl, because the connoisseur judges win

24 / 24

All the virtues of the perfect wine glass are paralleled in typography. There is the long, thin stem that obviates fingerprints on the bowl. Why? Because no cloud must come between your eyes and the fiery heart of the liquid. Are not the thousa

36 / 36

All the virtues of the perfect wine glass are paralleled in typography. There is the long, thin stem that obviate

Monotype Bembo Bold

6 / 7

All the virtues of the perfect wine glass are paralleled in typography. There is the long, thin stem that obviates fingerprints on the bowl. Why? Because no cloud must come between your eyes and the fiery heart of the liquid. Are not the margins on book pages similarly meant to obviate the necessity of fingering the type page? Again: the glass is colorless or at the most only faintly tinged in the bowl, because the connoisseur judges wine partly by its color and is impatient of anything that alters it. There are a thousand mannerisms in typography that are as impudent and arbitrary as putting port in tumblers of red or green glass! When a goblet has a base that looks too small for security, it does not matter how cleverly it is weighted; you feel nervous lest it should tip over. There are ways of setting lines of type which may work well enough, and yet keep the reader subconsciously worried by the fear of "doubling" lines, reading three words as one, and so forth. Now the man who first chose glass instead of clay or metal to hold his wine was a "modernist" in the sense in which I am going to use that term. That is, the first thing he asked of this particular object was not "How should it look?" but "What must it do?" and to that

8 / 9

All the virtues of the perfect wine glass are paralleled in typography. There is the long, thin stem that obviates fingerprints on the bowl. Why? Because no cloud must come between your eyes and the fiery heart of the liquid. Are not the margins on book pages similarly meant to obviate the necessity of fingering the type page? Again: the glass is colorless or at the most only faintly tinged in the bowl, because the connoisseur judges wine partly by its color and is impatient of anything that alters it. There are a thousand mannerisms in typography that are as impudent and arbitrary as putting port in tumblers of red or green glass! When a goblet has a base that looks too small for security, it does not matter how cleverl

10 / 11

All the virtues of the perfect wine glass are paralleled in typography. There is the long, thin stem that obviates fingerprints on the bowl. Why? Because no cloud must come between your eyes and the fiery heart of the liquid. Are not the margins on book pages similarly meant to obviate the necessity of fingering the type page? Again: the glass is colorless or at the most only faintly tinged in the bowl, because the connoisseur judges wine partly by its color and is impatient of anything that alters it. There are a thou

12 / 13

All the virtues of the perfect wine glass are paralleled in typography. There is the long, thin stem that obviates fingerprints on the bowl. Why? Because no cloud must come between your eyes and the fiery heart of the liquid. Are not the margins on book pages similarly meant to obviate the necessity of fingering the type page? Again: the

14 / 15

All the virtues of the perfect wine glass are paralleled in typography. There is the long, thin stem that obviates fingerprints on the bowl. Why? Because no cloud must come between your eyes and the fiery heart of the liquid. Are not the margins on book pages similarly meant to obviate the necessity of fingering the type page? Again: the glass is colorless or at the most only faintly tinged in the bowl, because the connoisseur judges wine partly by its color and is impatient of anything that alters it. There are a thousand mannerisms in typography that are as impud

18 / 19

All the virtues of the perfect wine glass are paralleled in typography. There is the long, thin stem that obviates fingerprints on the bowl. Why? Because no cloud must come between your eyes and the fiery heart of the liquid. Are not the margins on book pages similarly meant to obviate the necessity of fingering the type page? Again: the glass is colorless or a

24 / 24

All the virtues of the perfect wine glass are paralleled in typography. There is the long, thin stem that obviates fingerprints on the bowl. Why? Because no cloud must come between your eyes and the

36 / 36

All the virtues of the perfect wine glass are paralleled in typography. There is the long, thi

Monotype Bembo Bold Italic

6 / 7

All the virtues of the perfect wine glass are paralleled in typography. There is the long, thin stem that obviates fingerprints on the bowl. Why? Because no cloud must come between your eyes and the fiery heart of the liquid. Are not the margins on book pages similarly meant to obviate the necessity of fingering the type page? Again: the glass is colorless or at the most only faintly tinged in the bowl, because the connoisseur judges wine partly by its color and is impatient of anything that alters it. There are a thousand mannerisms in typography that are as impudent and arbitrary as putting port in tumblers of red or green glass! When a goblet has a base that looks too small for security, it does not matter how cleverly it is weighted; you feel nervous lest it should tip over. There are ways of setting lines of type which may work well enough, and yet keep the reader subconsciously worried by the fear of "doubling" lines, reading three words as one, and so forth. Now the man who first chose glass instead of clay or metal to hold his wine was a "modernist" in the sense in which I am going to use that term. That is, the first thing he asked of this particular object was not "How should it look?" but "What must it do?" and to that extent all good typography is modernist. Wine is so strange and potent a thing that it has been used in the central ritual of religion in one place and time, and attacked by a virago with a hatchet

8 / 9

All the virtues of the perfect wine glass are paralleled in typography. There is the long, thin stem that obviates fingerprints on the bowl. Why? Because no cloud must come between your eyes and the fiery heart of the liquid. Are not the margins on book pages similarly meant to obviate the necessity of fingering the type page? Again: the glass is colorless or at the most only faintly tinged in the bowl, because the connoisseur judges wine partly by its color and is impatient of anything that alters it. There are a thousand mannerisms in typography that are as impudent and arbitrary as putting port in tumblers of red or green glass! When a goblet has a base that looks too small for security, it does not matter how cleverly it is weighted; you feel nervous lest it should tip over. There are ways of setting lines of type which may work well enou

10 / 11

All the virtues of the perfect wine glass are paralleled in typography. There is the long, thin stem that obviates fingerprints on the bowl. Why? Because no cloud must come between your eyes and the fiery heart of the liquid. Are not the margins on book pages similarly meant to obviate the necessity of fingering the type page? Again: the glass is colorless or at the most only faintly tinged in the bowl, because the connoisseur judges wine partly by its color and is impatient of anything that alters it. There are a thousand mannerisms in typography that are as impudent and arbitrary as putting port in

12 / 13

All the virtues of the perfect wine glass are paralleled in typography. There is the long, thin stem that obviates fingerprints on the bowl. Why? Because no cloud must come between your eyes and the fiery heart of the liquid. Are not the margins on book pages similarly meant to obviate the necessity of fingering the type page? Again: the glass is colorless or at the most only faintly tinged in the bowl, bec

14 / 15

All the virtues of the perfect wine glass are paralleled in typography. There is the long, thin stem that obviates fingerprints on the bowl. Why? Because no cloud must come between your eyes and the fiery heart of the liquid. Are not the margins on book pages similarly meant to obviate the necessity of fingering the type page? Again: the glass is colorless or at the most only faintly tinged in the bowl, because the connoisseur judges wine partly by its color and is impatient of anything that alters it. There are a thousand mannerisms in typography that are as impudent and arbitrary as putting port in tumblers of red or green glass! When a goblet has a base that loo

18 / 19

All the virtues of the perfect wine glass are paralleled in typography. There is the long, thin stem that obviates fingerprints on the bowl. Why? Because no cloud must come between your eyes and the fiery heart of the liquid. Are not the margins on book pages similarly meant to obviate the necessity of fingering the type page? Again: the glass is colorless or at the most only faintly tinged in the bowl, because the connoiss

24 / 24

All the virtues of the perfect wine glass are paralleled in typography. There is the long, thin stem that obviates fingerprints on the bowl. Why? Because no cloud must come between your eyes and the fiery heart of the liquid. Are not the tho

36 / 36

All the virtues of the perfect wine glass are paralleled in typography. There is the long, thin stem that obviates fi

MONOTYPE BEMBO (CAPS) & BEMBO EXPERT (SMALL CAPS)

6/7

ALL THE VIRTUES OF THE PERFECT WINE GLASS ARE PARALLELED IN TYPOGRAPHY. THERE IS THE LONG, THIN STEM THAT OBVIATES FINGERPRINTS ON THE BOWL. WHY? BECAUSE NO CLOUD MUST COME BETWEEN YOUR EYES AND THE FIERY HEART OF THE LIQUID. ARE NOT THE MARGINS ON BOOK PAGES SIMILARLY MEANT TO OBVIATE THE NECESSITY OF FINGERING THE TYPE PAGE? AGAIN: THE GLASS IS COLORLESS OR AT THE MOST ONLY FAINTLY TINGED IN THE BOWL, BECAUSE THE CONNOISSEUR JUDGES WINE PARTLY BY ITS COLOR AND IS IMPATIENT OF ANYTHING THAT ALTERS IT. THERE ARE A THOUSAND MANNERISMS IN TYPOGRAPHY THAT ARE AS IMPUDENT AND ARBITRARY AS PUTTING PORT IN TUMBLERS OF RED OR GREEN GLASS! WHEN A GOBLET HAS A BASE THAT LOOKS TOO SMALL FOR SECURITY, IT DOES NOT MATTER HOW CLEVERLY IT IS WEIGHTED; YOU FEEL NERVOUS LEST IT SHOULD TIP OVER. THERE ARE WAYS OF SETTING LINES OF TYPE WHICH MAY WORK WELL ENOUGH, AND YET KEEP THE READER SUBCONSCIOUSLY WORRIED BY THE FEAR OF DOUBLING LINES, READING THREE WORDS AS ONE, AND SO FORTH. NOW THE MAN WHO FIRST CHOSE GLASS INSTEAD OF CLAY OR METAL TO HOLD HIS WINE WAS A MODERNIST IN THE SENSE IN WHICH I AM GOING TO USE THAT TERM. THAT IS, THE FIRST THING HE ASKED OF THIS PARTICULAR OBJECT WAS NOT HOW SHOULD IT LOOK? BUT W

8/9

ALL THE VIRTUES OF THE PERFECT WINE GLASS ARE PARALLELED IN TYPOGRAPHY. THERE IS THE LONG, THIN STEM THAT OBVIATES FINGERPRINTS ON THE BOWL. WHY? BECAUSE NO CLOUD MUST COME BETWEEN YOUR EYES AND THE FIERY HEART OF THE LIQUID. ARE NOT THE MARGINS ON BOOK PAGES SIMILARLY MEANT TO OBVIATE THE NECESSITY OF FINGERING THE TYPE PAGE? AGAIN: THE GLASS IS COLORLESS OR AT THE MOST ONLY FAINTLY TINGED IN THE BOWL, BECAUSE THE CONNOISSEUR JUDGES WINE PARTLY BY ITS COLOR AND IS IMPATIENT OF ANYTHING THAT ALTERS IT. THERE ARE A THOUSAND MANNERISMS IN TYPOGRAPHY THAT ARE AS IMPUDENT AND ARBITRARY AS PUTTING PORT IN TUMBLERS OF RED OR GREEN GLASS! WHEN A GOBLET HAS A BASE THAT LOOKS TOO SMALL FOR SECURITY, IT DOES NO

10/11

ALL THE VIRTUES OF THE PERFECT WINE GLASS ARE PARALLELED IN TYPOGRAPHY. THERE IS THE LONG, THIN STEM THAT OBVIATES FINGERPRINTS ON THE BOWL. WHY? BECAUSE NO CLOUD MUST COME BETWEEN YOUR EYES AND THE FIERY HEART OF THE LIQUID. ARE NOT THE MARGINS ON BOOK PAGES SIMILARLY MEANT TO OBVIATE THE NECESSITY OF FINGERING THE TYPE PAGE? AGAIN: THE GLASS IS COLORLESS OR AT THE MOST ONLY FAINTLY TINGED IN THE BOWL, BECAUSE THE CONNOISSEUR JUDGES WINE PARTLY BY ITS COLOR A

12/13

ALL THE VIRTUES OF THE PERFECT WINE GLASS ARE PARALLELED IN TYPOGRAPHY. THERE IS THE LONG, THIN STEM THAT OBVIATES FINGERPRINTS ON THE BOWL. WHY? BECAUSE NO CLOUD MUST COME BETWEEN YOUR EYES AND THE FIERY HEART OF THE LIQUID. ARE NOT THE MARGINS ON BOOK PAGES SIMILARLY MEANT TO OBVIATE THE NECESSITY OF FINGERING THE TYPE PAGE? AGA

14/15

ALL THE VIRTUES OF THE PERFECT WINE GLASS ARE PARALLELED IN TYPOGRAPHY. THERE IS THE LONG, THIN STEM THAT OBVIATES FINGERPRINTS ON THE BOWL. WHY? BECAUSE NO CLOUD MUST COME BETWEEN YOUR EYES AND THE FIERY HEART OF THE LIQUID. ARE NOT THE MARGINS ON BOOK PAGES SIMILARLY MEANT TO OBVIATE THE NECESSITY OF FINGERING THE TYPE PAGE? AGAIN: THE GLASS IS COLORLESS OR AT THE MOST ONLY FAINTLY TINGED IN THE BOWL, BECAUSE THE CONNOISSEUR JUDGES WINE PARTLY BY ITS COLOR AND IS IMPATIENT OF ANYTHING THAT ALTERS IT. THERE ARE A THOUSAND MANNERISMS IN TYPOGRAPHY THAT A

18/19

ALL THE VIRTUES OF THE PERFECT WINE GLASS ARE PARALLELED IN TYPOGRAPHY. THERE IS THE LONG, THIN STEM THAT OBVIATES FINGERPRINTS ON THE BOWL. WHY? BECAUSE NO CLOUD MUST COME BETWEEN YOUR EYES AND THE FIERY HEART OF THE LIQUID. ARE NOT THE MARGINS ON BOOK PAGES SIMILARLY MEANT TO OBVIATE THE NECESSITY OF FINGERING THE TYPE PAGE? AGAIN: THE GLA

24/24

ALL THE VIRTUES OF THE PERFECT WINE GLASS ARE PARALLELED IN TYPOGRAPHY. THERE IS THE LONG, THIN STEM THAT OBVIATES FINGERPRINTS ON THE BOWL. WHY? BECAUSE NO CLOUD MUST COME BETWEEN YOUR EYES AND T

36/36

ALL THE VIRTUES OF THE PERFECT WINE GLASS ARE PARALLELED IN TYPOGRAPHY. THERE IS THE LONG, T

Janson

Gj

Monotype Janson

Foundry:	*Monotype Typography*
Supplier:	*Monotype Typography*
Letterform authenticity:	*Excellent*
Digital outline:	*Good*
Side bearings:	*Good*
Kerning:	*Fair*
Hinting:	*Excellent*
Expert editions:	*Yes*
Multiple masters:	*No*
Family completeness:	*Good*
Formats:	*Type 1*
Platforms:	*Mac / PC*

While this digital rendition by Monotype varies a bit from the early metal recuts of this 17th-century typeface, it comes closest to Janson's famed sharpness and clarity.

Monotype Janson & Janson Expert

72 points

ABCDEFGHIJ
KLMNOPQRST
UVWXYZ&
1234567890$£
ABCDEFGHIJKLMNO
PQRSTUVWXYZ&!?
abcdefghijklm
nopqrstuvwxyz
1234567890$
fi ff fl ffi ffl ß (!?,.-:;)"

Monotype Janson Italic & Expert Italic

*ABCDEFGHIJKLM
NOPQRSTUVWX
YZ&1234567890$£
abcdefghijklmnopqrstu
vwxyz1234567890$
fi ff fl ffi ffl ß (!?,.-:;)"*

Monotype Janson

6/7

All the virtues of the perfect wine glass are paralleled in typography. There is the long, thin stem that obviates fingerprints on the bowl. Why? Because no cloud must come between your eyes and the fiery heart of the liquid. Are not the margins on book pages similarly meant to obviate the necessity of fingering the type page? Again: the glass is colorless or at the most only faintly tinged in the bowl, because the connoisseur judges wine partly by its color and is impatient of anything that alters it. There are a thousand mannerisms in typography that are as impudent and arbitrary as putting port in tumblers of red or green glass! When a goblet has a base that looks too small for security, it does not matter how cleverly it is weighted; you feel nervous lest it should tip over. There are ways of setting lines of type which may work well enough, and yet keep the reader subconsciously worried by the fear of "doubling" lines, reading three words as one, and so forth. Now the man who first chose glass instead of clay or metal to hold his wine was a "modernist" in the sense in which I am going to use that term. That is, the first thing he asked of this particular object was not "How should it look?" but "What must it do?" and to that extent all good typography is modernist. Wine is so strange and potent a thing that it has been used in the central ritual of religion in one place and time, and attacked by a virago with a

8/9

All the virtues of the perfect wine glass are paralleled in typography. There is the long, thin stem that obviates fingerprints on the bowl. Why? Because no cloud must come between your eyes and the fiery heart of the liquid. Are not the margins on book pages similarly meant to obviate the necessity of fingering the type page? Again: the glass is colorless or at the most only faintly tinged in the bowl, because the connoisseur judges wine partly by its color and is impatient of anything that alters it. There are a thousand mannerisms in typography that are as impudent and arbitrary as putting port in tumblers of red or green glass! When a goblet has a base that looks too small for security, it does not matter how cleverly it is weighted; you feel nervous lest it should tip over. There are ways of setting lines of type which may

10/11

All the virtues of the perfect wine glass are paralleled in typography. There is the long, thin stem that obviates fingerprints on the bowl. Why? Because no cloud must come between your eyes and the fiery heart of the liquid. Are not the margins on book pages similarly meant to obviate the necessity of fingering the type page? Again: the glass is colorless or at the most only faintly tinged in the bowl, because the connoisseur judges wine partly by its color and is impatient of anything that alters it. There are a thousand mannerisms in typography that are as

12/13

All the virtues of the perfect wine glass are paralleled in typography. There is the long, thin stem that obviates fingerprints on the bowl. Why? Because no cloud must come between your eyes and the fiery heart of the liquid. Are not the margins on book pages similarly meant to obviate the necessity of fingering the type page? Again: the glass is colorless or at the most only faintly tinged in the bo

14/15

All the virtues of the perfect wine glass are paralleled in typography. There is the long, thin stem that obviates fingerprints on the bowl. Why? Because no cloud must come between your eyes and the fiery heart of the liquid. Are not the margins on book pages similarly meant to obviate the necessity of fingering the type page? Again: the glass is colorless or at the most only faintly tinged in the bowl, because the connoisseur judges wine partly by its color and is impatient of anything that alters it. There are a thousand mannerisms in typography that are as impudent and arbitrary as putting port in tumblers of red or green glass! When a

18/19

All the virtues of the perfect wine glass are paralleled in typography. There is the long, thin stem that obviates fingerprints on the bowl. Why? Because no cloud must come between your eyes and the fiery heart of the liquid. Are not the margins on book pages similarly meant to obviate the necessity of fingering the type page? Again: the glass is colorless or at the most only faintly tinged in the bowl, because

24/24

All the virtues of the perfect wine glass are paralleled in typography. There is the long, thin stem that obviates fingerprints on the bowl. Why? Because no cloud must come between your eyes and the fiery heart of the liquid. Are no

36/36

All the virtues of the perfect wine glass are paralleled in typography. There is the long, thin stem that obv

Monotype Janson Italic

6 / 7

All the virtues of the perfect wine glass are paralleled in typography. There is the long, thin stem that obviates fingerprints on the bowl. Why? Because no cloud must come between your eyes and the fiery heart of the liquid. Are not the margins on book pages similarly meant to obviate the necessity of fingering the type page? Again: the glass is colorless or at the most only faintly tinged in the bowl, because the connoisseur judges wine partly by its color and is impatient of anything that alters it. There are a thousand mannerisms in typography that are as impudent and arbitrary as putting port in tumblers of red or green glass! When a goblet has a base that looks too small for security, it does not matter how cleverly it is weighted; you feel nervous lest it should tip over. There are ways of setting lines of type which may work well enough, and yet keep the reader subconsciously worried by the fear of "doubling" lines, reading three words as one, and so forth. Now the man who first chose glass instead of clay or metal to hold his wine was a "modernist" in the sense in which I am going to use that term. That is, the first thing to be asked of this particular object was not "How should it look?" but "What must it do?" and to that extent all good typography is modernist. Wine is so strange and potent a thing that it has been used in the central ritual of religion in one place and time, and attacked by a virago with a hatchet in another. There is only one other thing in the world that is capable of stirring and altering men's minds to the same extent, and that is the coherent expression of thought. That is man's chief miracle, unique to man. There

8 / 9

All the virtues of the perfect wine glass are paralleled in typography. There is the long, thin stem that obviates fingerprints on the bowl. Why? Because no cloud must come between your eyes and the fiery heart of the liquid. Are not the margins on book pages similarly meant to obviate the necessity of fingering the type page? Again: the glass is colorless or at the most only faintly tinged in the bowl, because the connoisseur judges wine partly by its color and is impatient of anything that alters it. There are a thousand mannerisms in typography that are as impudent and arbitrary as putting port in tumblers of red or green glass! When a goblet has a base that looks too small for security, it does not matter how cleverly it is weighted; you feel nervous lest it should tip over. There are ways of setting lines of type which may work well enough, and yet keep the reader subconsciously worried by the fear of "doubling" lines, reading three words as one, and so forth. Now

10 / 11

All the virtues of the perfect wine glass are paralleled in typography. There is the long, thin stem that obviates fingerprints on the bowl. Why? Because no cloud must come between your eyes and the fiery heart of the liquid. Are not the margins on book pages similarly meant to obviate the necessity of fingering the type page? Again: the glass is colorless or at the most only faintly tinged in the bowl, because the connoisseur judges wine partly by its color and is impatient of anything that alters it. There are a thousand mannerisms in typography that are as impudent and arbitrary as putting port in tumblers of red or green glass! When a goblet has a

12 / 13

All the virtues of the perfect wine glass are paralleled in typography. There is the long, thin stem that obviates fingerprints on the bowl. Why? Because no cloud must come between your eyes and the fiery heart of the liquid. Are not the margins on book pages similarly meant to obviate the necessity of fingering the type page? Again: the glass is colorless or at the most only faintly tinged in the bowl, because the connoisseur judges wine partly by its color an

14 / 15

All the virtues of the perfect wine glass are paralleled in typography. There is the long, thin stem that obviates fingerprints on the bowl. Why? Because no cloud must come between your eyes and the fiery heart of the liquid. Are not the margins on book pages similarly meant to obviate the necessity of fingering the type page? Again: the glass is colorless or at the most only faintly tinged in the bowl, because the connoisseur judges wine partly by its color and is impatient of anything that alters it. There are a thousand mannerisms in typography that are as impudent and arbitrary as putting port in tumblers of red or green glass! When a goblet has a base that looks too small for security, it does not matter how cleverly it is weighted; you feel nervous lest it

18 / 19

All the virtues of the perfect wine glass are paralleled in typography. There is the long, thin stem that obviates fingerprints on the bowl. Why? Because no cloud must come between your eyes and the fiery heart of the liquid. Are not the margins on book pages similarly meant to obviate the necessity of fingering the type page? Again: the glass is colorless or at the most only faintly tinged in the bowl, because the connoisseur judges wine partly by its color and is impatient of

24 / 24

All the virtues of the perfect wine glass are paralleled in typography. There is the long, thin stem that obviates fingerprints on the bowl. Why? Because no cloud must come between your eyes and the fiery heart of the liquid. Are not the margins on book pages similarly me

36 / 36

All the virtues of the perfect wine glass are paralleled in typography. There is the long, thin stem that obviates fingerprints o

Monotype Janson Bold

6 / 7

All the virtues of the perfect wine glass are paralleled in typography. There is the long, thin stem that obviates fingerprints on the bowl. Why? Because no cloud must come between your eyes and the fiery heart of the liquid. Are not the margins on book pages similarly meant to obviate the necessity of fingering the type page? Again: the glass is colorless or at the most only faintly tinged in the bowl, because the connoisseur judges wine partly by its color and is impatient of anything that alters it. There are a thousand mannerisms in typography that are as impudent and arbitrary as putting port in tumblers of red or green glass! When a goblet has a base that looks too small for security, it does not matter how cleverly it is weighted; you feel nervous lest it should tip over. There are ways of setting lines of type which may work well enough, and yet keep the reader subconsciously worried by the fear of "doubling" lines, reading three words as one, and so forth. Now the man who first chose glass instead of clay or metal to hold his wine was a "modernist" in the sense in which I am going to use that term. That is, the first thing he asked of this particular object was not "How should it look?" but "What must it do?" and to that extent all good typography is modernist. Wine is so strange and potent a thing that it

8 / 9

All the virtues of the perfect wine glass are paralleled in typography. There is the long, thin stem that obviates fingerprints on the bowl. Why? Because no cloud must come between your eyes and the fiery heart of the liquid. Are not the margins on book pages similarly meant to obviate the necessity of fingering the type page? Again: the glass is colorless or at the most only faintly tinged in the bowl, because the connoisseur judges wine partly by its color and is impatient of anything that alters it. There are a thousand mannerisms in typography that are as impudent and arbitrary as putting port in tumblers of red or green glass! When a goblet has a base that looks too small for security, it does not matter how cleverly it is weighted; you feel nervous lest it should tip over. There are

10 / 11

All the virtues of the perfect wine glass are paralleled in typography. There is the long, thin stem that obviates fingerprints on the bowl. Why? Because no cloud must come between your eyes and the fiery heart of the liquid. Are not the margins on book pages similarly meant to obviate the necessity of fingering the type page? Again: the glass is colorless or at the most only faintly tinged in the bowl, because the connoisseur judges wine partly by its color and is impatient of anything that alters it. There are a thousand manneris

12 / 13

All the virtues of the perfect wine glass are paralleled in typography. There is the long, thin stem that obviates fingerprints on the bowl. Why? Because no cloud must come between your eyes and the fiery heart of the liquid. Are not the margins on book pages similarly meant to obviate the necessity of fingering the type page? Again: the glass is colorless or at the mos

14 / 15

All the virtues of the perfect wine glass are paralleled in typography. There is the long, thin stem that obviates fingerprints on the bowl. Why? Because no cloud must come between your eyes and the fiery heart of the liquid. Are not the margins on book pages similarly meant to obviate the necessity of fingering the type page? Again: the glass is colorless or at the most only faintly tinged in the bowl, because the connoisseur judges wine partly by its color and is impatient of anything that alters it. There are a thousand mannerisms in typography that are as impudent and arbitrary as putting port in tumblers of red

18 / 19

All the virtues of the perfect wine glass are paralleled in typography. There is the long, thin stem that obviates fingerprints on the bowl. Why? Because no cloud must come between your eyes and the fiery heart of the liquid. Are not the margins on book pages similarly meant to obviate the necessity of fingering the type page? Again: the glass is colorless or at the most only faintly

24 / 24

All the virtues of the perfect wine glass are paralleled in typography. There is the long, thin stem that obviates fingerprints on the bowl. Why? Because no cloud must come between your eyes and the fiery heart of the l

36 / 36

All the virtues of the perfect wine glass are paralleled in typography. There is the long, thin stem th

Monotype Janson Bold Italic

6 / 7

All the virtues of the perfect wine glass are paralleled in typography. There is the long, thin stem that obviates fingerprints on the bowl. Why? Because no cloud must come between your eyes and the fiery heart of the liquid. Are not the margins on book pages similarly meant to obviate the necessity of fingering the type page? Again: the glass is colorless or at the most only faintly tinged in the bowl, because the connoisseur judges wine partly by its color and is impatient of anything that alters it. There are a thousand mannerisms in typography that are as impudent and arbitrary as putting port in tumblers of red or green glass! When a goblet has a base that looks too small for security, it does not matter how cleverly it is weighted; you feel nervous lest it should tip over. There are ways of setting lines of type which may work well enough, and yet keep the reader subconsciously worried by the fear of "doubling" lines, reading three words as one, and so forth. Now the man who first chose glass instead of clay or metal to hold his wine was a "modernist" in the sense in which I am going to use that term. That is, the first thing he asked of this particular object was not "How should it look?" but "What must it do?" and to that extent all good typography is modernist. Wine is so strange and potent a thing that it has been used in the central ritual of religion in one place and time, and attacked by a virago with a hatchet in another. There is only one other

8 / 9

All the virtues of the perfect wine glass are paralleled in typography. There is the long, thin stem that obviates fingerprints on the bowl. Why? Because no cloud must come between your eyes and the fiery heart of the liquid. Are not the margins on book pages similarly meant to obviate the necessity of fingering the type page? Again: the glass is colorless or at the most only faintly tinged in the bowl, because the connoisseur judges wine partly by its color and is impatient of anything that alters it. There are a thousand mannerisms in typography that are as impudent and arbitrary as putting port in tumblers of red or green glass! When a goblet has a base that looks too small for security, it does not matter how cleverly it is weighted; you feel nervous lest it should tip over. There are ways of setting lines of type which may work well enough, and yet keep the

10 / 11

All the virtues of the perfect wine glass are paralleled in typography. There is the long, thin stem that obviates fingerprints on the bowl. Why? Because no cloud must come between your eyes and the fiery heart of the liquid. Are not the margins on book pages similarly meant to obviate the necessity of fingering the type page? Again: the glass is colorless or at the most only faintly tinged in the bowl, because the connoisseur judges wine partly by its color and is impatient of anything that alters it. There are a thousand mannerisms in typography that are as impudent and arbitrary as put

12 / 13

All the virtues of the perfect wine glass are paralleled in typography. There is the long, thin stem that obviates fingerprints on the bowl. Why? Because no cloud must come between your eyes and the fiery heart of the liquid. Are not the margins on book pages similarly meant to obviate the necessity of fingering the type page? Again: the glass is colorless or at the most only faintly tinged in the bowl, because the connoi

14 / 15

All the virtues of the perfect wine glass are paralleled in typography. There is the long, thin stem that obviates fingerprints on the bowl. Why? Because no cloud must come between your eyes and the fiery heart of the liquid. Are not the margins on book pages similarly meant to obviate the necessity of fingering the type page? Again: the glass is colorless or at the most only faintly tinged in the bowl, because the connoisseur judges wine partly by its color and is impatient of anything that alters it. There are a thousand mannerisms in typography that are as impudent and arbitrary as putting port in tumblers of red or green glass! When a goblet has a base that looks too small for secu

18 / 19

All the virtues of the perfect wine glass are paralleled in typography. There is the long, thin stem that obviates fingerprints on the bowl. Why? Because no cloud must come between your eyes and the fiery heart of the liquid. Are not the margins on book pages similarly meant to obviate the necessity of fingering the type page? Again: the glass is colorless or at the most only faintly tinged in the bowl, because the connoisseur judges

24 / 24

All the virtues of the perfect wine glass are paralleled in typography. There is the long, thin stem that obviates fingerprints on the bowl. Why? Because no cloud must come between your eyes and the fiery heart of the liquid. Are not the margi

36 / 36

All the virtues of the perfect wine glass are paralleled in typography. There is the long, thin stem that obviates fi

MONOTYPE JANSON (CAPS) & JANSON EXPERT (SMALL CAPS)

6/7

ALL THE VIRTUES OF THE PERFECT WINE GLASS ARE PARALLELED IN TYPOGRAPHY. THERE IS THE LONG, THIN STEM THAT OBVIATES FINGERPRINTS ON THE BOWL. WHY? BECAUSE NO CLOUD MUST COME BETWEEN YOUR EYES AND THE FIERY HEART OF THE LIQUID. ARE NOT THE MARGINS ON BOOK PAGES SIMILARLY MEANT TO OBVIATE THE NECESSITY OF FINGERING THE TYPE PAGE? AGAIN: THE GLASS IS COLORLESS OR AT THE MOST ONLY FAINTLY TINGED IN THE BOWL, BECAUSE THE CONNOISSEUR JUDGES WINE PARTLY BY ITS COLOR AND IS IMPATIENT OF ANYTHING THAT ALTERS IT. THERE ARE A THOUSAND MANNERISMS IN TYPOGRAPHY THAT ARE AS IMPUDENT AND ARBITRARY AS PUTTING PORT IN TUMBLERS OF RED OR GREEN GLASS! WHEN A GOBLET HAS A BASE THAT LOOKS TOO SMALL FOR SECURITY, IT DOES NOT MATTER HOW CLEVERLY IT IS WEIGHTED; YOU FEEL NERVOUS LEST IT SHOULD TIP OVER. THERE ARE WAYS OF SETTING LINES OF TYPE WHICH MAY WORK WELL ENOUGH, AND YET KEEP THE READER SUBCONSCIOUSLY WORRIED BY THE FEAR OF DOUBLING LINES, READING THREE WORDS AS ONE, AND SO FORTH. NOW THE MAN WHO FIRST CHOSE GLASS INSTEAD OF CLAY OR METAL TO HOLD HIS WINE W AS A MODERNIST IN THE SENSE IN WHICH I AM GOING TO USE THAT TERM. THAT IS, THE FIRST THING HE ASKED OF THIS PARTICULAR OBJECT WAS NOT HOW SHOULD IT LOOK? BUT WHAT MUST IT DO? A

8/9

ALL THE VIRTUES OF THE PERFECT WINE GLASS ARE PARALLELED IN TYPOGRAPHY. THERE IS THE LONG, THIN STEM THAT OBVIATES FINGERPRINTS ON THE BOWL. WHY? BECAUSE NO CLOUD MUST COME BETWEEN YOUR EYES AND THE FIERY HEART OF THE LIQUID. ARE NOT THE MARGINS ON BOOK PAGES SIMILARLY MEANT TO OBVIATE THE NECESSITY OF FINGERING THE TYPE PAGE? AGAIN: THE GLASS IS COLORLESS OR AT THE MOST ONLY FAINTLY TINGED IN THE BOWL, BECAUSE THE CONNOISSEUR JUDGES WINE PARTLY BY ITS COLOR AND IS IMPATIENT OF ANYTHING THAT ALTERS IT. THERE ARE A THOUSAND MANNERISMS IN TYPOGRAPHY THAT ARE AS IMPUDENT AND ARBITRARY AS PUTTING PORT IN TUMBLERS OF RED OR GREEN GLASS! WHEN A GOBLET HAS A BASE THAT LOOKS TOO SMALL FOR SECURITY, IT DOES NOT

10/11

ALL THE VIRTUES OF THE PERFECT WINE GLASS ARE PARALLELED IN TYPOGRAPHY. THERE IS THE LONG, THIN STEM THAT OBVIATES FINGERPRINTS ON THE BOWL. WHY? BECAUSE NO CLOUD MUST COME BETWEEN YOUR EYES AND THE FIERY HEART OF THE LIQUID. ARE NOT THE MARGINS ON BOOK PAGES SIMILARLY MEANT TO OBVIATE THE NECESSITY OF FINGERING THE TYPE PAGE? AGAIN: THE GLASS IS COLORLESS OR AT THE MOST ONLY FAINTLY TINGED IN THE BOWL, BECAUSE THE CONNOISSEUR JUDGES WINE PARTLY BY ITS

12/13

ALL THE VIRTUES OF THE PERFECT WINE GLASS ARE PARALLELED IN TYPOGRAPHY. THERE IS THE LONG, THIN STEM THAT OBVIATES FINGERPRINTS ON THE BOWL. WHY? BECAUSE NO CLOUD MUST COME BETWEEN YOUR EYES AND THE FIERY HEART OF THE LIQUID. ARE NOT THE MARGINS ON BOOK PAGES SIMILARLY MEANT TO OBVIATE THE NECESSITY OF FINGERING THE TYPE PAGE? AGAIN:

14/15

ALL THE VIRTUES OF THE PERFECT WINE GLASS ARE PARALLELED IN TYPOGRAPHY. THERE IS THE LONG, THIN STEM THAT OBVIATES FINGERPRINTS ON THE BOWL. WHY? BECAUSE NO CLOUD MUST COME BETWEEN YOUR EYES AND THE FIERY HEART OF THE LIQUID. ARE NOT THE MARGINS ON BOOK PAGES SIMILARLY MEANT TO OBVIATE THE NECESSITY OF FINGERING THE TYPE PAGE? AGAIN: THE GLASS IS COLORLESS OR AT THE MOST ONLY FAINTLY TINGED IN THE BOWL, BECAUSE THE CONNOISSEUR JUDGES WINE PARTLY BY ITS COLOR AND IS IMPATIENT OF ANYTHING THAT ALTERS IT. THERE ARE A THOUSAND MANNERISMS IN TYPOGRAPHY THAT ARE AS

18/19

ALL THE VIRTUES OF THE PERFECT WINE GLASS ARE PARALLELED IN TYPOGRAPHY. THERE IS THE LONG, THIN STEM THAT OBVIATES FINGERPRINTS ON THE BOWL. WHY? BECAUSE NO CLOUD MUST COME BETWEEN YOUR EYES AND THE FIERY HEART OF THE LIQUID. ARE NOT THE MARGINS ON BOOK PAGES SIMILARLY MEANT TO OBVIATE THE NECESSITY OF FINGERING THE TYPE PAGE? AGAIN: THE GLA

24/24

ALL THE VIRTUES OF THE PERFECT WINE GLASS ARE PARALLELED IN TYPOGRAPHY. THERE IS THE LONG, THIN STEM THAT OBVIATES FINGERPRINTS ON THE BOWL. WHY? BECAUSE NO CLOUD MUST COME BETWEEN YOUR EYES AND TH

36/36

ALL THE VIRTUES OF THE PERFECT WINE GLASS ARE PARALLELED IN TYPOGRAPHY. THERE IS THE LONG, T

Caslon

T&w.

Lynotype Caslon 540/3

Foundry:	*Adobe Systems*
Supplier:	*Adobe Systems*
Letterform authenticity:	*Excellent*
Digital outline:	*Fair*
Side bearings:	*Excellent*
Kerning:	*Good*
Hinting:	*Excellent*
Expert editions:	*Yes*
Multiple masters:	*No*
Family completeness:	*Good*
Formats:	*Type 1*
Platforms:	*Mac/PC*

Lynotype Caslon 540 & Caslon 540 Small Caps

72 points

ABCDEFGHIJ
KLMNOPQRST
UVWXYZ&
1234567890$£
ABCDEFGHIJKLMNO
PQRSTUVWXYZ&
abcdefghijklmno
pqrstuvwxyz
1234567890
fi ß (! ?, . - : ;) ' '

Lynotype Caslon 540 Italic & Caslon 540 Italic Old Style Figures

72 points

*ABCDEFGHIJ
KLMNOPQRSTU
VWXYZ&
1234567890$£
abcdefghijklmnop
qrstuvwxyz
1234567890
fiß(!?,.-:;)"*

Lynotype Caslon 540

6/8

All the virtues of the perfect wine glass are paralleled in typog raphy. There is the long, thin stem that obviates fingerprints on the bowl. Why? Because no cloud must come between your eyes and the fiery heart of the liquid. Are not the margins on bo ok pages similarly meant to obviate the necessity of fingering the type page? Again: the glass is colorless or at the most only faintly tinged in the bowl, because the connoisseur judges wi ne partly by its color and is impatient of anything that alters it. There are a thousand mannerisms in typography that are as im pudent and arbitrary as putting port in tumblers of red or green glass! When a goblet has a base that looks too small for securi ty, it does not matter how cleverly it is weighted; you feel ner vous lest it should tip over. There are ways of setting lines of type which may work well enough, and yet keep the reader sub consciously worried by the fear of "doubling" lines, reading three words as one, and so forth. Now the man who first chose glass instead of clay or metal to hold his wine was a "moder nist" in the sense in which I am going to use that term. That is

8/10

All the virtues of the perfect wine glass are paral leled in typography. There is the long, thin stem that obviates fingerprints on the bowl. Why? Be cause no cloud must come between your eyes and the fiery heart of the liquid. Are not the marg ins on book pages similarly meant to obviate the necessity of fingering the type page? Again: the glass is colorless or at the most only faintly tin ged in the bowl, because the connoisseur judges wine partly by its color and is impatient of anyt hing that alters it. There are a thousand manneri sms in typography that are as impudent and arb itrary as putting port in tumblers of red or green glass! When a goblet has a base that looks too sm

10/12

All the virtues of the perfect wine glass are paralleled in typography. There is the long, thin stem that obviates finger prints on the bowl. Why? Because no clo ud must come between your eyes and the fiery heart of the liquid. Are not the margins on book pages similarly meant to obviate the necessity of fingering the type page? Again: the glass is colorless or at the most only faintly tinged in the bowl, because the connoisseur judges wine partly by its color and is impatient

12/14

All the virtues of the perfect win e glass are paralleled in typograp hy. There is the long, thin stem th at obviates fingerprints on the bo wl. Why? Because no cloud must come between your eyes and the fiery heart of the liquid. Are not t he margins on book pages similar ly meant to obviate the necessity of fingering the type page? Again:

14/16

All the virtues of the perfect wine glass are paralleled in typo graphy. There is the long, thin stem that obviates fingerprin ts on the bowl. Why? Because no cloud must come between your eyes and the fiery heart of the liquid. Are not the marg ins on book pages similarly meant to obviate the necessity of fingering the type page? Again: the glass is colorless or at the most only faintly tinged in the bowl, because the connoisse ur judges wine partly by its color and is impatient of anythi ng that alters it. There are a thousand mannerisms in typogra

18/20

All the virtues of the perfect wine glass are para lleled in typography. There is the long, thin ste m that obviates fingerprints on the bowl. Why? Because no cloud must come between your eye s and the fiery heart of the liquid. Are not the ma rgins on book pages similarly meant to obviate the necessity of fingering the type page? Again:

24/25

All the virtues of the perfect wine gl ass are paralleled in typography. Th ere is the long, thin stem that obviat es fingerprints on the bowl. Why? Be cause no cloud must come between your eyes and the fiery heart of the

36/37

All the virtues of the per fect wine glass are parall eled in typography. Ther e is the long, thin stem th

Lynotype Caslon 540 Italic

6 / 8

All the virtues of the perfect wine glass are paralleled in typography. There is the long, thin stem that obviates fingerprints on the bowl. Why? Because no cloud must come between your eyes and the fiery heart of the liquid. Are not the margins on book pages similarly meant to obviate the necessity of fingering the type page? Again: the glass is colorless or at the most only faintly tinged in the bowl, because the connoisseur judges wine partly by its color and is impatient of anything that alters it. There are a thousand mannerisms in typography that are as impudent and arbitrary as putting port in tumblers of red or green glass! When a goblet has a base that looks too small for security, it does not matter how cleverly it is weighted; you feel nervous lest it should tip over. There are ways of setting lines of type which may work well enough, and yet keep the reader subconsciously worried by the fear of "doubling" lines, reading three words as one, and so forth. Now the man who first chose glass instead of clay or metal to hold his wine was a "modernist" in the sense in which I am going to use that term. That is, the first thing he asked of this particular object was not "How should it look?" but "What must it do?" and to that extent all good typog

8 / 10

All the virtues of the perfect wine glass are paralleled in typography. There is the long, thin stem that obviates fingerprints on the bowl. Why? Because no cloud must come between your eyes and the fiery heart of the liquid. Are not the margins on book pages similarly meant to obviate the necessity of fingering the type page? Again: the glass is colorless or at the most only faintly tinged in the bowl, because the connoisseur judges wine partly by its color and is impatient of anything that alters it. There are a thousand mannerisms in typography that are as impudent and arbitrary as putting port in tumblers of red or green glass! When a goblet has a base that looks too small for security, it does not matter how cleverly it is weighted; you feel nervous

10 / 12

All the virtues of the perfect wine glass are paralleled in typography. There is the long, thin stem that obviates fingerprints on the bowl. Why? Because no cloud must come between your eyes and the fiery heart of the liquid. Are not the margins on book pages similarly meant to obviate the necessity of fingering the type page? Again: the glass is colorless or at the most only faintly tinged in the bowl, because the connoisseur judges wine partly by its color and is impatient of anything that alters it. There are a thousand mannerisms in typo

12 / 14

All the virtues of the perfect wine glass are paralleled in typography. There is the long, thin stem that obviates fingerprints on the bowl. Why? Because no cloud must come between your eyes and the fiery heart of the liquid. Are not the margins on book pages similarly meant to obviate the necessity of fingering the type page? Again: the glass is colorless or at the most only fa

14 / 16

All the virtues of the perfect wine glass are paralleled in typography. There is the long, thin stem that obviates fingerprints on the bowl. Why? Because no cloud must come between your eyes and the fiery heart of the liquid. Are not the margins on book pages similarly meant to obviate the necessity of fingering the type page? Again: the glass is colorless or at the most only faintly tinged in the bowl, because the connoisseur judges wine partly by its color and is impatient of anything that alters it. There are a thousand mannerisms in typography that are as impudent and arbitrary as putting port in tumblers of red

18 / 20

All the virtues of the perfect wine glass are paralleled in typography. There is the long, thin stem that obviates fingerprints on the bowl. Why? Because no cloud must come between your eyes and the fiery heart of the liquid. Are not the margins on book pages similarly meant to obviate the necessity of fingering the type page? Again: the glass is colorless or at the most only

24 / 25

All the virtues of the perfect wine glass are paralleled in typography. There is the long, thin stem that obviates fingerprints on the bowl. Why? Because no cloud must come between your eyes and the fiery heart of the liquid. Are not the thousand m

36 / 37

All the virtues of the perfect wine glass are paralleled in typography. There is the long, thin stem that obviates

Lynotype Caslon 3

6/8

All the virtues of the perfect wine glass are paralleled in typography. There is the long, thin stem that obviates fingerprints on the bowl. Why? Because no cloud must come between your eyes and the fiery heart of the liquid. Are not the margins on book pages similarly meant to obviate the necessity of fingering the type page? Again: the glass is colorless or at the most only faintly tinged in the bowl, because the connoisseur judges wine partly by its color and is impatient of anything that alters it. There are a thousand mannerisms in typography that are as impudent and arbitrary as putting port in tumblers of red or green glass! When a goblet has a base that looks too small for security, it does not matter how cleverly it is weighted; you feel nervous lest it should tip over. There are ways of setting lines of type which may work well enough, and yet keep the reader subconsciously worried by the fear of "doubling" lines, reading three words as one, and so forth. Now the man who first chose glass instead of clay or met-

8/10

All the virtues of the perfect wine glass are paralleled in typography. There is the long, thin stem that obviates fingerprints on the bowl. Why? Because no cloud must come between your eyes and the fiery heart of the liquid. Are not the margins on book pages similarly meant to obviate the necessity of fingering the type page? Again: the glass is colorless or at the most only faintly tinged in the bowl, because the connoisseur judges wine partly by its color and is impatient of anything that alters it. There are a thousand mannerisms in typography that are as impu dent and arbitrary as putting port in tumb

10/12

All the virtues of the perfect wine gla ss are paralleled in typography. Ther e is the long, thin stem that obviates fi ngerprints on the bowl. Why? Becau se no cloud must come between your eyes and the fiery heart of the liquid. Are not the margins on book pages similarly meant to obviate the necess ity of fingering the type page? Again: the glass is colorless or at the most only faintly tinged in the bowl, becau se the connoisseur judges wine partl

12/14

All the virtues of the perfect wi ne glass are paralleled in typog raphy. There is the long, thin st em that obviates fingerprints on the bowl. Why? Because no cloud must come between you r eyes and the fiery heart of the liquid. Are not the margins on book pages similarly meant to obviate the necessity of fingeri

14/16

All the virtues of the perfect wine glass are paralleled in typography. There is the long, thin stem that obviates fin gerprints on the bowl. Why? Because no cloud must co me between your eyes and the fiery heart of the liquid. Are not the margins on book pages similarly meant to obviate the necessity of fingering the type page? Again: the glass is colorless or at the most only faintly tinged in the bowl, because the connoisseur judges wine partly by its color and is impatient of anything that alters it.

18/20

All the virtues of the perfect wine glass are paralleled in typography. There is the long, thin stem that obviates fingerprints on the bowl. Why? Because no cloud must come be tween your eyes and the fiery heart of the li quid. Are not the margins on book pages si milarly meant to obviate the necessity of fin

24/25

All the virtues of the perfect win e glass are paralleled in typograp hy. There is the long, thin stem th at obviates fingerprints on the bo wl. Why? Because no cloud must come between your eyes and the

36/37

All the virtues of the p erfect wine glass are p aralleled in typograph y. There is the long, thi

Lynotype Caslon 3 Italic

6 / 8

All the virtues of the perfect wine glass are paralleled in typography. There is the long, thin stem that obviates fingerprints on the bowl. Why? Because no cloud must come between your eyes and the fiery heart of the liquid. Are not the margins on book pages similarly meant to obviate the necessity of fingering the type page? Again: the glass is colorless or at the most only faintly tinged in the bowl, because the connoisseur judges wine partly by its color and is impatient of anything that alters it. There are a thousand mannerisms in typography that are as impudent and arbitrary as putting port in tumblers of red or green glass! When a goblet has a base that looks too small for security, it does not matter how cleverly it is weighted; you feel nervous lest it should tip over. There are ways of setting lines of type which may work well enough, and yet keep the reader subconsciously worried by the fear of "doubling" lines, reading three words as one, and so forth. Now the man who first chose glass instead of clay or metal to hold his wine was a "modernist" in the sense in which I am going to use that term. That is,

8 / 10

All the virtues of the perfect wine glass are paralleled in typography. There is the long, thin stem that obviates fingerprints on the bowl. Why? Because no cloud must come between your eyes and the fiery heart of the liquid. Are not the margins on book pages similarly meant to obviate the necessity of fingering the type page? Again: the glass is colorless or at the most only faintly tinged in the bowl, because the connoisseur judges wine partly by its color and is impatient of anything that alters it. There are a thousand mannerisms in typography that are as impudent and arbitrary as putting port in tumblers of red or green glass! When a goblet has a base that looks too small

10 / 12

All the virtues of the perfect wine glass are paralleled in typography. There is the long, thin stem that obviates fingerprints on the bowl. Why? Because no cloud must come between your eyes and the fiery heart of the liquid. Are not the margins on book pages similarly meant to obviate the necessity of fingering the type page? Again: the glass is colorless or at the most only faintly tinged in the bowl, because the connoisseur judges wine partly by its color and is impatient

12 / 14

All the virtues of the perfect wine glass are paralleled in typography. There is the long, thin stem that obviates fingerprints on the bowl. Why? Because no cloud must come between your eyes and the fiery heart of the liquid. Are not the margins on book pages similarly meant to obviate the necessity of fingering the type page? Again

14 / 16

All the virtues of the perfect wine glass are paralleled in typography. There is the long, thin stem that obviates fingerprints on the bowl. Why? Because no cloud must come between your eyes and the fiery heart of the liquid. Are not the margins on book pages similarly meant to obviate the necessity of fingering the type page? Again: the glass is colorless or at the most only faintly tinged in the bowl, because the connoisseur judges wine partly by its color and is impatient of anything that alters it. There are a thousand mannerisms in typograp

18 / 20

All the virtues of the perfect wine glass are paralleled in typography. There is the long, thin stem that obviates fingerprints on the bowl. Why? Because no cloud must come between your eyes and the fiery heart of the liquid. Are not the margins on book pages similarly meant to obviate the necessity of fingering the type page? Again:

24 / 25

All the virtues of the perfect wine glass are paralleled in typography. There is the long, thin stem that obviates fingerprints on the bowl. Why? Because no cloud must come between your eyes and the fiery heart of the li

36 / 37

All the virtues of the perfect wine glass are paralleled in typography. There is the long, thin stem t

LYNOTYPE CASLON 540 SMALL CAPS

6/8

ALL THE VIRTUES OF THE PERFECT WINE GLASS ARE PARALLEL
ED IN TYPOGRAPHY. THERE IS THE LONG, THIN STEM THAT OBVI
ATES FINGERPRINTS ON THE BOWL. WHY? BECAUSE NO CLOUD
MUST COME BETWEEN YOUR EYES AND THE FIERY HEART OF THE
LIQUID. ARE NOT THE MARGINS ON BOOK PAGES SIMILARLY MEA
NT TO OBVIATE THE NECESSITY OF FINGERING THE TYPE PAGE?
AGAIN: THE GLASS IS COLORLESS OR AT THE MOST ONLY FAINT
LY TINGED IN THE BOWL, BECAUSE THE CONNOISSEUR JUDGES
WINE PARTLY BY ITS COLOR AND IS IMPATIENT OF ANYTHING TH
AT ALTERS IT. THERE ARE A THOUSAND MANNERISMS IN TYPOGR
APHY THAT ARE AS IMPUDENT AND ARBITRARY AS PUTTING PORT
IN TUMBLERS OF RED OR GREEN GLASS! WHEN A GOBLET HAS A
BASE THAT LOOKS TOO SMALL FOR SECURITY, IT DOES NOT MATT
ER HOW CLEVERLY IT IS WEIGHTED; YOU FEEL NERVOUS LEST IT
SHOULD TIP OVER. THERE ARE WAYS OF SETTING LINES OF TYPE
WHICH MAY WORK WELL ENOUGH, AND YET KEEP THE READER SU
BCONSCIOUSLY WORRIED BY THE FEAR OF "DOUBLING" LINES,
READING THREE WORDS AS ONE, AND SO FORTH. NOW THE MAN
WHO FIRST CHOSE GLASS INSTEAD OF CLAY OR METAL TO HOLD
HIS WINE WAS A "MODERNIST" IN THE SENSE IN WHICH I AM GOI
NG TO USE THAT TERM. THAT IS, THE FIRST THING HE ASKED OF

8/10

ALL THE VIRTUES OF THE PERFECT WINE GLASS
ARE PARALLELED IN TYPOGRAPHY. THERE IS THE
LONG, THIN STEM THAT OBVIATES FINGERPRINTS
ON THE BOWL. WHY? BECAUSE NO CLOUD MUST
COME BETWEEN YOUR EYES AND THE FIERY HEA
RT OF THE LIQUID. ARE NOT THE MARGINS ON
BOOK PAGES SIMILARLY MEANT TO OBVIATE THE
NECESSITY OF FINGERING THE TYPE PAGE? AGA
IN: THE GLASS IS COLORLESS OR AT THE MOST
ONLY FAINTLY TINGED IN THE BOWL, BECAUSE
THE CONNOISSEUR JUDGES WINE PARTLY BY ITS
COLOR AND IS IMPATIENT OF ANYTHING THAT AL
TERS IT. THERE ARE A THOUSAND MANNERISMS
IN TYPOGRAPHY THAT ARE AS IMPUDENT AND ARB
ITRARY AS PUTTING PORT IN TUMBLERS OF RED
OR GREEN GLASS! WHEN A GOBLET HAS A BASE

10/12

ALL THE VIRTUES OF THE PERFECT WI
NE GLASS ARE PARALLELED IN TYPOGRA
PHY. THERE IS THE LONG, THIN STEM
THAT OBVIATES FINGERPRINTS ON THE
BOWL. WHY? BECAUSE NO CLOUD MUST
COME BETWEEN YOUR EYES AND THE FIE
RY HEART OF THE LIQUID. ARE NOT THE
MARGINS ON BOOK PAGES SIMILARLY ME
ANT TO OBVIATE THE NECESSITY OF FIN
GERING THE TYPE PAGE? AGAIN: THE
GLASS IS COLORLESS OR AT THE MOST
ONLY FAINTLY TINGED IN THE BOWL, BE
CAUSE THE CONNOISSEUR JUDGES WINE

12/14

ALL THE VIRTUES OF THE PERFE
CT WINE GLASS ARE PARALLELED
IN TYPOGRAPHY. THERE IS THE
LONG, THIN STEM THAT OBVIATES
FINGERPRINTS ON THE BOWL. WH
Y? BECAUSE NO CLOUD MUST CO
ME BETWEEN YOUR EYES AND THE
FIERY HEART OF THE LIQUID. ARE
NOT THE MARGINS ON BOOK PAGE
S SIMILARLY MEANT TO OBVIATE T
HE NECESSITY OF FINGERING THE

14/16

ALL THE VIRTUES OF THE PERFECT WINE GLASS ARE PARALLE
LED IN TYPOGRAPHY. THERE IS THE LONG, THIN STEM THAT O
BVIATES FINGERPRINTS ON THE BOWL. WHY? BECAUSE NO CL
OUD MUST COME BETWEEN YOUR EYES AND THE FIERY HEART
OF THE LIQUID. ARE NOT THE MARGINS ON BOOK PAGES SIMIL
ARLY MEANT TO OBVIATE THE NECESSITY OF FINGERING THE
TYPE PAGE? AGAIN: THE GLASS IS COLORLESS OR AT THE MO
ST ONLY FAINTLY TINGED IN THE BOWL, BECAUSE THE CONNO
ISSEUR JUDGES WINE PARTLY BY ITS COLOR AND IS IMPATIENT
OF ANYTHING THAT ALTERS IT. THERE ARE A THOUSAND MAN

18/20

ALL THE VIRTUES OF THE PERFECT WINE GLASS
ARE PARALLELED IN TYPOGRAPHY. THERE IS TH
E LONG, THIN STEM THAT OBVIATES FINGERPRIN
TS ON THE BOWL. WHY? BECAUSE NO CLOUD MU
ST COME BETWEEN YOUR EYES AND THE FIERY H
EART OF THE LIQUID. ARE NOT THE MARGINS O
N BOOK PAGES SIMILARLY MEANT TO OBVIATE T
HE NECESSITY OF FINGERING THE TYPE PAGE? A

24/25

ALL THE VIRTUES OF THE PERFECT
WINE GLASS ARE PARALLELED IN TYP
OGRAPHY. THERE IS THE LONG, THIN
STEM THAT OBVIATES FINGERPRINTS
ON THE BOWL. WHY? BECAUSE NO C
LOUD MUST COME BETWEEN YOUR E

36/37

ALL THE VIRTUES OF THE
PERFECT WINE GLASS ARE
PARALLELED IN TYPOGRA
PHY. THERE IS THE LONG,

Baskerville

Gg

Monotype Baskerville

Foundry:	*Monotype Typography*
Supplier:	*Monotype Typography*
Letterform authenticity:	*Excellent*
Digital outline:	*Good*
Side bearings:	*Excellent*
Kerning:	*Good*
Hinting:	*Excellent*
Expert editions:	*Yes*
Multiple masters:	*No*
Family completeness:	*Excellent*
Formats:	*Type 1 / partial TrueType*
Platforms:	*Mac / PC*

Monotype Baskerville & Baskerville Expert

72 points

ABCDEFGHIJ
KLMNOPQRST
UVWXYZ&
1234567890$£
ABCDEFGHIJKLMNO
PQRSTUVWXYZ&!?
abcdefghijklm
nopqrstuvwxyz
1234567890$
fi ff ffi ffl ß (!?,.-:;)''

Monotype Baskerville Italic & Expert Italic

72 points

ABCDEFGHIJ
KLMNOPQRST
UVWXYZ&
1234567890$£
abcdefghijklmnopqr
stuvwxyz
1234567890$
fi ff fl ffi ffl ß (!?,.-:;) "

Monotype Baskerville

6 / 7

All the virtues of the perfect wine glass are paralleled in typography. There is the long, thin stem that obviates fingerprints on the bowl. Why? Because no cloud must come between your eyes and the fiery heart of the liquid. Are not the margins on book pages similarly meant to obviate the necessity of fingering the type page? Again: the glass is colorless or at the most only faintly tinged in the bowl, because the connoisseur judges wine partly by its color and is impatient of anything that alters it. There are a thousand mannerisms in typography that are as impudent and arbitrary as putting port in tumblers of red or green glass! When a goblet has a base that looks too small for security, it does not matter how cleverly it is weighted; you feel nervous lest it should tip over. There are ways of setting lines of type which may work well enough, and yet keep the reader subconsciously worried by the fear of "doubling" lines, reading three words as one, and so forth. Now the man who first chose glass instead of clay or metal to hold his wine was a "modernist" in the sense in which I am going to use that term. That is, the first thing he asked of this particular object was not "How should it look?" but "What must it do?" and to that extent all good typography is modernist. Wine is so strange and potent a thing that it has been used in the central ritual of religion

8 / 9

All the virtues of the perfect wine glass are paralleled in typography. There is the long, thin stem that obviates fingerprints on the bowl. Why? Because no cloud must come between your eyes and the fiery heart of the liquid. Are not the margins on book pages similarly meant to obviate the necessity of fingering the type page? Again: the glass is colorless or at the most only faintly tinged in the bowl, because the connoisseur judges wine partly by its color and is impatient of anything that alters it. There are a thousand mannerisms in typography that are as impudent and arbitrary as putting port in tumblers of red or green glass! When a goblet has a base that looks too small for security, it does not matter how cleverly it is weighted; you feel nervous lest it should tip over. There are ways of setting lines of type

10 / 11

All the virtues of the perfect wine glass are paralleled in typography. There is the long, thin stem that obviates fingerprints on the bowl. Why? Because no cloud must come between your eyes and the fiery heart of the liquid. Are not the margins on book pages similarly meant to obviate the necessity of fingering the type page? Again: the glass is colorless or at the most only faintly tinged in the bowl, because the connoisseur judges wine partly by its color and is impatient of anything that alters it. There are a thousand mannerisms in typ

12 / 13

All the virtues of the perfect wine glass are paralleled in typography. There is the long, thin stem that obviates fingerprints on the bowl. Why? Because no cloud must come between your eyes and the fiery heart of the liquid. Are not the margins on book pages similarly meant to obviate the necessity of fingering the type page? Again: the glass is colorless or at the most only faintly ting

14 / 15

All the virtues of the perfect wine glass are paralleled in typography. There is the long, thin stem that obviates fingerprints on the bowl. Why? Because no cloud must come between your eyes and the fiery heart of the liquid. Are not the margins on book pages similarly meant to obviate the necessity of fingering the type page? Again: the glass is colorless or at the most only faintly tinged in the bowl, because the connoisseur judges wine partly by its color and is impatient of anything that alters it. There are a thousand mannerisms in typography that are as impudent and arbitrary as putting port in tumblers of red or green glass! When a

18 / 19

All the virtues of the perfect wine glass are paralleled in typography. There is the long, thin stem that obviates fingerprints on the bowl. Why? Because no cloud must come between your eyes and the fiery heart of the liquid. Are not the margins on book pages similarly meant to obviate the necessity of fingering the type page? Again: the glass is colorless or at the most only faintly tinged in the

24 / 24

All the virtues of the perfect wine glass are paralleled in typography. There is the long, thin stem that obviates fingerprints on the bowl. Why? Because no cloud must come between your eyes and the fiery heart of the liquid.

36 / 36

All the virtues of the perfect wine glass are paralleled in typography. There is the long, thin stem that ob

Monotype Baskerville Italic

6 / 7

All the virtues of the perfect wine glass are paralleled in typography. There is the long, thin stem that obviates fingerprints on the bowl. Why? Because no cloud must come between your eyes and the fiery heart of the liquid. Are not the margins on book pages similarly meant to obviate the necessity of fingering the type page? Again: the glass is colorless or at the most only faintly tinged in the bowl, because the connoisseur judges wine partly by its color and is impatient of anything that alters it. There are a thousand mannerisms in typography that are as impudent and arbitrary as putting port in tumblers of red or green glass! When a goblet has a base that looks too small for security, it does not matter how cleverly it is weighted; you feel nervous lest it should tip over. There are ways of setting lines of type which may work well enough, and yet keep the reader subconsciously worried by the fear of "doubling" lines, reading three words as one, and so forth. Now the man who first chose glass instead of clay or metal to hold his wine was a "modernist" in the sense in which I am going to use that term. That is, the first thing he asked of this particular object was not "How should it look?" but "What must it do?" and to that extent all good typography is modernist. Wine is so strange and potent a thing that it has been used in the central ritual of religion in one place and time, and attacked by a virago with a hatchet in another. There is only one other thing in the world that is capable of stirring and altering men's minds to the same extent, and that is the coherent expression of thought. That is man's chief miracle, unique to man.

8 / 9

All the virtues of the perfect wine glass are paralleled in typography. There is the long, thin stem that obviates finger prints on the bowl. Why? Because no cloud must come between your eyes and the fiery heart of the liquid. Are not the margins on book pages similarly meant to obviate the necessi ty of fingering the type page? Again: the glass is colorless or at the most only faintly tinged in the bowl, because the connois seur judges wine partly by its color and is impatient of any thing that alters it. There are a thousand mannerisms in typo graphy that are as impudent and arbitrary as putting port in tumblers of red or green glass! When a goblet has a base that looks too small for security, it does not matter how cleverly it is weighted; you feel nervous lest it should tip over. There are ways of setting lines of type which may work well enough, and yet keep the reader subconsciously worried by the fear of "doubling" lines, reading three words as one, and so forth.

10 / 11

All the virtues of the perfect wine glass are paralle led in typography. There is the long, thin stem th at obviates fingerprints on the bowl. Why? Becau se no cloud must come between your eyes and the fi ery heart of the liquid. Are not the margins on bo ok pages similarly meant to obviate the necessity of fingering the type page? Again: the glass is color less or at the most only faintly tinged in the bowl, because the connoisseur judges wine partly by its color and is impatient of anything that alters it. There are a thousand mannerisms in typography that are as impudent and arbitrary as putting port in tumblers of red or green glass! When a goblet

12 / 13

All the virtues of the perfect wine glass are paralleled in typography. There is the lo ng, thin stem that obviates fingerprints on the bowl. Why? Because no cloud must come between your eyes and the fiery heart of the liquid. Are not the margins on book pages similarly meant to obviate the nece ssity of fingering the type page? Again: the glass is colorless or at the most only faint ly tinged in the bowl, because the connoi sseur judges wine partly by its color and is

14 / 15

All the virtues of the perfect wine glass are paralleled in typography. There is the long, thin stem that obviates fingerprints on the bowl. Why? Because no cloud must come between your eyes and the fiery heart of the liquid. Are not the margins on book pages similarly meant to obviate the necessity of fingering the type page? Again: the glass is colorless or at the most only faintly tinged in the bowl, because the connoisseur judges wine partly by its color and is impatient of anything that alters it. There are a thousand mannerisms in typography that are as impudent and arbitrary as putting port in tumblers of red or green glass! When a goblet has a base that looks too small for security, it does not matter how cleverly it is weighted; you feel nervous lest it should tip over.

18 / 19

All the virtues of the perfect wine glass are paralleled in typo graphy. There is the long, thin stem that obviates fingerprints on the bowl. Why? Because no cloud must come between yo ur eyes and the fiery heart of the liquid. Are not the margins on book pages similarly meant to obviate the necessity of fing ering the type page? Again: the glass is colorless or at the mo st only faintly tinged in the bowl, because the connoisseur ju dges wine partly by its color and is impatient of anything th

24 / 24

All the virtues of the perfect wine glass are pa ralleled in typography. There is the long, thin stem that obviates fingerprints on the bowl. Why? Because no cloud must come between your eyes and the fiery heart of the liquid. Are not the margins on book pages similarly mean

36 / 36

All the virtues of the perfect wi ne glass are paralleled in typog raphy. There is the long, thin s tem that obviates fingerprints

Monotype Baskerville Semi Bold

6/7

All the virtues of the perfect wine glass are paralleled in typography. There is the long, thin stem that obviates fingerprints on the bowl. Why? Because no cloud must come between your eyes and the fiery heart of the liquid. Are not the margins on book pages similarly meant to obviate the necessity of fingering the type page? Again: the glass is colorless or at the most only faintly tinged in the bowl, because the connoisseur judges wine partly by its color and is impatient of anything that alters it. There are a thousand mannerisms in typography that are as impudent and arbitrary as putting port in tumblers of red or green glass! When a goblet has a base that looks too small for security, it does not matter how cleverly it is weighted; you feel nervous lest it should tip over. There are ways of setting lines of type which may work well enough, and yet keep the reader subconsciously worried by the fear of "doubling" lines, reading three words as one, and so forth. Now the man who first chose glass instead of clay or metal to hold his wine was a "modernist" in the sense in which I am going to use that term. That is, the first thing he asked of this particular object was not "H

8/9

All the virtues of the perfect wine glass are paralleled in typography. There is the long, thin stem that obviates fingerprints on the bowl. Why? Because no cloud must come between your eyes and the fiery heart of the liquid. Are not the margins on book pages similarly meant to obviate the necessity of fingering the type page? Again: the glass is colorless or at the most only faintly tinged in the bowl, because the connoisseur judges wine partly by its color and is impatient of anything that alters it. There are a thousand mannerisms in typography that are as impudent and arbitrary as putting port in tumblers of red or green glass! When a goblet has a base that looks too small for security, it

10 / 11

All the virtues of the perfect wine glass are paralleled in typography. There is the long, thin stem that obviates fingerprints on the bowl. Why? Because no cloud must come between your eyes and the fiery heart of the liquid. Are not the margins on book pages similarly meant to obviate the necessity of fingering the type page? Again: the glass is colorless or at the most only faintly tinged in the bowl, because the connoisseur judges wine partly by its

12 / 13

All the virtues of the perfect wine glass are paralleled in typography. There is the long, thin stem that obviates fingerprints on the bowl. Why? Because no cloud must come between your eyes and the fiery heart of the liquid. Are not the margins on book pages similarly meant to obviate the necessity of fingering the type page? Agai

14/15

All the virtues of the perfect wine glass are paralleled in typography. There is the long, thin stem that obviates fingerprints on the bowl. Why? Because no cloud must come between your eyes and the fiery heart of the liquid. Are not the margins on book pages similarly meant to obviate the necessity of fingering the type page? Again: the glass is colorless or at the most only faintly tinged in the bowl, because the connoisseur judges wine partly by its color and is impatient of anything that alters it. There are a thousand mannerisms

18 / 19

All the virtues of the perfect wine glass are paralleled in typography. There is the long, thin stem that obviates fingerprints on the bowl. Why? Because no cloud must come between your eyes and the fiery heart of thel iquid. Are not the margins on book pages similarly meant to obviate the necessity of fingering the type page? Again: the glass is co

24 / 24

All the virtues of the perfect wine glass are paralleled in typography. There is the long, thin stem that obviates fingerprints on the bowl. Why? Because no cloud must come between your eyes a

36 / 36

All the virtues of the perfect perfect wine glass are paralleled in typography. There is the long, t

Monotype Baskerville Semi Bold Italic

6 | 7

All the virtues of the perfect wine glass are paralleled in typography. There is the long, thin stem that obviates fingerprints on the bowl. Why? Because no cloud must come between your eyes and the fiery heart of the liquid. Are not the margins on book pages similarly meant to obviate the necessity of fingering the type page? Again: the glass is colorless or at the most only faintly tinged in the bowl, because the connoisseur judges wine partly by its color and is impatient of anything that alters it. There are a thousand mannerisms in typography that are as impudent and arbitrary as putting port in tumblers of red or green glass! When a goblet has a base that looks too small for security, it does not matter how cleverly it is weighted; you feel nervous lest it should tip over. There are ways of setting lines of type which may work well enough, and yet keep the reader subconsciously worried by the fear of "doubling" lines, reading three words as one, and so forth. Now the man who first chose glass instead of clay or metal to hold his wine was a "modernist" in the sense in which I am going to use that term. That is, the first thing he asked of this particular object was not "How should it look?" but "What must it

8 | 9

All the virtues of the perfect wine glass are paralleled in typography. There is the long, thin stem that obviates fingerprints on the bowl. Why? Because no cloud must come between your eyes and the fiery heart of the liquid. Are not the margins on book pages similarly meant to obviate the necessity of fingering the type page? Again: the glass is colorless or at the most only faintly tinged in the bowl, because the connoisseur judges wine partly by its color and is impatient of anything that alters it. There are a thousand mannerisms in typography that are as impudent and arbitrary as putting port in tumblers of red or green glass! When a goblet has a base that looks too small for security, it does not matter how cleverly it is

10 | 11

All the virtues of the perfect wine glass are paralleled in typography. There is the long, thin stem that obviates fingerprints on the bowl. Why? Because no cloud must come between your eyes and the fiery heart of the liquid. Are not the margins on book pages similarly meant to obviate the necessity of fingering the type page? Again: the glass is colorless or at the most only faintly tinged in the bowl, because the connoisseur judges wine partly by its color and is impatient of any

12 | 13

All the virtues of the perfect wine glass are paralleled in typography. There is the long, thin stem that obviates fingerprints on the bowl. Why? Because no cloud must come between your eyes and the fiery heart of the liquid. Are not the margins on book pages similarly meant to obviate the necessity of fingering the type page? Again: the glas

14 | 15

All the virtues of the perfect wine glass are paralleled in typography. There is the long, thin stem that obviates fingerprints on the bowl. Why? Because no cloud must come between your eyes and the fiery heart of the liquid. Are not the margins on book pages similarly meant to obviate the necessity of fingering the type page? Again: the glass is colorless or at the most only faintly tinged in the bowl, because the connoisseur judges wine partly by its color and is impatient of anything that alters it. There are a thousand mannerisms in typography that are as impude

18 | 19

All the virtues of the perfect wine glass are paralleled in typography. There is the long, thin stem that obviates fingerprints on the bowl. Why? Because no cloud must come between your eyes and the fiery heart of the liquid. Are not the margins on book pages similarly meant to obviate the necessity of fingering the type page? Again: the glass is colorless

24 | 24

All the virtues of the perfect wine glass are paralleled in typography. There is the long, thin stem that obviates fingerprints on the bowl. Why? Because no cloud must come between your eyes and the fiery h

36 | 36

All the virtues of the perfect wine glass are paralleled in typography. There is the long, thin s

Monotype Baskerville Bold

6 / 7

All the virtues of the perfect wine glass are paralleled in typography. There is the long, thin stem that obviates fingerprints on the bowl. Why? Because no cloud must come between your eyes and the fiery heart of the liqui d. Are not the margins on book pages similarly meant to obviate the necessity of fingering the type page? Again: the glass is colorless or at the most only faintly tinge d in the bowl, because the connoisseur judges wine part ly by its color and is impatient of anything that alters it. There are a thousand mannerisms in typography that are as impudent and arbitrary as putting port in tumble rs of red or green glass! When a goblet has a base that lo oks too small for security, it does not matter how clever ly it is weighted; you feel nervous lest it should tip over. There are ways of setting lines of type which may work well enough, and yet keep the reader subconsciously wo rried by the fear of "doubling" lines, reading three wor ds as one, and so forth. Now the man who first chose gla ss instead of clay or metal to hold his wine was a "mode rnist" in the sense in which I am going to use that term. That is, the first thing he asked of this particular object

8 / 9

All the virtues of the perfect wine glass are paralleled in typography. There is the long, thin stem that obviates fingerprints on the bowl. Why? Because no cloud must come be tween your eyes and the fiery heart of the li quid. Are not the margins on book pages si milarly meant to obviate the necessity of fi ngering the type page? Again: the glass is colorless or at the most only faintly tinged in the bowl, because the connoisseur judg es wine partly by its color and is impatient of anything that alters it. There are a thou sand mannerisms in typography that are as impudent and arbitrary as putting port in tumblers of red or green glass! When a goblet has a base that looks too small for

10 / 11

All the virtues of the perfect wine glass are paralleled in typography. There is the long, thin stem that ob viates fingerprints on the bowl. Wh y? Because no cloud must come be tween your eyes and the fiery heart of the liquid. Are not the margins on book pages similarly meant to obviate the necessity of fingering the type page? Again: the glass is colorless or at the most only faint ly tinged in the bowl, because the connoisseur judges wine partly by

12 / 13

All the virtues of the perfect wine glass are paralleled in typography. There is the lon g, thin stem that obviates fin gerprints on the bowl. Why? Because no cloud must come between your eyes and the fie ry heart of the liquid. Are not the margins on book pages si milarly meant to obviate the necessity of fingering the ty

14 / 15

All the virtues of the perfect wine glass are paralleled in typography. There is the long, thin stem that obvia tes fingerprints on the bowl. Why? Because no cloud must come between your eyes and the fiery heart of the liquid. Are not the margins on book pages similar ly meant to obviate the necessity of fingering the type page? Again: the glass is colorless or at the most only faintly tinged in the bowl, because the connoisseur judges wine partly by its color and is impatient of any thing that alters it. There are a thousand mannerism

18 / 19

All the virtues of the perfect wine glass ar e paralleled in typography. There is the lo ng, thin stem that obviates fingerprints on the bowl. Why? Because no cloud must co me between your eyes and the fiery heart of the liquid. Are not the margins on book pages similarly meant to obviate the nece ssity of fingering the type page? Again: the

24 / 24

All the virtues of the perfect wi ne glass are paralleled in typog raphy. There is the long, thin st em that obviates fingerprints o n the bowl. Why? Because no cl oud must come between your e

36 / 36

All the virtues of the p erfect wine glass are paralleled in typogra phy. There is the long

Monotype Baskerville Bold Italic

6 / 7

All the virtues of the perfect wine glass are paralleled in typography. There is the long, thin stem that obviates fingerprints on the bowl. Why? Because no cloud must come between your eyes and the fiery heart of the liquid. Are not the margins on book pages similarly meant to obviate the necessity of fingering the type page? Again: the glass is colorless or at the most only faintly tinged in the bowl, because the connoisseur judges wine partly by its color and is impatient of anything that alters it. There are a thousand mannerisms in typography that are as impudent and arbitrary as putting port in tumblers of red or green glass! When a goblet has a base that looks too small for security, it does not matter how cleverly it is weighted; you feel nervous lest it should tip over. There are ways of setting lines of type which may work well enough, and yet keep the reader subconsciously worried by the fear of "doubling" lines, reading three words as one, and so forth. Now the man who first chose glass instead of clay or metal to hold his wine was a "modernist" in the sense in which I am going to use that term. That is, the first thing he asked of this particular object was not "How should it look?" but "What must it do?" and to that

8 / 9

All the virtues of the perfect wine glass are paralleled in typography. There is the long, thin stem that obviates fingerprints on the bowl. Why? Because no cloud must come between your eyes and the fiery heart of the liquid. Are not the margins on book pages similarly meant to obviate the necessity of fingering the type page? Again: the glass is colorless or at the most only faintly tinged in the bowl, because the connoisseur judges wine partly by its color and is impatient of anything that alters it. There are a thousand mannerisms in typography that are as impudent and arbitrary as putting port in tumblers of red or green glass! When a goblet has a base that looks too small for security, it does not matter how cleverly it is weig

10 / 11

All the virtues of the perfect wine glass are paralleled in typography. There is the long, thin stem that obviates fingerprints on the bowl. Why? Because no cloud must come between your eyes and the fiery heart of the liquid. Are not the margins on book pages similarly meant to obviate the necessity of fingering the type page? Again: the glass is colorless or at the most only faintly tinged in the bowl, because the connoisseur judges wine partly by its color and is impatient of

12 / 13

All the virtues of the perfect wine glass are paralleled in typography. There is the long, thin stem that obviates fingerprints on the bowl. Why? Because no cloud must come between your eyes and the fiery heart of the liquid. Are not the margins on book pages similarly meant to obviate the necessity of fingering the type page? Again: the glass

14 / 15

All the virtues of the perfect wine glass are paralleled in typography. There is the long, thin stem that obviates fingerprints on the bowl. Why? Because no cloud must come between your eyes and the fiery heart of the liquid. Are not the margins on book pages similarly meant to obviate the necessity of fingering the type page? Again: the glass is colorless or at the most only faintly tinged in the bowl, because the connoisseur judges wine partly by its color and is impatient of anything that alters it. There are a thousand mannerisms in

18 / 19

All the virtues of the perfect wine glass are paralleled in typography. There is the long, thin stem that obviates fingerprints on the bowl. Why? Because no cloud must come between your eyes and the fiery heart of the liquid. Are not the margins on book pages similarly meant to obviate the necessity of fingering the type page? Again: the glass is

24 / 24

All the virtues of the perfect wine glass are paralleled in typography. There is the long, thin stem that obviates fingerprints on the bowl. Why? Because no cloud must come between your eyes

36 / 36

All the virtues of the perfect wine glass are paralleled in typography. There is the long, th

Monotype Baskerville (Caps) & Baskerville Expert (Small Caps)

6/7

All the virtues of the perfe f wine glass are paralleled in typography. There is the long, t n stem that obviates fingerprints on the bowl. Why? Because no cloud must come between your eyes and the fiery heart of the liquid. Are not the margins on book pages similarly meant to obviate the necessity of fingering the type page? Again: the glass is colorless or at the most only faintly tinged in the bowl, because the connoisseur judges wine partly by its color and is impatient of anything that alters it. There are a thousand mannerisms in typography that are as impudent and arbitrary as putting port in tumblers of red or green glass! When a goblet has a base that looks too small for security, it does not matter how cleverly it is weighted; you feel nervous lest it should tip over. There are ways of setting lines of type which may work well enough, and yet keep the reader subconsciously worried by the fear of doubling lines, reading three words as one, and so forth. Now the man who first chose glass instead of clay or metal to hold his wine was a modernist in the sense in which I am going to use that term. That is, the first thing he asked of this particular object was not How should it look?

8/9

All the virtues of the perfect wine glass are paralleled in typography. There is the long, thin stem that obviates fingerprints on the bowl. Why? Because no cloud must come between your eyes and the fiery heart of the liquid. Are not the margins on book pages similarly meant to obviate the necessity of fingering the type page? Again: the glass is colorless or at the most only faintly tinged in the bowl, because the connoisseur judges wine partly by its color and is impatient of anything that alters it. There are a thousand mannerisms in typography that are as impudent and arbitrary as putting port in tumblers of red or green glass! When a goblet has a base that looks too small for security

10/11

All the virtues of the perfect wine glass are paralleled in typography. There is the long, thin stem that obviates fingerprints on the bowl. Why? Because no cloud must come between your eyes and the fiery heart of the liquid. Are not the margins on book pages similarly meant to obviate the necessity of fingering the type page? Again: the glass is colorless or at the most only faintly tinged in the bowl, because the connoisseur judges wine partly by its color and is i

12/13

All the virtues of the perfect wine glass are paralleled in typography. There is the long, thin stem that obviates finger prints on the bowl. Why? Because no cloud must come between your eyes and the fiery heart of the liquid. Are not the margins on book pages similarly meant to obviate the necessity of fingering the type page? Ag

14/15

All the virtues of the perfect wine glass are paralleled in typography. There is the long, thin stem that obviates fingerprints on the bowl. Why? Because no cloud must come between your eyes and the fiery heart of the liquid. Are not the margins on book pages similarly meant to obviate the necessity of fingering the type page? Aga in: the glass is colorless or at the most only faintly tinged in the bowl, because the connoisseur judges wine partly by its color and is impatient of anything that alters it. There are a thousand mannerisms in typography that

18/19

All the virtues of the perfect wine glass are paralleled in typography. There is the long, thin stem that obviates fingerprints on the bowl. Why? Because no cloud must come between your eyes and the fiery heart of the liquid. Are not the margins on book pages similarly meant to obviate the necessity of fingering the type page? Again: the

24/24

All the virtues of the perfect wine glass are paralleled in typography. There is the long, thin stem that obviates fingerprints on the bowl. Why? Because no cloud must come between your eyes and

36/36

All the virtues of the perfect wine glass are paralleled in typography. There is the long

Times New Roman

GgT

Monotype Times New Roman

Foundry:	*Monotype Typography*
Supplier:	*Monotype Typography*
Letterform authenticity:	*Excellent*
Digital outline:	*Good*
Side bearings:	*Fair*
Kerning:	*Fair*
Hinting:	*Excellent*
Expert editions:	*Yes*
Multiple masters:	*No*
Family completeness:	*Excellent*
Formats:	*Type 1 / partial TrueType*
Platforms:	*Mac / PC*

This very well developed family features a special Small Text version for setting text in very small sizes.

72 points

ABCDEFGHIJ
KLMNOPQRST
UVWXYZ&
1234567890$£
ABCDEFGHIJKLMNO
PQRSTUVWXYZ&!?
abcdefghijklm
nopqrstuvwxyz
1234567890$
fi ff fl ffi ffl ß (!?,.-:;)''

72 points

*ABCDEFGHIJ
KLMNOPQRST
UVWXYZ&
1234567890$£
abcdefghijkl
mnopqrstuvwxyz
1234567890$
fifffliffifflß(!?,.-:;)"*

Monotype Times New Roman

6/7

All the virtues of the perfect wine glass are paralleled in typography. There is the long, thin stem that obviates fingerprints on the bowl. Why? Because no cloud must come between your eyes and the fiery heart of the liquid. Are not the margins on book pages similarly meant to obviate the necessity of fingering the type page? Again: the glass is colorless or at the most only faintly tinged in the bowl, because the connoisseur judges wine partly by its color and is impatient of anything that alters it. There are a thousand mannerisms in typography that are as impudent and arbitrary as putting port in tumblers of red or green glass! When a goblet has a base that looks too small for security, it does not matter how cleverly it is weighted; you feel nervous lest it should tip over. There are ways of setting lines of type which may work well enough, and yet keep the reader subconsciously worried by the fear of "doubling" lines, reading three words as one, and so forth. Now the man who first chose glass instead of clay or metal to hold his wine was a "modernist" in the sense in which I am going to use that term. That is, the first thing he asked of this particular object was not "How should it look?" but "What must it do?" and to that extent all good typography is modernist. Wine is so strange and potent a thing that it has be

8/9

All the virtues of the perfect wine glass are paralleled in typography. There is the long, thin stem that obviates fingerprints on the bowl. Why? Because no cloud must come between your eyes and the fiery heart of the liquid. Are not the margins on book pages similarly meant to obviate the necessity of fingering the type page? Again: the glass is colorless or at the most only faintly tinged in the bowl, because the connoisseur judges wine partly by its color and is impatient of anything that alters it. There are a thousand mannerisms in typography that are as impudent and arbitrary as putting port in tumblers of red or green glass! When a goblet has a base that looks too small for security, it does not matter how cleverly it is weighted; you feel nervous lest it should tip over.

10/11

All the virtues of the perfect wine glass are paralleled in typography. There is the long, thin stem that obviates fingerprints on the bowl. Why? Because no cloud must come between your eyes and the fiery heart of the liquid. Are not the margins on book pages similarly meant to obviate the necessity of fingering the type page? Again: the glass is colorless or at the most only faintly tinged in the bowl, because the connoisseur judges wine partly by its color and is impatient of anything that alters it. There are a thousand

12/13

All the virtues of the perfect wine glass are paralleled in typography. There is the long, thin stem that obviates fingerprints on the bowl. Why? Because no cloud must come between your eyes and the fiery heart of the liquid. Are not the margins on book pages similarly meant to obviate the necessity of fingering the type page? Again: the glass is colorless or at the mo

14/15

All the virtues of the perfect wine glass are paralleled in typography. There is the long, thin stem that obviates fingerprints on the bowl. Why? Because no cloud must come between your eyes and the fiery heart of the liquid. Are not the margins on book pages similarly meant to obviate the necessity of fingering the type page? Again: the glass is colorless or at the most only faintly tinged in the bowl, because the connoisseur judges wine partly by its color and is impatient of anything that alters it. There are a thousand mannerisms in typography that are as impudent and arbitrary as putting port in tu

18/19

All the virtues of the perfect wine glass are paralleled in typography. There is the long, thin stem that obviates fingerprints on the bowl. Why? Because no cloud must come between your eyes and the fiery heart of the liquid. Are not the margins on book pages similarly meant to obviate the necessity of fingering the type page? Again: the glass is colorless or at the most only faintly

24/25

All the virtues of the perfect wine glass are paralleled in typography. There is the long, thin stem that obviates fingerprints on the bowl. Why? Because no cloud must come between your eyes and the fiery heart of the li

36/36

All the virtues of the perfect wine glass are paralleled in typography. There is the long, thin ste

Monotype Times Italic

6 / 7

All the virtues of the perfect wine glass are paralleled in typography. There is the long, thin stem that obviates fingerprints on the bowl. Why? Because no cloud must come between your eyes and the fiery heart of the liquid. Are not the margins on book pages similarly meant to obviate the necessity of fingering the type page? Again: the glass is colorless or at the most only faintly tinged in the bowl, because the connoisseur judges wine partly by its color and is impatient of anything that alters it. There are a thousand mannerisms in typography that are as impudent and arbitrary as putting port in tumblers of red or green glass! When a goblet has a base that looks too small for security, it does not matter how cleverly it is weighted; you feel nervous lest it should tip over. There are ways of setting lines of type which may work well enough, and yet keep the reader subconsciously worried by the fear of "doubling" lines, reading three words as one, and so forth. Now the man who first chose glass instead of clay or metal to hold his wine was a "modernist" in the sense in which I am going to use that term. That is, the first thing he asked of this particular object was not "How should it look?" but "What must it do?" and to that extent all good typography is modernist. Wine is so strange and potent a thing that it has been used in the central ritual of religion in one pl

8 / 9

All the virtues of the perfect wine glass are paralleled in typography. There is the long, thin stem that obviates fingerprints on the bowl. Why? Because no cloud must come between your eyes and the fiery heart of the liquid. Are not the margins on book pages similarly meant to obviate the necessity of fingering the type page? Again: the glass is colorless or at the most only faintly tinged in the bowl, because the connoisseur judges wine partly by its color and is impatient of anything that alters it. There are a thousand mannerisms in typography that are as impudent and arbitrary as putting port in tumblers of red or green glass! When a goblet has a base that looks too small for security, it does not matter how cleverly it is weighted; you feel nervous lest it should tip over. There are ways of setting lines of ty

10 / 11

All the virtues of the perfect wine glass are paralleled in typography. There is the long, thin stem that obviates fingerprints on the bowl. Why? Because no cloud must come between your eyes and the fiery heart of the liquid. Are not the margins on book pages similarly meant to obviate the necessity of fingering the type page? Again: the glass is colorless or at the most only faintly tinged in the bowl, because the connoisseur judges wine partly by its color and is impatient of anything that alters it. There are a thousand mannerisms in ty

12 / 13

All the virtues of the perfect wine glass are paralleled in typography. There is the long, thin stem that obviates fingerprints on the bowl. Why? Because no cloud must come between your eyes and the fiery heart of the liquid. Are not the margins on book pages similarly meant to obviate the necessity of fingering the type page? Again: the glass is colorless or at the most only faintly ting

14 / 15

All the virtues of the perfect wine glass are paralleled in typography. There is the long, thin stem that obviates fingerprints on the bowl. Why? Because no cloud must come between your eyes and the fiery heart of the liquid. Are not the margins on book pages similarly meant to obviate the necessity of fingering the type page? Again: the glass is colorless or at the most only faintly tinged in the bowl, because the connoisseur judges wine partly by its color and is impatient of anything that alters it. There are a thousand mannerisms in typography that are as impudent and arbitrary as putting port in tumblers of red or green glass!

18 / 19

All the virtues of the perfect wine glass are paralleled in typography. There is the long, thin stem that obviates fingerprints on the bowl. Why? Because no cloud must come between your eyes and the fiery heart of the liquid. Are not the margins on book pages similarly meant to obviate the necessity of fingering the type page? Again: the glass is colorless or at the most only faintly tinged in the bowl,

24 / 25

All the virtues of the perfect wine glass are paralleled in typography. There is the long, thin stem that obviates fingerprints on the bowl. Why? Because no cloud must come between your eyes and the fiery heart of the liquid. Are no

36 / 36

All the virtues of the perfect wine glass are paralleled in typography. There is the long, thin stem that obviate

Monotype Times New Roman Medium

6 / 7

All the virtues of the perfect wine glass are paralleled in typography. There is the long, thin stem that obviates fingerprints on the bowl. Why? Because no cloud must come between your eyes and the fiery heart of the liquid. Are not the margins on book pages similarly meant to obviate the necessity of fingering the type page? Again: the glass is colorless or at the most only faintly tinged in the bowl, because the connoisseur judges wine partly by its color and is impatient of anything that alters it. There are a thousand mannerisms in typography that are as impudent and arbitrary as putting port in tumblers of red or green glass! When a goblet has a base that looks too small for security, it does not matter how cleverly it is weighted; you feel nervous lest it should tip over. There are ways of setting lines of type which may work well enough, and yet keep the reader subconsciously worried by the fear of "doubling" lines, reading three words as one, and so forth. Now the man who first chose glass instead of clay or metal to hold his wine was a "modernist" in the sense in which I am going to use that term. That is, the first thing he asked of this particular object was not "How should it look?" but "What must it do?" and to that extent all good typography is modernist. Wine is so strange and potent a thing that

8 / 9

All the virtues of the perfect wine glass are paralleled in typography. There is the long, thin stem that obviates fingerprints on the bowl. Why? Because no cloud must come between your eyes and the fiery heart of the liquid. Are not the margins on book pages similarly meant to obviate the necessity of fingering the type page? Again: the glass is colorless or at the most only faintly tinged in the bowl, because the connoisseur judges wine partly by its color and is impatient of anything that alters it. There are a thousand mannerisms in typography that are as impudent and arbitrary as putting port in tumblers of red or green glass! When a goblet has a base that looks too small for security, it does not matter how cleverly it is weighted; you feel nervous lest it should ti

10 / 11

All the virtues of the perfect wine glass are paralleled in typography. There is the long, thin stem that obviates fingerprints on the bowl. Why? Because no cloud must come between your eyes and the fiery heart of the liquid. Are not the margins on book pages similarly meant to obviate the necessity of fingering the type page? Again: the glass is colorless or at the most only faintly tinged in the bowl, because the connoisseur judges wine partly by its color and is impatient of anything that alters it. There are a tho

12 / 13

All the virtues of the perfect wine glass are paralleled in typography. There is the long, thin stem that obviates fingerprints on the bowl. Why? Because no cloud must come between your eyes and the fiery heart of the liquid. Are not the margins on book pages similarly meant to obviate the necessity of fingering the type page? Again: the glass is colorless or at the

14 / 15

All the virtues of the perfect wine glass are paralleled in typography. There is the long, thin stem that obviates fingerprints on the bowl. Why? Because no cloud must come between your eyes and the fiery heart of the liquid. Are not the margins on book pages similarly meant to obviate the necessity of fingering the type page? Again: the glass is colorless or at the most only faintly tinged in the bowl, because the connoisseur judges wine partly by its color and is impatient of anything that alters it. There are a thousand mannerisms in typography that are as impudent and arbitrary as putting port in

18 / 19

All the virtues of the perfect wine glass are paralleled in typography. There is the long, thin stem that obviates fingerprints on the bowl. Why? Because no cloud must come between your eyes and the fiery heart of the liquid. Are not the margins on book pages similarly meant to obviate the necessity of fingering the type page? Again: the glass is colorless or at the most

24 / 25

All the virtues of the perfect wine glass are paralleled in typography. There is the long, thin stem that obviates fingerprints on the bowl. Why? Because no cloud must come between your eyes and the fiery heart of th

36 / 36

All the virtues of the perfect wine glass are paralleled in typography. There is the long, thin stem

Monotype Times Medium Italic

6 / 7

All the virtues of the perfect wine glass are paralleled in typography. There is the long, thin stem that obviates fingerprints on the bowl. Why? Because no cloud must come between your eyes and the fiery heart of the liquid. Are not the margins on book pages similarly meant to obviate the necessity of fingering the type page? Again: the glass is colorless or at the most only faintly tinged in the bowl, because the connoisseur judges wine partly by its color and is impatient of anything that alters it. There are a thousand mannerisms in typography that are as impudent and arbitrary as putting port in tumblers of red or green glass! When a goblet has a base that looks too small for security, it does not matter how cleverly it is weighted; you feel nervous lest it should tip over. There are ways of setting lines of type which may work well enough, and yet keep the reader subconsciously worried by the fear of "doubling" lines, reading three words as one, and so forth. Now the man who first chose glass instead of clay or metal to hold his wine was a "modernist" in the sense in which I am going to use that term. That is, the first thing he asked of this particular object was not "How should it look?" but "What must it do?" and to that extent all good typography is modernist. Wine is so strange and potent a thing that it has been used in the central ritual of religion in one place and time, and attacked by a

8 / 9

All the virtues of the perfect wine glass are paralleled in typography. There is the long, thin stem that obviates fingerprints on the bowl. Why? Because no cloud must come between your eyes and the fiery heart of the liquid. Are not the margins on book pages similarly meant to obviate the necessity of fingering the type page? Again: the glass is colorless or at the most only faintly tinged in the bowl, because the connoisseur judges wine partly by its color and is impatient of anything that alters it. There are a thousand mannerisms in typography that are as impudent and arbitrary as putting port in tumblers of red or green glass! When a goblet has a base that looks too small for security, it does not matter how cleverly it is weighted; you feel nervous lest it should tip over. There are ways of setting lines of type whi

10 / 11

All the virtues of the perfect wine glass are paralleled in typography. There is the long, thin stem that obviates fingerprints on the bowl. Why? Because no cloud must come between your eyes and the fiery heart of the liquid. Are not the margins on book pages similarly meant to obviate the necessity of fingering the type page? Again: the glass is colorless or at the most only faintly tinged in the bowl, because the connoisseur judges wine partly by its color and is impatient of anything that alters it. There are a thousand mannerisms in typography that

12 / 13

All the virtues of the perfect wine glass are paralleled in typography. There is the long, thin stem that obviates fingerprints on the bowl. Why? Because no cloud must come between your eyes and the fiery heart of the liquid. Are not the margins on book pages similarly meant to obviate the necessity of fingering the type page? Again: the glass is colorless or at the most only faintly tinged

14 / 15

All the virtues of the perfect wine glass are paralleled in typography. There is the long, thin stem that obviates fingerprints on the bowl. Why? Because no cloud must come between your eyes and the fiery heart of the liquid. Are not the margins on book pages similarly meant to obviate the necessity of fingering the type page? Again: the glass is colorless or at the most only faintly tinged in the bowl, because the connoisseur judges wine partly by its color and is impatient of anything that alters it. There are a thousand mannerisms in typography that are as impudent and arbitrary as putting port in tumblers of red or green glass! When a gobl

18 / 19

All the virtues of the perfect wine glass are paralleled in typography. There is the long, thin stem that obviates fingerprints on the bowl. Why? Because no cloud must come between your eyes and the fiery heart of the liquid. Are not the margins on book pages similarly meant to obviate the necessity of fingering the type page? Again: the glass is colorless or at the most only faintly tinged in the bowl, beca

24 / 25

All the virtues of the perfect wine glass are paralleled in typography. There is the long, thin stem that obviates fingerprints on the bowl. Why? Because no cloud must come between your eyes and the fiery heart of the liquid. Are not t

36 / 36

All the virtues of the perfect wine glass are paralleled in typography. There is the long, thin stem that

Monotype Times New Roman Semi Bold

6/7

All the virtues of the perfect wine glass are paralleled in typography. There is the long, thin stem that obviates fingerprints on the bowl. Why? Because no cloud must come between your eyes and the fiery heart of the liquid. Are not the margins on book pages similarly meant to obviate the necessity of fingering the type page? Again: the glass is colorless or at the most only faintly tinged in the bowl, because the connoisseur judges wine partly by its color and is impatient of anything that alters it. There are a thousand mannerisms in typography that are as impudent and arbitrary as putting port in tumblers of red or green glass! When a goblet has a base that looks too small for security, it does not matter how cleverly it is weighted; you feel nervous lest it should tip over. There are ways of setting lines of type which may work well enough, and yet keep the reader subconsciously worried by the fear of "doubling" lines, reading three words as one, and so forth. Now the man who first chose glass instead of clay or metal to hold his wine was a "modernist" in the sense in which I am going to use that term. That is, the first thing he asked of this particular object was not "How should it look?" but "What must it do?" and to

8/9

All the virtues of the perfect wine glass are paralleled in typography. There is the long, thin stem that obviates fingerprints on the bowl. Why? Because no cloud must come between your eyes and the fiery heart of the liquid. Are not the margins on book pages similarly meant to obviate the necessity of fingering the type page? Again: the glass is colorless or at the most only faintly tinged in the bowl, because the connoisseur judges wine partly by its color and is impatient of anything that alters it. There are a thousand mannerisms in typography that are as impudent and arbitrary as putting port in tumblers of red or green glass! When a goblet has a base that looks too small for security, it does not matter how cleverly it

10/11

All the virtues of the perfect wine glass are paralleled in typography. There is the long, thin stem that obviates fingerprints on the bowl. Why? Because no cloud must come between your eyes and the fiery heart of the liquid. Are not the margins on book pages similarly meant to obviate the necessity of fingering the type page? Again: the glass is colorless or at the most only faintly tinged in the bowl, because the connoisseur judges wine partly by its color and is impatient of anything that alters it. There are a thousand

12/13

All the virtues of the perfect wine glass are paralleled in typography. There is the long, thin stem that obviates fingerprints on the bowl. Why? Because no cloud must come between your eyes and the fiery heart of the liquid. Are not the margins on book pages similarly meant to obviate the necessity of fingering the type page? Again: the gl

14/15

All the virtues of the perfect wine glass are paralleled in typography. There is the long, thin stem that obviates fingerprints on the bowl. Why? Because no cloud must come between your eyes and the fiery heart of the liquid. Are not the margins on book pages similarly meant to obviate the necessity of fingering the type page? Again: the glass is colorless or at the most only faintly tinged in the bowl, because the connoisseur judges wine partly by its color and is impatient of anything that alters it. There are a thousand mannerisms in typography that are as

18/19

All the virtues of the perfect wine glass are paralleled in typography. There is the long, thin stem that obviates fingerprints on the bowl. Why? Because no cloud must come between your eyes and the fiery heart of the liquid. Are not the margins on book pages similarly meant to obviate the necessity of fingering the type page? Again: the glass is colorles

24/25

All the virtues of the perfect wine glass are paralleled in typography. There is the long, thin stem that obviates fingerprints on the bowl. Why? Because no cloud must come between your eyes and the fi

36/36

All the virtues of the perfect wine glass are paralleled in typography. There is the long, thin

Monotype Times Semi Bold Italic

6 / 7

All the virtues of the perfect wine glass are paralleled in typography. There is the long, thin stem that obviates fingerprints on the bowl. Why? Because no cloud must come between your eyes and the fiery heart of the liquid. Are not the margins on book pages similarly meant to obviate the necessity of fingering the type page? Again: the glass is colorless or at the most only faintly tinged in the bowl, because the connoisseur judges wine partly by its color and is impatient of anything that alters it. There are a thousand mannerisms in typography that are as impudent and arbitrary as putting port in tumblers of red or green glass! When a goblet has a base that looks too small for security, it does not matter how cleverly it is weighted; you feel nervous lest it should tip over. There are ways of setting lines of type which may work well enough, and yet keep the reader subconsciously worried by the fear of "doubling" lines, reading three words as one, and so forth. Now the man who first chose glass instead of clay or metal to hold his wine was a "modernist" in the sense in which I am going to use that term. That is, the first thing he asked of this particular object was not "How should it look?" but "What must it do?" and to that extent all good typography is modernist. Wi

8 / 9

All the virtues of the perfect wine glass are paralleled in typography. There is the long, thin stem that obviates fingerprints on the bowl. Why? Because no cloud must come between your eyes and the fiery heart of the liquid. Are not the margins on book pages similarly meant to obviate the necessity of fingering the type page? Again: the glass is colorless or at the most only faintly tinged in the bowl, because the connoisseur judges wine partly by its color and is impatient of anything that alters it. There are a thousand mannerisms in typography that are as impudent and arbitrary as putting port in tumblers of red or green glass! When a goblet has a base that looks too small for security, it does not matter how cleverly it is weighted; you feel nervous lest

10 / 11

All the virtues of the perfect wine glass are paralleled in typography. There is the long, thin stem that obviates fingerprints on the bowl. Why? Because no cloud must come between your eyes and the fiery heart of the liquid. Are not the margins on book pages similarly meant to obviate the necessity of fingering the type page? Again: the glass is colorless or at the most only faintly tinged in the bowl, because the connoisseur judges wine partly by its color and is impatient of anything that alters it. There are a thousand mannerisms in typogra

12 / 13

All the virtues of the perfect wine glass are paralleled in typography. There is the long, thin stem that obviates fingerprints on the bowl. Why? Because no cloud must come between your eyes and the fiery heart of the liquid. Are not the margins on book pages similarly meant to obviate the necessity of fingering the type page? Again: the glass is colorless or at

14 / 15

All the virtues of the perfect wine glass are paralleled in typography. There is the long, thin stem that obviates fingerprints on the bowl. Why? Because no cloud must come between your eyes and the fiery heart of the liquid. Are not the margins on book pages similarly meant to obviate the necessity of fingering the type page? Again: the glass is colorless or at the most only faintly tinged in the bowl, because the connoisseur judges wine partly by its color and is impatient of anything that alters it. There are a thousand mannerisms in typography that are as impudent and arbitrary as puttin

18 / 19

All the virtues of the perfect wine glass are paralleled in typography. There is the long, thin stem that obviates fingerprints on the bowl. Why? Because no cloud must come between your eyes and the fiery heart of the liquid. Are not the margins on book pages similarly meant to obviate the necessity of fingering the type page? Again: the glass is colorless or at the most onl

24 / 25

All the virtues of the perfect wine glass are paralleled in typography. There is the long, thin stem that obviates fingerprints on the bowl. Why? Because no cloud must come between your eyes and the fiery heart of the liquid. Are

36 / 36

All the virtues of the perfect wine glass are paralleled in typography. There is the long, thin stem that

Monotype Times New Roman Bold

6 / 7

All the virtues of the perfect wine glass are paralleled in typography. There is the long, thin stem that obviates fingerprints on the bowl. Why? Because no cloud must come between your eyes and the fiery heart of the liquid. Are not the margins on book pages similarly meant to obviate the necessity of fingering the type page? Again: the glass is colorless or at the most only faintly tinged in the bowl, because the connoisseur judges wine partly by its color and is impatient of anything that alters it. There are a thousand mannerisms in typography that are as impudent and arbitrary as putting port in tumblers of red or green glass! When a goblet has a base that looks too small for security, it does not matter how cleverly it is weighted; you feel nervous lest it should tip over. There are ways of setting lines of type which may work well enough, and yet keep the reader subconsciously worried by the fear of "doubling" lines, reading three words as one, and so forth. Now the man who first chose glass instead of clay or metal to hold his wine was a "modernist" in the sense in which I am going to use that term. That is, the first thing he asked of this particular object was not "How should it look?" but "What must it do?" and to that extent all good typography is modernist. Wine is so strange and potent a thing that it has been used in the central ritual of religion in one pl

8 / 9

All the virtues of the perfect wine glass are paralleled in typography. There is the long, thin stem that obviates fingerprints on the bowl. Why? Because no cloud must come between your eyes and the fiery heart of the liquid. Are not the margins on book pages similarly meant to obviate the necessity of fingering the type page? Again: the glass is colorless or at the most only faintly tinged in the bowl, because the connoisseur judges wine partly by its color and is impatient of anything that alters it. There are a thousand mannerisms in typography that are as impudent and arbitrary as putting port in tumblers of red or green glass! When a goblet has a base that looks too small for security, it does not matter how cleverly it is weighted; you feel nervous lest it should tip over. There are ways of setting lines of ty

10 / 11

All the virtues of the perfect wine glass are paralleled in typography. There is the long, thin stem that obviates fingerprints on the bowl. Why? Because no cloud must come between your eyes and the fiery heart of the liquid. Are not the margins on book pages similarly meant to obviate the necessity of fingering the type page? Again: the glass is colorless or at the most only faintly tinged in the bowl, because the connoisseur judges wine partly by its color and is impatient of anything that alters it. There are a thousand manneri

12 / 13

All the virtues of the perfect wine glass are paralleled in typography. There is the long, thin stem that obviates fingerprints on the bowl. Why? Because no cloud must come between your eyes and the fiery heart of the liquid. Are not the margins on book pages similarly meant to obviate the necessity of fingering the type page? Again: the glass is colorless or at the most only fain

14 / 15

All the virtues of the perfect wine glass are paralleled in typography. There is the long, thin stem that obviates fingerprints on the bowl. Why? Because no cloud must come between your eyes and the fiery heart of the liquid. Are not the margins on book pages similarly meant to obviate the necessity of fingering the type page? Again: the glass is colorless or at the most only faintly tinged in the bowl, because the connoisseur judges wine partly by its color and is impatient of anything that alters it. There are a thousand mannerisms in typography that are as impudent and arbitrary as putting port in tumblers of red or green glas

18 / 19

All the virtues of the perfect wine glass are paralleled in typography. There is the long, thin stem that obviates fingerprints on the bowl. Why? Because no cloud must come between your eyes and the fiery heart of the liquid. Are not the margins on book pages similarly meant to obviate the necessity of fingering the type page? Again: the glass is colorless or at the most only faintly tinged in the bo

24 / 25

All the virtues of the perfect wine glass are paralleled in typography. There is the long, thin stem that obviates fingerprints on the bowl. Why? Because no cloud must come between your eyes and the fiery heart of the liquid. Are

36 / 36

All the virtues of the perfect wine glass are paralleled in typography. There is the long, thin stem that

Monotype Times Bold Italic

6 | 7

All the virtues of the perfect wine glass are paralleled in typography. There is the long, thin stem that obviates fingerprints on the bowl. Why? Because no cloud must come between your eyes and the fiery heart of the liquid. Are not the margins on book pages similarly meant to obviate the necessity of fingering the type page? Again: the glass is colorless or at the most only faintly tinged in the bowl, because the connoisseur judges wine partly by its color and is impatient of anything that alters it. There are a thousand mannerisms in typography that are as impudent and arbitrary as putting port in tumblers of red or green glass! When a goblet has a base that looks too small for security, it does not matter how cleverly it is weighted; you feel nervous lest it should tip over. There are ways of setting lines of type which may work well enough, and yet keep the reader subconsciously worried by the fear of "doubling" lines, reading three words as one, and so forth. Now the man who first chose glass instead of clay or metal to hold his wine was a "modernist" in the sense in which I am going to use that term. That is, the first thing he asked of this particular object was not "How should it look?" but "What must it do?" and to that extent all good typography is modernist. Wine is so strange and potent a thing that it has been used in the central ritual of religion in one pl

8 | 9

All the virtues of the perfect wine glass are paralleled in typography. There is the long, thin stem that obviates fingerprints on the bowl. Why? Because no cloud must come between your eyes and the fiery heart of the liquid. Are not the margins on book pages similarly meant to obviate the necessity of fingering the type page? Again: the glass is colorless or at the most only faintly tinged in the bowl, because the connoisseur judges wine partly by its color and is impatient of anything that alters it. There are a thousand mannerisms in typography that are as impudent and arbitrary as putting port in tumblers of red or green glass! When a goblet has a base that looks too small for security, it does not matter how cleverly it is weighted; you feel nervous lest it should tip over. There are ways of setting lines of

10 | 11

All the virtues of the perfect wine glass are paralleled in typography. There is the long, thin stem that obviates fingerprints on the bowl. Why? Because no cloud must come between your eyes and the fiery heart of the liquid. Are not the margins on book pages similarly meant to obviate the necessity of fingering the type page? Again: the glass is colorless or at the most only faintly tinged in the bowl, because the connoisseur judges wine partly by its color and is impatient of anything that alters it. There are a thousand mannerisms in

12 | 13

All the virtues of the perfect wine glass are paralleled in typography. There is the long, thin stem that obviates fingerprints on the bowl. Why? Because no cloud must come between your eyes and the fiery heart of the liquid. Are not the margins on book pages similarly meant to obviate the necessity of fingering the type page? Again: the glass is colorless or at the most only fain

14 | 15

All the virtues of the perfect wine glass are paralleled in typography. There is the long, thin stem that obviates fingerprints on the bowl. Why? Because no cloud must come between your eyes and the fiery heart of the liquid. Are not the margins on book pages similarly meant to obviate the necessity of fingering the type page? Again: the glass is colorless or at the most only faintly tinged in the bowl, because the connoisseur judges wine partly by its color and is impatient of anything that alters it. There are a thousand mannerisms in typography that are as impudent and arbitrary as putting port in tumblers of red or green glass!

18 | 19

All the virtues of the perfect wine glass are paralleled in typography. There is the long, thin stem that obviates fingerprints on the bowl. Why? Because no cloud must come between your eyes and the fiery heart of the liquid. Are not the margins on book pages similarly meant to obviate the necessity of fingering the type page? Again: the glass is colorless or at the most only faintly tinged in the

24 | 25

All the virtues of the perfect wine glass are paralleled in typography. There is the long, thin stem that obviates fingerprints on the bowl. Why? Because no cloud must come between your eyes and the fiery heart of the liquid. Ar

36 | 36

All the virtues of the perfect wine glass are paralleled in typography. There is the long, thin stem that obvi

MONOTYPE TIMES NEW ROMAN (CAPS) & TIMES NEW ROMAN EXPERT (SMALL CAPS)

6/7

ALL THE VIRTUES OF THE PERFECT WINE GLASS ARE PARALLEL ED IN TYPOGRAPHY. THERE IS THE LONG, THIN STEM THAT OBV IATES FINGERPRINTS ON THE BOWL. WHY? BECAUSE NO CLOUD MUST COME BETWEEN YOUR EYES AND THE FIERY HEART OF THE LIQUID. ARE NOT THE MARGINS ON BOOK PAGES SIMILARLY ME ANT TO OBVIATE THE NECESSITY OF FINGERING THE TYPE PAGE? AGAIN: THE GLASS IS COLORLESS OR AT THE MOST ONLY FAINT LY TINGED IN THE BOWL, BECAUSE THE CONNOISSEUR JUDGES WINE PARTLY BY ITS COLOR AND IS IMPATIENT OF ANYTHING THAT ALTERS IT. THERE ARE A THOUSAND MANNERISMS IN TYP OGRAPHY THAT ARE AS IMPUDENT AND ARBITRARY AS PUTTI NG PORT IN TUMBLERS OF RED OR GREEN GLASS! WHEN A GOBL ET HAS A BASE THAT LOOKS TOO SMALL FOR SECURITY, IT DOES NOT MATTER HOW CLEVERLY IT IS WEIGHTED; YOU FEEL NERVO US LEST IT SHOULD TIP OVER. THERE ARE WAYS OF SETTING LIN ES OF TYPE WHICH MAY WORK WELL ENOUGH, AND YET KEEP THE READER SUBCONSCIOUSLY WORRIED BY THE FEAR OF DOU BLING LINES, READING THREE WORDS AS ONE, AND SO FORTH. NOW THE MAN WHO FIRST CHOSE GLASS INSTEAD OF CLAY OR METAL TO HOLD HIS WINE WAS A MODERNIST IN THE SENSE IN WHICH I AM GOING TO USE THAT TERM. THAT IS, THE FIRST THI

8/9

ALL THE VIRTUES OF THE PERFECT WINE GLASS ARE PARALLELED IN TYPOGRAPHY. THERE IS THE LONG, THIN STEM THAT OBVIATES FINGERPR INTS ON THE BOWL. WHY? BECAUSE NO CLOUD MUST COME BETWEEN YOUR EYES AND THE FIERY HEART OF THE LIQUID. ARE NOT THE MARGINS ON BOOK PAGES SIMILARLY MEANT TO OBVIATE THE NECESSITY OF FINGERING THE TYPE PAGE? AGAIN: THE GLASS IS COLORLESS OR AT THE MO ST ONLY FAINTLY TINGED IN THE BOWL, BECAU SE THE CONNOISSEUR JUDGES WINE PARTLY BY ITS COLOR AND IS IMPATIENT OF ANYTHING TH AT ALTERS IT. THERE ARE A THOUSAND MANNER ISMS IN TYPOGRAPHY THAT ARE AS IMPUDENT AND ARBITRARY AS PUTTING PORT IN TUMBLE RS OF RED OR GREEN GLASS! WHEN A GOBLET H

10/11

ALL THE VIRTUES OF THE PERFECT WI NE GLASS ARE PARALLELED IN TYPOGR APHY. THERE IS THE LONG, THIN STEM THAT OBVIATES FINGERPRINTS ON THE BOWL. WHY? BECAUSE NO CLOUD MUST COME BETWEEN YOUR EYES AND THE FI ERY HEART OF THE LIQUID. ARE NOT T HE MARGINS ON BOOK PAGES SIMILAR LY MEANT TO OBVIATE THE NECESSITY OF FINGERING THE TYPE PAGE? AGAIN: THE GLASS IS COLORLESS OR AT THE MO ST ONLY FAINTLY TINGED IN THE BOWL, BECAUSE THE CONNOISSEUR JUDGES

12/13

ALL THE VIRTUES OF THE PERFEC T WINE GLASS ARE PARALLELED IN TYPOGRAPHY. THERE IS THE L ONG, THIN STEM THAT OBVIATES FINGERPRINTS ON THE BOWL. W HY? BECAUSE NO CLOUD MUST C OME BETWEEN YOUR EYES AND T HE FIERY HEART OF THE LIQUID. ARE NOT THE MARGINS ON BOOK PAGES SIMILARLY MEANT TO OBVI ATE THE NECESSITY OF FINGERIN

14/15

ALL THE VIRTUES OF THE PERFECT WINE GLASS ARE PARALL ELED IN TYPOGRAPHY. THERE IS THE LONG, THIN STEM THAT OBVIATES FINGERPRINTS ON THE BOWL. WHY? BECAUSE NO C LOUD MUST COME BETWEEN YOUR EYES AND THE FIERY HEA RT OF THE LIQUID. ARE NOT THE MARGINS ON BOOK PAGES SI MILARLY MEANT TO OBVIATE THE NECESSITY OF FINGERING THE TYPE PAGE? AGAIN: THE GLASS IS COLORLESS OR AT THE MOST ONLY FAINTLY TINGED IN THE BOWL, BECAUSE THE CO NNOISSEUR JUDGES WINE PARTLY BY ITS COLOR AND IS IMPA TIENT OF ANYTHING THAT ALTERS IT. THERE ARE A THOUSAN

18/19

ALL THE VIRTUES OF THE PERFECT WINE GLASS ARE PARALLELED IN TYPOGRAPHY. THERE IS TH E LONG, THIN STEM THAT OBVIATES FINGERPRI NTS ON THE BOWL. WHY? BECAUSE NO CLOUD MUST COME BETWEEN YOUR EYES AND THE FIER Y HEART OF THE LIQUID. ARE NOT THE MARGIN S ON BOOK PAGES SIMILARLY MEANT TO OBVIAT E THE NECESSITY OF FINGERING THE TYPE PAGE

24/25

ALL THE VIRTUES OF THE PERFECT WINE GLASS ARE PARALLELED IN TY POGRAPHY. THERE IS THE LONG, THI N STEM THAT OBVIATES FINGERPRIN TS ON THE BOWL. WHY? BECAUSE N O CLOUD MUST COME BETWEEN YOU

36/36

ALL THE VIRTUES OF TH E PERFECT WINE GLASS ARE PARALLELED IN TY POGRAPHY. THERE IS T

Cheltenham

gh

Berthold Cheltenham ATF Old Style

Foundry:	*H. Berthold AG*
Supplier:	*FontShop*
Letterform authenticity:	*Excellent*
Digital outline:	*Fair*
Side bearings:	*Excellent*
Kerning:	*Poor*
Hinting:	*Excellent*
Expert editions:	*No*
Multiple masters:	*No*
Family completeness:	*Fair*
Formats:	*Type 1*
Platforms:	*Mac/PC/UNIX*

Berthold Cheltenham ATF Old Style

72 points

ABCDEFGHIJ
KLMNOPQRST
UVWXYZ&
1234567890$£
abcdefghijklmno
pqrstuvwxyz
ß(!?,.-:;)"

Berthold Cheltenham ATF Old Style Italic

72 points

ABCDEFGHIJ KLMNOPQRST UVWXYZ& 1234567890$£ abcdefghijklmno pqrstuvwxyz ß(!?,.-:;)"

Berthold Cheltenham ATF Old Style

6/7

All the virtues of the perfect wine glass are paralleled in typography. There is the long, thin stem that obviates fingerprints on the bowl. Why? Because no cloud must come between your eyes and the fiery heart of the liquid. Are not the margins on book pages similarly meant to obviate the necessity of fingering the type page? Again: the glass is colorless or at the most only faintly tinged in the bowl, because the connoisseur judges wine partly by its color and is impatient of anything that alters it. There are a thousand mannerisms in typography that are as impudent and arbitrary as putting port in tumblers of red or green glass! When a goblet has a base that looks too small for security, it does not matter how cleverly it is weighted; you feel nervous lest it should tip over. There are ways of setting lines of type which may work well enough, and yet keep the reader subconsciously worried by the fear of "doubling" lines, reading three words as one, and so forth. Now the man who first chose glass instead of clay or metal to hold his wine was a "modernist" in the sense in which I am going to use that term. That is, the first thing he asked of this particular object was not "How should it look?" but "What must it do?" and to that extent all good typography is modernist. Wine is so strange and potent that it has been used in the central ritual of religion in one place and time, and attacked by a virago with a hatchet in another. There is only one other thing in the world that is capable of stirring and altering men's minds to the same extent, and that is the coherent expre

8/9

All the virtues of the perfect wine glass are paralleled in typography. There is the long, thin stem that obviates fingerprints on the bowl. Why? Because no cloud must come between your eyes and the fiery heart of the liquid. Are not the margins on book pages similarly meant to obviate the necessity of fingering the type page? Again: the glass is colorless or at the most only faintly tinged in the bowl, because the connoisseur judges wine partly by its color and is impatient of anything that alters it. There are a thousand mannerisms in typography that are as impudent and arbitrary as putting port in tumblers of red or green glass! When a goblet has a base that looks too small for security, it does not matter how cleverly it is weighted; you feel nervous lest it should tip over. There are ways of setting lines of type which may work well enough, and yet keep the read

10/11

All the virtues of the perfect wine glass are paralleled in typography. There is the long, thin stem that obviates fingerprints on the bowl. Why? Because no cloud must come between your eyes and the fiery heart of the liquid. Are not the margins on book pages similarly meant to obviate the necessity of fingering the type page? Again: the glass is colorless or at the most only faintly tinged in the bowl, because the connoisseur judges wine partly by its color and is impatient of anything that alters it. There are a thousand mannerisms in typography that are as impudent and arbitrary as putting port in tumblers of

12/13

All the virtues of the perfect wine glass are paralleled in typography. There is the long, thin stem that obviates fingerprints on the bowl. Why? Because no cloud must come between your eyes and the fiery heart of the liquid. Are not the margins on book pages similarly meant to obviate the necessity of fingering the type page? Again: the glass is colorless or at the most only faintly tinged in the bowl, because the connoisseur j

14/15

All the virtues of the perfect wine glass are paralleled in typography. There is the long, thin stem that obviates fingerprints on the bowl. Why? Because no cloud must come between your eyes and the fiery heart of the liquid. Are not the margins on book pages similarly meant to obviate the necessity of fingering the type page? Again: the glass is colorless or at the most only faintly tinged in the bowl, because the connoisseur judges wine partly by its color and is impatient of anything that alters it. There are a thousand mannerisms in typography that are as impudent and arbitrary as putting port in tumblers of red or green glass! When a goblet has a base that looks too small for security, it does not matter how cleverly it is weight

18/18

All the virtues of the perfect wine glass are paralleled in typography. There is the long, thin stem that obviates fingerprints on the bowl. Why? Because no cloud must come between your eyes and the fiery heart of the liquid. Are not the margins on book pages similarly meant to obviate the necessity of fingering the type page? Again: the glass is colorless or at the most only faintly tinged in the bowl, because the connoisseur judges wine partly by its color an

24/24

All the virtues of the perfect wine glass are paralleled in typography. There is the long, thin stem that obviates fingerprints on the bowl. Why? Because no cloud must come between your eyes and the fiery heart of the liquid. Are not the margins on book pages si

36/36

All the virtues of the perfect wine glass are paralleled in typography. There is the long, thin stem that obviates fingerp

Berthold Cheltenham ATF Old Style Italic

6/7

All the virtues of the perfect wine glass are paralleled in typography. There is the long, thin stem that obviates fingerprints on the bowl. Why? Because no cloud must come between your eyes and the fiery heart of the liquid. Are not the margins on book pages similarly meant to obviate the necessity of fingering the type page? Again: the glass is colorless or at the most only faintly tinged in the sense in which I am going to use that term. That is, the first thing he asked of this particular object was not "How should it look?" but "What must it do?" and to that extent all good typography is modernist. Wine is so strange and potent a thing that it has been used in the central ritual of religion in one place and time, and attacked by a virago with a hatchet in another. There is only one other thing in the world that is capable of stirring and altering men's minds to the same extent, and that is the coherent expression

8/9

All the virtues of the perfect wine glass are paralleled in typography. There is the long, thin stem that obviates fingerprints on the bowl. Why? Because no cloud must come between your eyes and the fiery heart of the liquid. Are not the margins on book pages similarly meant to obviate the necessity of fingering the type page? Again: the glass is colorless or at the most only faintly tinged in the bowl, because the connoisseur judges wine partly by its color and is impatient of anything that alters it. There are a thousand mannerisms in typography that are as impudent and arbitrary as putting port in tumblers of red or green glass! When a goblet has a base that looks too small for security, it does not matter how cleverly it is weighted; you feel nervous lest it should tip over. There are ways of setting lines of type which may work well enough, and yet keep the reader

10/11

All the virtues of the perfect wine glass are paralleled in typography. There is the long, thin stem that obviates fingerprints on the bowl. Why? Because no cloud must come between your eyes and the fiery heart of the liquid. Are not the margins on book pages similarly meant to obviate the necessity of fingering the type page? Again: the glass is colorless or at the most only faintly tinged in the bowl, because the connoisseur judges wine partly by its color and is impatient of anything that alters it. There are a thousand mannerisms in typography that are as impudent and arbitrary as putting port in tumblers of red or

12/13

All the virtues of the perfect wine glass are paralleled in typography. There is the long, thin stem that obviates fingerprints on the bowl. Why? Because no cloud must come between your eyes and the fiery heart of the liquid. Are not the margins on book pages similarly meant to obviate the necessity of fingering the type page? Again: the glass is colorless or at the most only faintly tinged in the bowl, because the connoisseur judges

14/15

All the virtues of the perfect wine glass are paralleled in typography. There is the long, thin stem that obviates fingerprints on the bowl. Why? Because no cloud must come between your eyes and the fiery heart of the liquid. Are not the margins on book pages similarly meant to obviate the necessity of fingering the type page? Again: the glass is colorless or at the most only faintly tinged in the bowl, because the connoisseur judges wine partly by its color and is impatient of anything that alters it. There are a thousand mannerisms in typography that are as impudent and arbitrary as putting port in tumblers of red or green glass! When a goblet has a base that looks too small for security, it does not matter how cleverly it is weight

18/18

All the virtues of the perfect wine glass are paralleled in typography. There is the long, thin stem that obviates fingerprints on the bowl. Why? Because no cloud must come between your eyes and the fiery heart of the liquid. Are not the margins on book pages similarly meant to obviate the necessity of fingering the type page? Again: the glass is colorless or at the most only faintly tinged in the bowl, because the connoisseur judges wine partly by its color and is i

24/24

All the virtues of the perfect wine glass are paralleled in typography. There is the long, thin stem that obviates fingerprints on the bowl. Why? Because no cloud must come between your eyes and the fiery heart of the liquid. Are not the margins on book pages simi

36/36

All the virtues of the perfect wine glass are paralleled in typography. There is the long, thin stem that obviates fingerpri

Berthold Cheltenham ATF Old Style Condensed

6 / 7

All the virtues of the perfect wine glass are paralleled in typography. There is the long, thin stem that obviates fingerprints on the bowl. Why? Because no cloud must come between your eyes and the fiery heart of the liquid. Are not the margins on book pages similarly meant to obviate the necessity of fingering the type page? Again: the glass is colorless or at the most only faintly tinged in the bowl, because the connoisseur judges wine partly by its color and is impatient of anything that alters it. There are a thousand mannerisms in typography that are as impudent and arbitrary as putting port in tumblers of red or green glass! When a goblet has a base that looks too small for security, it does not matter how cleverly it is weighted; you feel nervous lest it should tip over. There are ways of setting lines of type which may work well enough, and yet keep the reader subconsciously worried by the fear of "doubling" lines, reading three words as one, and so forth. Now the man who first chose glass instead of clay or metal to hold his wine was a "modernist" in the sense in which I am going to use that term. That is, the first thing he asked of this particular object was not "How should it look?" but "What must it do?" and to that extent all good typography is modernist. Wine is so strange and potent a thing that it has been used in the central ritual of religion in one place and time, and attacked by a virago with a hatchet in another. There is only one other thing in the world that is capable of stirring and altering men's minds to the same extent, and that is the coherent expression of thought. That is man's chief miracle, unique to man. There is no "explanation" whatever of the fact that I can make arbitrary sounds which will lead a total stranger to think my own thought. It is sheer magic that I should be able to hold a one

8 / 9

All the virtues of the perfect wine glass are paralleled in typography. Tre is the long, thin stem that obviates fingerprints on the bowl. Why? Because no cloud must come between your eyes and the fiery heart of the liquid. Are not the margins on book pages similarly meant to obviate the necessity of fingering the type page? Again: the glass is colorless or at the most only faintly tinged in the bowl, because the connoisseur judges wine partly by its color and is impatient of anything that alters it. There are a thousand mannerisms in typography that are as impudent and arbitrary as putting port in tumblers of red or green glass! When a goblet has a base that looks too small for security, it does not matter how cleverly it is weighted; you feel nervous lest it should tip over. There are ways of setting lines of type which may work well enough, and yet keep the reader subconsciously worried by the fear of "doubling" lines, reading three words as one, and so forth. Now the man who first chose glass

10 / 11

All the virtues of the perfect wine glass are paralleled in typography. There is the long, thin stem that obviates fingerprints on the bowl. Why? Because no cloud must come between your eyes and the fiery heart of the liquid. Are not the margins on book pages similarly meant to obviate the necessity of fingering the type page? Again: the glass is colorless or at the most only faintly tinged in the bowl, because the connoisseur judges wine partly by its color and is impatient of anything that alters it. There are a thousand mannerisms in typography that are as impudent and arbitrary as putting port in tumblers of red or green glass! When a goblet has a base that looks too small for security, it does not matter

12 / 13

All the virtues of the perfect wine glass are paralleled in typography. There is the long, thin stem that obviates fingerprints on the bowl. Why? Because no cloud must come between your eyes and the fiery heart of the liquid. Are not the margins on book pages similarly meant to obviate the necessity of fingering the type page? Again: the glass is colorless or at the most only faintly tinged in the bowl, because the connoisseur judges wine partly by its color and is impatient of anything that alters it.

14 / 15

All the virtues of the perfect wine glass are paralleled in typography. There is the long, thin stem that obviates fingerprints on the bowl. Why? Because no cloud must come between your eyes and the fiery heart of the liquid. Are not the margins on book pages similarly meant to obviate the necessity of fingering the type page? Again: the glass is colorless or at the most only faintly tinged in the bowl, because the connoisseur judges wine partly by its color and is impatient of anything that alters it. There are a thousand mannerisms in typography that are as impudent and arbitrary as putting port in tumblers of red or green glass! When a goblet has a base that looks too small for security, it does not matter how cleverly it is weighted; you feel nervous lest it should tip over. There are ways of setting lines of type which may work well enough,

18 / 18

All the virtues of the perfect wine glass are paralleled in typography. There is the long, thin stem that obviates fingerprints on the bowl. Why? Because no cloud must come between your eyes and the fiery heart of the liquid. Are not the margins on book pages similarly meant to obviate the necessity of fingering the type page? Again: the glass is colorless or at the most only faintly tinged in the bowl, because the connoisseur judges wine partly by its color and is impatient of anything that alters it. There are a thousand manneri

24 / 24

All the virtues of the perfect wine glass are paralleled in typography. There is the long, thin stem that obviates fingerprints on the bowl. Why? Because no cloud must come between your eyes and the fiery heart of the liquid. Are not the margins on book pages similarly meant to obviate the necessity of fi

36 / 36

All the virtues of the perfect wine glass are paralleled in typography. There is the long, thin stem that obviates fingerprints on the bowl. W

Berthold Cheltenham ATF Old Style Condensed Bold

6 / 7

All the virtues of the perfect wine glass are paralleled in typography. There is the long, thin stem that obviates fingerprints on the bowl. Why? Because no cloud must come between your eyes and the fiery heart of the liquid. Are not the margins on book pages similarly meant to obviate the necessity of fingering the type page? Again: the glass is colorless or at the most only faintly tinged in the bowl, because the connoisseur judges wine partly by its color and is impatient of anything that alters it. There are a thousand mannerisms in typography that are as impudent and arbitrary as putting port in tumblers of red or green glass! When a goblet has a base that looks too small for security, it does not matter how cleverly it is weighted; you feel nervous lest it should tip over. There are ways of setting lines of type which may work well enough, and yet keep the reader subconsciously worried by the fear of "doubling" lines, reading three words as one, and so forth. Now the man who first chose glass instead of clay or metal to hold his wine was a "modernist" in the sense in which I am going to use that term. That is, the first thing he asked of this particular object was not "How should it look?" but "What must it do?" and to that extent all good typography is modernist. Wine is so strange and potent a thing that it has been used in the central ritual of religion in one place and time, and attacked by a virago with a hatchet in another. There is only one other thing in the world that is capable of stirring and altering men's minds to the same extent, and that is the coherent expression of thought. That is man's chief miracle, unique to man. There is no "explanation" whatever of the fact that I can make arbi

8 / 9

All the virtues of the perfect wine glass are paralleled in typography. There is the long, thin stem that obviates fingerprints on the bowl. Why? Because no cloud must come between your eyes and the fiery heart of the liquid. Are not the margins on book pages similarly meant to obviate the necessity of fingering the type page? Again: the glass is colorless or at the most only faintly tinged in the bowl, because the connoisseur judges wine partly by its color and is impatient of anything that alters it. There are a thousand mannerisms in typography that are as impudent and arbitrary as putting port in tumblers of red or green glass! When a goblet has a base that looks too small for security, it does not matter how cleverly it is weighted; you feel nervous lest it should tip over. There are ways of setting lines of type which may work well enough, and yet keep the reader subconsciously worried by the fear of "doubling" lines, reading

10 / 11

All the virtues of the perfect wine glass are paralleled in typography. There is the long, thin stem that obviates fingerprints on the bowl. Why? Because no cloud must come between your eyes and the fiery heart of the liquid. Are not the margins on book pages similarly meant to obviate the necessity of fingering the type page? Again: the glass is colorless or at the most only faintly tinged in the bowl, because the connoisseur judges wine partly by its color and is impatient of anything that alters it. There are a thousand mannerisms in typography that are as impudent and arbitrary as putting port in tumblers of red or green glass! When a goblet has

12 / 13

All the virtues of the perfect wine glass are paralleled in typography. There is the long, thin stem that obviates fingerprints on the bowl. Why? Because no cloud must come between your eyes and the fiery heart of the liquid. Are not the margins on book pages similarly meant to obviate the necessity of fingering the type page? Again: the glass is colorless or at the most only faintly tinged in the bowl, because the connoisseur judges wine partly by its color and is impatient of an

14 / 15

All the virtues of the perfect wine glass are paralleled in typography. There is the long, thin stem that obviates fingerprints on the bowl. Why? Because no cloud must come between your eyes and the fiery heart of the liquid. Are not the margins on book pages similarly meant to obviate the necessity of fingering the type page? Again: the glass is colorless or at the most only faintly tinged in the bowl, because the connoisseur judges wine partly by its color and is impatient of anything that alters it. There are a thousand mannerisms in typography that are as impudent and arbitrary as putting port in tumblers of red or green glass! When a goblet has a base that looks too small for security, it does not matter how cleverly it is weighted; you feel nervous lest it should tip over. There are

18 / 18

All the virtues of the perfect wine glass are paralleled in typo graphy. There is the long, thin stem that obviates fingerprints on the bowl. Why? Because no cloud must come between your eyes and the fiery heart of the liquid. Are not the margins on book pages similarly meant to obviate the necessity of finger ing the type page? Again: the glass is colorless or at the most only faintly tinged in the bowl, because the connoisseur judges wine partly by its color and is impatient of anything that alters

24 / 24

All the virtues of the perfect wine glass are par alleled in typography. There is the long, thin st em that obviates fingerprints on the bowl. Wh y? Because no cloud must come between your eyes and the fiery heart of the liquid. Are not the margins on book pages similarly meant to obvi

36 / 36

All the virtues of the perfect wi ne glass are paralleled in typog raphy. There is the long, thin st em that obviates fingerprints on

Century

5rE2

Berthold Century ATF

Foundry:	*H. Berthold*
Supplier:	*FontShop*
Letterform authenticity:	*Excellent*
Digital outline:	*Fair*
Side bearings:	*Good*
Kerning:	*Poor*
Hinting:	*Excellent*
Expert editions:	*No*
Multiple masters:	*No*
Family completeness:	*Fair*
Formats:	*Type 1*
Platforms:	*Mac / PC / UNIX*

Berthold Century ATF Expanded

72 points

ABCDEFGHIJ
KLMNOPQRST
UVWXYZ&
1234567890$£
abcdefghijklmno
pqrstuvwxyz
ß(!?,.-:;)"

Berthold Century ATF Expanded Italic

72 points

ABCDEFGHIJ KLMNOPQRST UVWXYZ& 1234567890$£ abcdefghijklmno pqrstuvwxyz ß(!?,.-:;)''

Berthold Century ATF Expanded

6 / 8

All the virtues of the perfect wine glass are paralleled in typography. There is the long, thin stem that obviates fingerprints on the bowl. Why? Because no cloud must come between your eyes and the fiery heart of the liquid. Are not the margins on book pages similarly meant to obviate the necessity of fingering the type page? Again: the glass is colorless or at the most only faintly tinged in the bowl, because the connoisseur judges wine partly by its color and is impatient of anything that alters it. There are a thousand mannerisms in typography that are as impudent and arbitrary as putting port in tumblers of red or green glass! When a goblet has a base that looks too small for security, it does not matter how cleverly it is weighted; you feel nervous lest it should tip over. There are ways of setting lines of type which may work well enough, and yet keep the reader subconsciously worried by the fear of "doubling" lines, reading three words as one, and so forth. Now the man who first chose glass instead of clay or metal to hold his wine was a "modernist" in the sense in which I am going to use that term. That

8 / 10

All the virtues of the perfect wine glass are paralleled in typography. There is the long, thin stem that obviates fingerprints on the bowl. Why? Because no cloud must come between your eyes and the fiery heart of the liquid. Are not the margins on book pages similarly meant to obviate the necessity of fingering the type page? Again: the glass is colorless or at the most only faintly tinged in the bowl, because the connoisseur judges wine partly by its color and is impatient of anything that alters it. There are a thousand mannerisms in typography that are as impudent and arbitrary as putting port in tumblers of red or green glass! When a goblet has a base tha

10 / 12

All the virtues of the perfect wine glass are paralleled in typography. There is the long, thin stem that obviates finger prints on the bowl. Why? Because no cl oud must come between your eyes and the fiery heart of the liquid. Are not the margins on book pages similarly meant to obviate the necessity of fingering the type page? Again: the glass is colorless or at the most only faintly tinged in the bowl, because the connoisseur judges wine partly by its color and is impatient

12 / 14

All the virtues of the perfect wine glass are paralleled in typograp hy. There is the long, thin stem that obviates fingerprints on the bowl. Why? Because no cloud must come between your eyes and the fiery heart of the liquid. Are not the ma rgins on book pages similarly me ant to obviate the necessity of fin gering the type page? Again: the

14 / 16

All the virtues of the perfect wine glass are paralleled in typo graphy. There is the long, thin stem that obviates fingerprints on the bowl. Why? Because no cloud must come between your eyes and the fiery heart of the liquid. Are not the margins on book pages similarly meant to obviate the necessity of fin gering the type page? Again: the glass is colorless or at the m ost only faintly tinged in the bowl, because the connoisseur judges wine partly by its color and is impatient of anything that alters it. There are a thousand mannerisms in typogra

18 / 20

All the virtues of the perfect wine glass are pa ralleled in typography. There is the long, thin stem that obviates fingerprints on the bowl. Why? Because no cloud must come between your eyes and the fiery heart of the liquid. Ar e not the margins on book pages similarly m eant to obviate the necessity of fingering the

24 / 25

All the virtues of the perfect wine g lass are paralleled in typography. T here is the long, thin stem that obvi ates fingerprints on the bowl. Why? Because no cloud must come betw een your eyes and the fiery heart of

36 / 36

All the virtues of the per fect wine glass are paral leled in typography. The re is the long, thin stem t

Berthold Century ATF Expanded Italic

6/8

All the virtues of the perfect wine glass are paralleled in typography. There is the long, thin stem that obviates fingerprints on the bowl. Why? Because no cloud must come between your eyes and the fiery heart of the liquid. Are not the margins on book pages similarly meant to obviate the necessity of fingering the type page? Again: the glass is colorless or at the most only faintly tinged in the bowl, because the connoisseur judges wine partly by its color and is impatient of anything that alters it. There are a thousand mannerisms in typography that are as impudent and arbitrary as putting port in tumblers of red or green glass! When a goblet has a base that looks too small for security, it does not matter how cleverly it is weighted; you feel nervous lest it should tip over. There are ways of setting lines of type which may work well enough, and yet keep the reader subconsciously worried by the fear of "doubling" lines, reading three words as one, and so forth. Now the man who first chose glass instead of clay or metal to hold his wine was a "modernist" in the sense in which I am going to use that term. That is, the first thing he asked of this

8/10

All the virtues of the perfect wine glass are paralleled in typography. There is the long, thin stem that obviates fingerprints on the bowl. Why? Because no cloud must come between your eyes and the fiery heart of the liquid. Are not the margins on book pages similarly meant to obviate the necessity of fingering the type page? Again: the glass is colorless or at the most only faintly tinged in the bowl, because the connoisseur judges wine partly by its color and is impatient of anything that alters it. There are a thousand mannerisms in typography that are as impudent and arbitrary as putting port in tumblers of red or green glass! When a goblet has a base that looks too small for

10/12

All the virtues of the perfect wine glass are paralleled in typography. There is the long, thin stem that obviates finger prints on the bowl. Why? Because no cloud must come between your eyes and the fiery heart of the liquid. Are not the margins on book pages similarly meant to obviate the necessity of fingering the type page? Again: the glass is colorless or at the most only faintly tinged in the bowl, because the connoisseur judges wine partly by its color and is impatient

12/14

All the virtues of the perfect wine glass are paralleled in typography. There is the long, thin stem that obviates fingerprints on the bowl. Why? Because no cloud must come e between your eyes and the fiery heart of the liquid. Are not the margins on book pages similarly meant to obviate the necessity of fingering the type page? Again: the glass

14/16

All the virtues of the perfect wine glass are paralleled in typography. There is the long, thin stem that obviates fingerprints on the bowl. Why? Because no cloud must come between your eyes and the fiery heart of the liquid. Are not the margins on book pages similarly meant to obviate the necessity of fingering the type page? Again: the glass is colorless or at the most only faintly tinged in the bowl, because the connoisseur judges wine partly by its color and is impatient of anything that alters it. There are a thousand mannerisms in typogr

18/20

All the virtues of the perfect wine glass are paralleled in typography. There is the long, thin stem that obviates fingerprints on the bowl. Why? Because no cloud must come between your eyes and the fiery heart of the liquid. Are not the margins on book pages similarly meant to obviate the necessity of fingering the type page? A

24/25

All the virtues of the perfect wine glass are paralleled in typography. There is the long, thin stem that obviates fingerprints on the bowl. Why? Because no cloud must come between your eyes and the fiery heart of th

36/36

All the virtues of the perfect wine glass are paralleled in typography. There is the long, thin stem th

Berthold Century ATF Bold

6 / 8

All the virtues of the perfect wine glass are paralleled in typography. There is the long, thin stem that obviates fingerprints on the bowl. Why? Because no cloud must come between your eyes and the fiery heart of the liquid. Are not the margins on book pages similarly meant to obviate the necessity of fingering the type page? Again: the glass is colorless or at the most only faintly tinged in the bowl, because the connoisseur judges wine partly by its color and is impatient of anything that alters it. There are a thousand mannerisms in typography that are as impudent and arbitrary as putting port in tumblers of red or green glass! When a goblet has a base that looks too small for security, it does not matter how cleverly it is weighted; you feel nervous lest it should tip over. There are ways of setting lines of type which may work well enough, and yet keep the reader subconsciously worried by the fear of "doubling" lines, reading three words as one, and so forth. Now the man who first chose glass instead of clay or metal to hold his wine was a "modernist" in the sense in which I am going to use that term. That is, the first thing he asked of this par

8 / 10

All the virtues of the perfect wine glass are paralleled in typography. There is the long, thin stem that obviates fingerprints on the bowl. Why? Because no cloud must come between your eyes and the fiery heart of the liquid. Are not the margins on book pages similarly meant to obviate the necessity of fingering the type page? Again: the glass is colorless or at the most only faintly tinged in the bowl, because the connoisseur judges wine partly by its color and is impatient of anything that alters it. There are a thousand mannerisms in typography that are as impudent and arbitrary as putting port in tumblers of red or green glass! When a goblet has a base that looks too small for securi

10 / 12

All the virtues of the perfect wine glass are paralleled in typography. There is the long, thin stem that obviates fingerprints on the bowl. Why? Because no cloud must come between your eyes and the fiery heart of the liquid. Are not the margins on book pages similarly meant to obviate the necessity of fingering the type page? Again: the glass is colorless or at the most only faintly tinged in the bowl, because the connoisseur judges wine partly by its color and is impatient of anything that al

12 / 14

All the virtues of the perfect wine glass are paralleled in typography. There is the long, thin stem that obviates fingerprints on the bowl. Why? Because no cloud must come between your eyes and the fiery heart of the liquid. Are not the margins on book pages similarly meant to obviate the necessity of fingering the type page? Again: the glass is

14 / 16

All the virtues of the perfect wine glass are paralleled in typography. There is the long, thin stem that obviates fingerprints on the bowl. Why? Because no cloud must come between your eyes and the fiery heart of the liquid. Are not the margins on book pages similarly meant to obviate the necessity of fingering the type page? Again: the glass is colorless or at the most only faintly tinged in the bowl, because the connoisseur judges wine partly by its color and is impatient of anything that alters it. There are a thousand mannerisms in typogra

18 / 20

All the virtues of the perfect wine glass are paralleled in typography. There is the long, thin stem that obviates fingerprints on the bowl. Why? Because no cloud must come between your eyes and the fiery heart of the liquid. Are not the margins on book pages similarly meant to obviate the necessity of fingering the type page? Again: the gla

24 / 25

All the virtues of the perfect wine glass are paralleled in typography. There is the long, thin stem that obviates fingerprints on the bowl. Why? Because no cloud must come between your eyes and the fiery heart of the li

36 / 36

All the virtues of the perfect wine glass are paralleled in typography. There is the long, thin stem th

Berthold Century ATF Bold Italic

6/8

All the virtues of the perfect wine glass are paralleled in typography. There is the long, thin stem that obviates fingerprints on the bowl. Why? Because no cloud must come between your eyes and the fiery heart of the liquid. Are not the margins on book pages similarly meant to obviate the necessity of fingering the type page? Again: the glass is colorless or at the most only faintly tinged in the bowl, because the connoisseur judges wine partly by its color and is impatient of anything that alters it. There are a thousand mannerisms in typography that are as impudent and arbitrary as putting port in tumblers of red or green glass! When a goblet has a base that looks too small for security, it does not matter how cleverly it is weighted; you feel nervous lest it should tip over. There are ways of setting lines of type which may work well enough, and yet keep the reader subconsciously worried by the fear of "doubling" lines, reading three words as one, and so forth. Now the man who first chose glass instead of clay or metal to hold his wine was a "modernist" in the sense in which I am going to use that term. That is, the first thing he asked of this

8/10

All the virtues of the perfect wine glass are paralleled in typography. There is the long, thin stem that obviates fingerprints on the bowl. Why? Because no cloud must come between your eyes and the fiery heart of the liquid. Are not the margins on book pages similarly meant to obviate the necessity of fingering the type page? Again: the glass is colorless or at the most only faintly tinged in the bowl, because the connoisseur judges wine partly by its color and is impatient of anything that alters it. There are a thousand mannerisms in typography that are as impudent and arbitrary as putting port in tumblers of red or green glass! When a goblet has a

10/12

All the virtues of the perfect wine glass are paralleled in typography. There is the long, thin stem that obviates fingerprints on the bowl. Why? Because no cloud must come between your eyes and the fiery heart of the liquid. Are not the margins on book pages similarly meant to obviate the necessity of fingering the type page? Again: the glass is colorless or at the most only faintly tinged in the bowl, because the connoisseur judges wine partly by its color and is imp

12/14

All the virtues of the perfect wine glass are paralleled in typography. There is the long, thin stem that obviates fingerprints on the bowl. Why? Because no cloud must come between your eyes and the fiery heart of the liquid. Are not the margins on book pages similarly meant to obviate the necessity of fingering the type page

11/16

All the virtues of the perfect wineglass are paralleled in typography. There is the long, thin stem that obviates fingerprints on the bowl. Why? Because no cloud must come between your eyes and the fiery heart of the liquid. Are not the margins on book pages similarly meant to obviate the necessity of fingering the type page? Again: the glass is colorless or at the most only faintly tinged in the bowl, because the connoisseur judges wine partly by its color and is impatient of anything that alters it. There are a thousand mannerisms in typo

18/20

All the virtues of the perfect wine glass are paralleled in typography. There is the long, thin stem that obviates fingerprints on the bowl. Why? Because no cloud must come between your eyes and the fiery heart of the liquid. Are not the margins on book pages similarly meant to obviate the necessity of fingering the type pag

24/25

All the virtues of the perfect wine glass are paralleled in typography. There is the long, thin stem that obviates fingerprints on the bowl. Why? Because no cloud must come between your eyes and the fiery heart of the

36/36

All the virtues of the perfect wine glass are paralleled in typography. There is the long, thin stem tha

Bodoni

igD4

Berthold Bodoni Antiqua

Foundry:	*H. Berthold AG*
Supplier:	*Adobe Systems*
Letterform authenticity:	*Excellent*
Digital outline:	*Good*
Side bearings:	*Excellent*
Kerning:	*Good*
Hinting:	*Excellent*
Expert editions:	*Yes*
Multiple masters:	*No*
Family completeness:	*Excellent*
Formats:	*Type 1*
Platforms:	*Mac/PC*

This rendition by Berthold manages to walk a tight rope between the high contrast, inherent to Bodoni, and good legibility. A fully developed set of condensed weights adds greatly to the versatility of this family. Due to the extremely fine thin elements, this typeface would really be improved by the Multiple Masters optical scaling.

72 points

ABCDEFGHIJ
KLMNOPQRST
UVWXYZ&
1234567890$£
ABCDEFGHIJKLMNO
PQRSTUVWXYZ&
abcdefghijklmn
opqrstuvwxyz
1234567890$
fi ß(!?,.-:;)"

Berthold Bodoni Antiqua Italic & Old Style Figs Italic

72 points

ABCDEFGHIJ
KLMNOPQRST
UVWXYZ&
1234567890$£
abcdefghijklmn
opqrstuvwxyz
1234567890o$
fiß(!?,.-:;)"

Berthold Bodoni Antiqua Light

6 / 8

All the virtues of the perfect wine glass are paralleled in typography. There is the long, thin stem that obviates fingerprints on the bowl. Why? Because no cloud must come between your eyes and the fiery heart of the liquid. Are not the margins on book pages similarly meant to obviate the necessity of fingering the type page? Again: the glass is colorless or at the most only faintly tinged in the bowl, because the connoisseur judges wine partly by its color and is impatient of anything that alters it. There are a thousand mannerisms in typography that are as impudent and arbitrary as putting port in tumblers of red or green glass! When a goblet has a base that looks too small for security, it does not matter how cleverly it is weighted; you feel nervous lest it should tip over. There are ways of setting lines of type which may work well enough, and yet keep the reader subconsciously worried by the fear of "doubling" lines, reading three words as one, and so forth. Now the man who first chose glass instead of clay or metal to hold his wine was a "modernist" in the sense in which I am going to use that term. That is, the first thing he ask

8 / 10

All the virtues of the perfect wine glass are paralleled in typography. There is the long, thin stem that obviates fingerprints on the bowl. Why? Because no cloud must come between your eyes and the fiery heart of the liquid. Are not the margins on book pages similarly meant to obviate the necessity of fingering the type page? Again: the glass is colorless or at the most only faintly tinged in the bowl, because the connoisseur judges wine partly by its color and is impatient of anything that alters it. There are a thousand mannerisms in typography that are as impudent and arbitrary as putting port in tumblers of red or green glass! When a goblet has a base that looks too small for sec

10 / 12

All the virtues of the perfect wine glass are paralleled in typography. There is the long, thin stem that obviates fingerprints on the bowl. Why? Because no cloud must come between your eyes and the fiery heart of the liquid. Are not the margins on book pages similarly meant to obviate the necessity of fingering the type page? Again: the glass is colorless or at the most only faintly tinged in the bowl, because the connoisseur judges wine partly by its color and is impatient of anything

12 / 14

All the virtues of the perfect wine glass are paralleled in typography. There is the long, thin stem that obviates fingerprints on the bowl. Why? Because no cloud must come between your eyes and the fiery heart of the liquid. Are not the margins on book pages similarly meant to obviate the necessity of fingering the type page? Again:

14 / 16

All the virtues of the perfect wine glass are paralleled in typography. There is the long, thin stem that obviates fingerprints on the bowl. Why? Because no cloud must come between your eyes and the fiery heart of the liquid. Are not the margins on book pages similarly meant to obviate the necessity of fingering the type page? Again: the glass is colorless or at the most only faintly tinged in the bowl, because the connoisseur judges wine partly by its color and is impatient of anything that alters it. There are a thousand mannerisms in typography that

18 / 20

All the virtues of the perfect wine glass are paralleled in typography. There is the long, thin stem that obviates fingerprints on the bowl. Why? Because no cloud must come between your eyes and the fiery heart of the liquid. Are not the margins on book pages similarly meant to obviate the necessity of fingering the type page? Again: the

24 / 25

All the virtues of the perfect wine glass are paralleled in typography. There is the long, thin stem that obviates fingerprints on the bowl. Why? Because no cloud must come between your eyes and the fiery heart of the liqu

36 / 37

All the virtues of the perfect wine glass are paralleled in typography. There is the long, thin stem tha

Berthold Bodoni Antiqua Light Italic

6 / 8

All the virtues of the perfect wine glass are paralleled in typography. There is the long, thin stem that obviates fingerprints on the bowl. Why? Because no cloud must come between your eyes and the fiery heart of the liquid. Are not the margins on book pages similarly meant to obviate the necessity of fingering the type page? Again: the glass is colorless or at the most only faintly tinged in the bowl, because the connoisseur judges wine partly by its color and is impatient of anything that alters it. There are a thousand mannerisms in typography that are as impudent and arbitrary as putting port in tumblers of red or green glass! When a goblet has a base that looks too small for security, it does not matter how cleverly it is weighted; you feel nervous lest it should tip over. There are ways of setting lines of type which may work well enough, and yet keep the reader subconsciously worried by the fear of "doubling" lines, reading three words as one, and so forth. Now the man who first chose glass instead of clay or metal to hold his wine was a "modernist" in the sense in which I am going to use that term. That is, the first thing he asked of this pa

8 / 10

All the virtues of the perfect wine glass are paralleled in typography. There is the long, thin stem that obviates fingerprints on the bowl. Why? Because no cloud must come between your eyes and the fiery heart of the liquid. Are not the margins on book pages similarly meant to obviate the necessity of fingering the type page? Again: the glass is colorless or at the most only faintly tinged in the bowl, because the connoisseur judges wine partly by its color and is impatient of anything that alters it. There are a thousand mannerisms in typography that are as impudent and arbitrary as putting port in tumblers of red or green glass! When a goblet has a base that looks too small for security, it does

10 / 12

All the virtues of the perfect wine glass are paralleled in typography. There is the long, thin stem that obviates fingerprints on the bowl. Why? Because no cloud must come between your eyes and the fiery heart of the liquid. Are not the margins on book pages similarly meant to obviate the necessity of fingering the type page? Again: the glass is colorless or at the most only faintly tinged in the bowl, because the connoisseur judges wine partly by its color and is impatient of anything that al

12 / 14

All the virtues of the perfect wine glass are paralleled in typography. There is the long, thin stem that obviates fingerprints on the bowl. Why? Because no cloud must come between your eyes and the fiery heart of the liquid. Are not the margins on book pages similarly meant to obviate the necessity of fingering the type page? Again: the

14 / 16

All the virtues of the perfect wine glass are paralleled in typography. There is the long, thin stem that obviates fingerprints on the bowl. Why? Because no cloud must come between your eyes and the fiery heart of the liquid. Are not the margins on book pages similarly meant to obviate the necessity of fingering the type page? Again: the glass is colorless or at the most only faintly tinged in the bowl, because the connoisseur judges wine partly by its color and is impatient of anything that alters it. There are a thousand mannerisms in typography that are a

18 / 20

All the virtues of the perfect wine glass are paralleled in typography. There is the long, thin stem that obviates fingerprints on the bowl. Why? Because no cloud must come between your eyes and the fiery heart of the liquid. Are not the margins on book pages similarly meant to obviate the necessity of fingering the type page? Again: the glass

24 / 25

All the virtues of the perfect wine glass are paralleled in typography. There is the long, thin stem that obviates fingerprints on the bowl. Why? Because no cloud must come between your eyes and the fiery heart of the liqu

36 / 37

All the virtues of the perfect wine glass are paralleled in typography. There is the long, thin stem th

Berthold Bodoni Antiqua

6 / 8

All the virtues of the perfect wine glass are paralleled in typography. There is the long, thin stem that obviates fingerprints on the bowl. Why? Because no cloud must come between your eyes and the fiery heart of the liquid. Are not the margins on book pages similarly meant to obviate the necessity of fingering the type page? Again: the glass is colorless or at the most only faintly tinged in the bowl, because the connoisseur judges wine partly by its color and is impatient of anything that alters it. There are a thousand mannerisms in typography that are as impudent and arbitrary as putting port in tumblers of red or green glass! When a goblet has a base that looks too small for security, it does not matter how cleverly it is weighted; you feel nervous lest it should tip over. There are ways of setting lines of type which may work well enough, and yet keep the reader subconsciously worried by the fear of "doubling" lines, reading three words as one, and so forth. Now the man who first chose glass instead of clay or metal to hold his wine was a "modernist" in the sense in which I am going to use that term. That is, the first thing

8 / 10

All the virtues of the perfect wine glass are paralleled in typography. There is the long, thin stem that obviates fingerprints on the bowl. Why? Because no cloud must come between your eyes and the fiery heart of the liquid. Are not the margins on book pages similarly meant to obviate the necessity of fingering the type page? Again: the glass is colorless or at the most only faintly tinged in the bowl, because the connoisseur judges wine partly by its color and is impatient of anything that alters it. There are a thousand mannerisms in typography that are as impudent and arbitrary as putting port in tumblers of red or green glass! When a goblet has a base that looks too small for sec

10 / 12

All the virtues of the perfect wine glass are paralleled in typography. There is the long, thin stem that obviates fingerprints on the bowl. Why? Because no cloud must come between your eyes and the fiery heart of the liquid. Are not the margins on book pages similarly meant to obviate the necessity of fingering the type page? Again: the glass is colorless or at the most only faintly tinged in the bowl, because the connoisseur judges wine partly by its color and is impatient of any

12 / 14

All the virtues of the perfect wine glass are paralleled in typography. There is the long, thin stem that obviates fingerprints on the bowl. Why? Because no cloud must come between your eyes and the fiery heart of the liquid. Are not the margins on book pages similarly meant to obviate the necessity of fingering the type page? Again:

14 / 16

All the virtues of the perfect wine glass are paralleled in typography. There is the long, thin stem that obviates fingerprints on the bowl. Why? Because no cloud must come between your eyes and the fiery heart of the liquid. Are not the margins on book pages similarly meant to obviate the necessity of fingering the type page? Again: the glass is colorless or at the most only faintly tinged in the bowl, because the connoisseur judges wine partly by its color and is impatient of anything that alters it. There are a thousand mannerisms in typography tha

18 / 20

All the virtues of the perfect wine glass are paralleled in typography. There is the long, thin stem that obviates fingerprints on the bowl. Why? Because no cloud must come between your eyes and the fiery heart of the liquid. Are not the margins on book pages similarly meant to obviate the necessity of fingering the type page? Again: the

24 / 25

All the virtues of the perfect wine glass are paralleled in typography. There is the long, thin stem that obviates fingerprints on the bowl. Why? Because no cloud must come between your eyes and the fiery heart of the liq

36 / 37

All the virtues of the perfect wine glass are paralleled in typography. There is the long, thin stem tha

6 / 8

All the virtues of the perfect wine glass are paralleled in typography. There is the long, thin stem that obviates fingerprints on the bowl. Why? Because no cloud must come between your eyes and the fiery heart of the liquid. Are not the margins on book pages similarly meant to obviate the necessity of fingering the type page? Again: the glass is colorless or at the most only faintly tinged in the bowl, because the connoisseur judges wine partly by its color and is impatient of anything that alters it. There are a thousand mannerisms in typography that are as impudent and arbitrary as putting port in tumblers of red or green glass! When a goblet has a base that looks too small for security, it does not matter how cleverly it is weighted; you feel nervous lest it should tip over. There are ways of setting lines of type which may work well enough, and yet keep the reader subconsciously worried by the fear of "doubling" lines, reading three words as one, and so forth. Now the man who first chose glass instead of clay or metal to hold his wine was a "modernist" in the sense in which I am going to use that term. That is, the first thing he asked of this

8 / 10

All the virtues of the perfect wine glass are paralleled in typography. There is the long, thin stem that obviates fingerprints on the bowl. Why? Because no cloud must come between your eyes and the fiery heart of the liquid. Are not the margins on book pages similarly meant to obviate the necessity of fingering the type page? Again: the glass is colorless or at the most only faintly tinged in the bowl, because the connoisseur judges wine partly by its color and is impatient of anything that alters it. There are a thousand mannerisms in typography that are as impudent and arbitrary as putting port in tumblers of red or green glass! When a goblet has a base that looks too small for security, it does not

10 / 12

All the virtues of the perfect wine glass are paralleled in typography. There is the long, thin stem that obviates fingerprints on the bowl. Why? Because no cloud must come between your eyes and the fiery heart of the liquid. Are not the margins on book pages similarly meant to obviate the necessity of fingering the type page? Again: the glass is colorless or at the most only faintly tinged in the bowl, because the connoisseur judges wine partly by its color and is impatient of anything that a

12 / 14

All the virtues of the perfect wine glass are paralleled in typography. There is the long, thin stem that obviates fingerprints on the bowl. Why? Because no cloud must come between your eyes and the fiery heart of the liquid. Are not the margins on book pages similarly meant to obviate the necessity of fingering the type page? Again: the

14 / 16

All the virtues of the perfect wine glass are paralleled in typography. There is the long, thin stem that obviates fingerprints on the bowl. Why? Because no cloud must come between your eyes and the fiery heart of the liquid. Are not the margins on book pages similarly meant to obviate the necessity of fingering the type page? Again: the glass is colorless or at the most only faintly tinged in the bowl, because the connoisseur judges wine partly by its color and is impatient of anything that alters it. There are a thousand mannerisms in typography that are

18 / 20

All the virtues of the perfect wine glass are paralleled in typography. There is the long, thin stem that obviates fingerprints on the bowl. Why? Because no cloud must come between your eyes and the fiery heart of the liquid. Are not the margins on book pages similarly meant to obviate the necessity of fingering the type page? Again: the glass is

24 / 25

All the virtues of the perfect wine glass are paralleled in typography. There is the long, thin stem that obviates fingerprints on the bowl. Why? Because no cloud must come between your eyes and the fiery heart of the liquid.

36 / 37

All the virtues of the perfect wine glass are paralleled in typography. There is the long, thin stem th

Berthold Bodoni Antiqua Medium

6 / 8

All the virtues of the perfect wine glass are paralleled in typography. There is the long, thin stem that obviates fingerprints on the bowl. Why? Because no cloud must come between your eyes and the fiery heart of the liquid. Are not the margins on book pages similarly meant to obviate the necessity of fingering the type page? Again: the glass is colorless or at the most only faintly tinged in the bowl, because the connoisseur judges wine partly by its color and is impatient of anything that alters it. There are a thousand mannerisms in typography that are as impudent and arbitrary as putting port in tumblers of red or green glass! When a goblet has a base that looks too small for security, it does not matter how cleverly it is weighted; you feel nervous lest it should tip over. There are ways of setting lines of type which may work well enough, and yet keep the reader subconsciously worried by the fear of "doubling" lines, reading three words as one, and so forth. Now the man who first chose glass instead of clay or metal to hold his wine was a

8 / 10

All the virtues of the perfect wine glass are paralleled in typography. There is the long, thin stem that obviates fingerprints on the bowl. Why? Because no cloud must come between your eyes and the fiery heart of the liquid. Are not the margins on book pages similarly meant to obviate the necessity of fingering the type page? Again: the glass is colorless or at the most only faintly tinged in the bowl, because the connoisseur judges wine partly by its color and is impatient of anything that alters it. There are a thousand mannerisms in typography that are as impudent and arbitrary as putting port in tumblers of red or green glass! W

10 / 12

All the virtues of the perfect wine glass are paralleled in typography. There is the long, thin stem that obviates fingerprints on the bowl. Why? Because no cloud must come between your eyes and the fiery heart of the liquid. Are not the margins on book pages similarly meant to obviate the necessity of fingering the type page? Again: the glass is colorless or at the most only faintly tinged in the bowl, because the connoisseur judges wine partly

12 / 14

All the virtues of the perfect wine glass are paralleled in typography. There is the long, thin stem that obviates fingerprints on the bowl. Why? Because no cloud must come between your eyes and the fiery heart of the liquid. Are not the margins on book pages similarly meant to obviate the necessity of fingeri

14 / 16

All the virtues of the perfect wine glass are paralleled in typography. There is the long, thin stem that obviates fingerprints on the bowl. Why? Because no cloud must come between your eyes and the fiery heart of the liquid. Are not the margins on book pages similarly meant to obviate the necessity of fingering the type page? Again: the glass is colorless or at the most only faintly tinged in the bowl, because the connoisseur judges wine partly by its color and is impatient of anything that alters it. There are

18 / 20

All the virtues of the perfect wine glass are paralleled in typography. There is the long, thin stem that obviates fingerprints on the bowl. Why? Because no cloud must come between your eyes and the fiery heart of the liquid. Are not the margins on book pages similarly meant to obviate the necessity of fingerin

24 / 25

All the virtues of the perfect wine glass are paralleled in typography. There is the long, thin stem that obviates fingerprints on the bowl. Why? Because no cloud must come between your eyes and the fier

36 / 37

All the virtues of the perfect wine glass are paralleled in typography. There is the long, thin

Berthold Bodoni Antiqua Medium Italic

6 / 8

All the virtues of the perfect wine glass are paralleled in typography. There is the long, thin stem that obviates fingerprints on the bowl. Why? Because no cloud must come between your eyes and the fiery heart of the liquid. Are not the margins on book pages similarly meant to obviate the necessity of fingering the type page? Again: the glass is colorless or at the most only faintly tinged in the bowl, because the connoisseur judges wine partly by its color and is impatient of anything that alters it. There are a thousand mannerisms in typography that are as impudent and arbitrary as putting port in tumblers of red or green glass! When a goblet has a base that looks too small for security, it does not matter how cleverly it is weighted; you feel nervous lest it should tip over. There are ways of setting lines of type which may work well enough, and yet keep the reader subconsciously worried by the fear of "doubling" lines, reading three words as one, and so forth. Now the man who first chose glass instead of clay or metal to hold his wine was a "mod-

8 / 10

All the virtues of the perfect wine glass are paralleled in typography. There is the long, thin stem that obviates fingerprints on the bowl. Why? Because no cloud must come between your eyes and the fiery heart of the liquid. Are not the margins on book pages similarly meant to obviate the necessity of fingering the type page? Again: the glass is colorless or at the most only faintly tinged in the bowl, because the connoisseur judges wine partly by its coor and is impatient of anything that alters it. There are a thousand mannerisms in typography that are as impudent and arbitrary as putting port in tumblers of red or green glass! When a

10 / 12

All the virtues of the perfect wine glass are paralleled in typography. There is the long, thin stem that obviates fingerprints on the bowl. Why? Because no cloud must come between your eyes and the fiery heart of the liquid. Are not the margins on book pages similarly meant to obviate the necessity of fingering the type page? Again: the glass is colorless or at the most only faintly tinged in the bowl, because the connoisseur judges wine partly by its

12 / 14

All the virtues of the perfect wine glass are paralleled in typography. There is the long, thin stem that obviates fingerprints on the bowl. Why? Because no cloud must come between your eyes and the fiery heart of the liquid. Are not the margins on book pages similarly meant to obviate the necessity of fingering th

14 / 16

All the virtues of the perfect wine glass are paralleled in typography. There is the long, thin stem that obviates fingerprints on the bowl. Why? Because no cloud must come between your eyes and the fiery heart of the liquid. Are not the margins on book pages similarly meant to obviate the necessity of fingering the type page? Again: the glass is colorless or at the most only faintly tinged in the bowl, because the connoisseur judges wine partly by its color and is impatient of anything that alters it. There are a

18 / 20

All the virtues of the perfect wine glass are paralleled in typography. There is the long, thin stem that obviates fingerprints on the bowl. Why? Because no cloud must come between your eyes and the fiery heart of the liquid. Are not the margins on book pages similarly meant to obviate the necessity of fingering the t

24 / 25

All the virtues of the perfect wine glass are paralleled in typography. There is the long, thin stem that obviates fingerprints on the bowl. Why? Because no cloud must come e between your eyes and the fiery

36 / 37

All the virtues of the perfect wine glass are paralleled in typography. There is the long, thin

Berthold Bodoni Antiqua Bold

6 / 8
All the virtues of the perfect wine glass are paralleled in typography. There is the long, thin stem that obviates fingerprints on the bowl. Why? Because no cloud must come between your eyes and the fiery heart of the liquid. Are not the margins on book pages similarly meant to obviate the necessity of fingering the type page? Again: the glass is colorless or at the most only faintly tinged in the bowl, because the connoisseur judges wine partly by its color and is impatient of anything that alters it. There are a thousand mannerisms in typography that are as impudent and arbitrary as putting port in tumblers of red or green glass! When a goblet has a base that looks too small for security, it does not matter how cleverly it is weighted; you feel nervous lest it should tip over. There are ways of setting lines of type which may work well enough, and yet keep the reader subconsciously worried by the fear of "dou

8 / 10
All the virtues of the perfect wine glass are paralleled in typography. There is the long, thin stem that obviates finger prints on the bowl. Why? Because no cloud must come between your eyes and the fiery heart of the liquid. Are not the margins on book pages similarly meant to obviate the necessity of fingering the type page? Again: the glass is colorless or at the most only faintly tinged in the bowl, because the connoisseur judges wine partly by its color and is impatient of anything that alters it. There are a thousand mannerisms in typography

10 / 12
All the virtues of the perfect wine glass are paralleled in typography. There is the long, thin stem that obviates fingerprints on the bowl. Why? Because no cloud must come between your eyes and the fiery heart of the liquid. Are not the margins on book pages similarly meant to obviate the necessity of fingering the type page? Again: the glass is colorless or at the most only faintly tinged

12 / 14
All the virtues of the perfect wine glass are paralleled in typography. There is the long, thin stem that obviates fingerprints on the bowl. Why? Because no cloud must come between your eyes and the fiery heart of the liquid. Are not the margins on book pages similarly m

14 / 16
All the virtues of the perfect wine glass are paralleled in typography. There is the long, thin stem that obviates fingerprints on the bowl. Why? Because no cloud must come between your eyes and the fiery heart of the liquid. Are not the margins on book pages similarly meant to obviate the necessity of fingering the type page? Again: the glass is colorless or at the most only faintly tinged in the bowl, because the connoisseur judges wine

18 / 20
All the virtues of the perfect wine glass are paralleled in typography. There is the long, thin stem that obviates finger prints on the bowl. Why? Because no cloud must come between your eyes and the fiery heart of the liquid. Are not the margins on book pages similarly m

24 / 25
All the virtues of the perfect wine glass are paralleled in typography. There is the long, thin stem that obviates finger prints on the bowl. Why? Because no cloud must come bet

36 / 37
All the virtues of the perfect wine glass are paralleled in typography. There is t

Berthold Bodoni Antiqua Bold Italic

6 / 8

All the virtues of the perfect wine glass are paralleled in typography. There is the long, thin stem that obviates fingerprints on the bowl. Why? Because no cloud must come between your eyes and the fiery heart of the liquid. Are not the margins on book pages similarly meant to obviate the necessity of fingering the type page? Again: the glass is colorless or at the most only faintly tinged in the bowl, because the connoisseur judges wine partly by its color and is impatient of anything that alters it. There are a thousand mannerisms in typography that are as impudent and arbitrary as putting port in tumblers of red or green glass! When a goblet has a base that looks too small for security, it does not matter how cleverly it is weighted; you feel nervous lest it should tip over. There are ways of setting lines of type which may work well enough, and yet keep the reader subconsciously worried by the fear of "doubling" lines,

8 / 10

All the virtues of the perfect wine glass are paralleled in typography. There is the long, thin stem that obviates fingerprints on the bowl. Why? Because no cloud must come between your eyes and the fiery heart of the liquid. Are not the margins on book pages similarly meant to obviate the necessity of fingering the type page? Again: the glass is colorless or at the most only faintly tinged in the bowl, because the connoisseur judges wine partly by its color and is impatient of anything that alters it. There are a thousand mannerisms in typography that are a

10 / 12

All the virtues of the perfect wine glass are paralleled in typography. There is the long, thin stem that obviates fingerprints on the bowl. Why? Because no cloud must come between your eyes and the fiery heart of the liquid. Are not the margins on book pages similarly meant to obviate the necessity of fingering the type page? Again: the glass is colorless or at the most only faintly tinged in the

12 / 14

All the virtues of the perfect wine glass are paralleled in typography. There is the long, thin stem that obviates fingerprints on the bowl. Why? Because no cloud must come between your eyes and the fiery heart of the liquid. Are not the margins on book pages similarly meant

11 / 16

All the virtues of the perfect wine glass are paralleled in typography. There is the long, thin stem that obviates fingerprints on the bowl. Why? Because no cloud must come between your eyes and the fiery heart of the liquid. Are not the margins on book pages similarly meant to obviate the necessity of fingering the type page? Again: the glass is colorless or at the most only faintly tinged in the bowl, because the connoisseur judges wine partly by

18 / 20

All the virtues of the perfect wine glass are paralleled in typography. There is the long, thin stem that obviates fingerprints on the bowl. Why? Because no cloud must come between your eyes and the fiery heart of the liquid. Are not the margins on book pages similarly mea

24 / 25

All the virtues of the perfect wine glass are paralleled in typography. There is the long, thin stem that obviates finge rprints on the bowl. Why? Because no cloud must come bet

36 / 37

All the virtues of the perfect wine glass are paralleled in typography. There is th

Berthold Bodoni Antiqua Small Caps

6 / 8

All the virtues of the perfect wine glass are paralleled in typography. There is the long, thin stem that obviates fingerprints on the bowl. Why? Because no cloud must come between your eyes and the fiery heart of the liquid. Are not the margins on book pages similarly meant to obviate the necessity of fingering the type page? Again: the glass is colorless or at the most only faintly tinged in the bowl, because the connoisseur judges wine partly by its color and is impatient of anything that alters it. There are a thousand mannerisms in typography that are as impudent and arbitrary as putting port in tumblers of red or green glass! When a goblet has a base that looks too small for security, it does not matter how cleverly it is weighted; you feel nervous lest it should tip over. There are ways of setting lines of type which may work well enough, and yet keep the reader subconsciously worried by the fear of "doubling" lines, reading three words as one, and so forth. Now the man who first chose glass instead of clay or metal to hold his wine was a "modernist" in the

8 / 10

All the virtues of the perfect wine glass are paralleled in typography. There is the long, thin stem that obviates fingerprints on the bowl. Why? Because no cloud must come between your eyes and the fiery heart of the liquid. Are not the margins on book pages similarly meant to obviate the necessity of fingering the type page? Again: the glass is colorless or at the most only faintly tinged in the bowl, because the connoisseur judges wine partly by its color and is impatient of anything that alters it. There are a thousand mannerisms in typography that are as impudent and arbitrary as putting port in tumblers of red or green glass! When a goblet

10 / 12

All the virtues of the perfect wine glass are paralleled in typography. There is the long, thin stem that obviates fingerprints on the bowl. Why? Because no cloud must come between your eyes and the fiery heart of the liquid. Are not the margins on book pages similarly meant to obviate the necessity of fingering the type page? Again: the glass is colorless or at the most only faintly tinged in the bowl, because the connoisseur judges wine partly by its color

12 / 14

All the virtues of the perfect wine glass are paralleled in typography. There is the long, thin stem that obviates fingerprints on the bowl. Why? Because no cloud must come between your eyes and the fiery heart of the liquid. Are not the margins on book pages similarly meant to obviate the necessity of fingering the

14 / 16

All the virtues of the perfect wine glass are paralleled in typography. There is the long, thin stem that obviates fingerprints on the bowl. Why? Because no cloud must come between your eyes and the fiery heart of the liquid. Are not the margins on book pages similarly meant to obviate the necessity of fingering the type page? Again: the glass is colorless or at the most only faintly tinged in the bowl, because the connoisseur judges wine partly by its color and is impatient of anything that alters it. There are a thousand

18 / 20

All the virtues of the perfect wine glass are paralleled in typography. There is the long, thin stem that obviates fingerprints on the bowl. Why? Because no cloud must come between your eyes and the fiery heart of the liquid. Are not the margins on book pages similarly meant to obviate the necessity of fingering the t

24 / 25

All the virtues of the perfect wine glass are paralleled in typography. There is the long, thin stem that obviates fingerprints on the bowl. Why? Because no cloud must come b etween your eyes and the fiery hea

36 / 37

All the virtues of the pe rfect wine glass are par alleled in typography. T here is the long, thin st

Didot

Linotype Didot

Foundry:	*Linotype-Hell AG*
Supplier:	*Adobe Systems*
Letterform authenticity:	*Excellent*
Digital outline:	*Excellent*
Side bearings:	*Good*
Kerning:	*Fair*
Hinting:	*Excellent*
Expert editions:	*Yes*
Multiple masters:	*No*
Family completeness:	*Good*
Formats:	*Type 1*
Platforms:	*Mac/PC*

This Linotype revival, despite very high contrast, is extremely legible in text. The family features special display and initials weights.

72 points

ABCDEFGHIJ
KLMNOPQRST
UVWXYZ&
1234567890$£
ABCDEFGHIJKLMN
OPQRSTUVWXYZ
abcdefghijklmn
opqrstuvwxyz
1234567890 0
fiß(!?,.-:;)''

Linotype Didot Italic & Italic Old Style Figures

72 points

ABCDEFGHIJ
KLMNOPQRST
UVWXYZ&
1234567890$£
abcdefghijklmno
pqrstuvwxyz
1234567890 0
fiß(!?,.-:;) ' '

Linotype Didot Roman

6 / 8

All the virtues of the perfect wine glass are paralleled in ty pography. There is the long, thin stem that obviates finger prints on the bowl. Why? Because no cloud must come be tween your eyes and the fiery heart of the liquid. Are not the margins on book pages similarly meant to obviate the necessity of fingering the type page? Again: the glass is col orless or at the most only faintly tinged in the bowl, becau se the connoisseur judges wine partly by its color and is impatient of anything that alters it. There are a thousand mannerisms in typography that are as impudent and arbi trary as putting port in tumblers of red or green glass! Wh en a goblet has a base that looks too small for security, it does not matter how cleverly it is weighted; you feel nervo us lest it should tip over. There are ways of setting lines of type which may work well enough, and yet keep the rea der subconsciously worried by the fear of "doubling" lin es, reading three words as one, and so forth. Now the man who first chose glass instead of clay or metal to hold his

8 / 10

All the virtues of the perfect wine glass are paralleled in typography. There is the long, thin stem that obviates fingerprints on the bowl. Why? Because no cloud must come bet ween your eyes and the fiery heart of the liqu id. Are not the margins on book pages simila rly meant to obviate the necessity of fingeri ng the type page? Again: the glass is colorless or at the most only faintly tinged in the bowl, because the connoisseur judges wine partly by its color and is impatient of anything that alters it. There are a thousand mannerisms in typography that are as impudent and arbit rary as putting port in tumblers of red or gre

10 / 12

All the virtues of the perfect wine gla ss are paralleled in typography. The re is the long, thin stem that obviates fingerprints on the bowl. Why? Beca use no cloud must come between yo ur eyes and the fiery heart of the liqu id. Are not the margins on book pag es similarly meant to obviate the nec essity of fingering the type page? Aga in: the glass is colorless or at the mo st only faintly tinged in the bowl, bec

12 / 14

All the virtues of the perfect wi ne glass are paralleled in typog raphy. There is the long, thin st em that obviates fingerprints on the bowl. Why? Because no cloud must come between yo ur eyes and the fiery heart of the liquid. Are not the margins on book pages similarly meant to obviate the necessity of fing

14 / 16

All the virtues of the perfect wine glass are paralleled in typography. There is the long, thin stem that obviates fi ngerprints on the bowl. Why? Because no cloud must co me between your eyes and the fiery heart of the liquid. Are not the margins on book pages similarly meant to obviate the necessity of fingering the type page? Again: the glass is colorless or at the most only faintly tinged in the bowl, because the connoisseur judges wine partly by its color and is impatient of anything that alters it. Th

18 / 20

All the virtues of the perfect wine glass are paralleled in typography. There is the long, t hin stem that obviates fingerprints on the b owl. Why? Because no cloud must come bet ween your eyes and the fiery heart of the liq uid. Are not the margins on book pages sim ilarly meant to obviate the necessity of finge

24 / 26

All the virtues of the perfect wine glass are paralleled in typograph y. There is the long, thin stem that obviates fingerprints on the bow l. Why? Because no cloud must c

36 / 39

All the virtues of the per fect wine glass are parall eled in typography. The re is the long, thin stem

Linotype Didot Italic

6 / 8

All the virtues of the perfect wine glass are paralleled in typography. There is the long, thin stem that obviates fingerprints on the bowl. Why? Because no cloud must come between your eyes and the fiery heart of the liquid. Are not the margins on book pages similarly meant to obviate the necessity of fingering the type page? Again: the glass is colorless or at the most only faintly tinged in the bowl, because the connoisseur judges wine partly by its color and so forth. Now the man who first chose glass instead of clay or metal to hold his wine was a "modernist" in the sense in which I am going to use that term. That is, the first thing he ask

8 / 10

All the virtues of the perfect wine glass are paralleled in typography. There is the long, thin stem that obviates fingerprints on the bowl. Why? Because no cloud must come between your eyes and the fiery heart of the liquid. Are not the margins on book pages similarly meant to obviate the necessity of fingering the type page? Again: the glass is colorless or at the most only faintly tinged in the bowl, because the connoisseur judges wine partly by its color and is impatient of anything that alters it. There are a thousand mannerisms in typography that are as impudent and arbitrary as putting port in tumblers of red or green glass! When a goblet has a base that looks too small for securit

10 / 12

All the virtues of the perfect wine glass are paralleled in typography. There is the long, thin stem that obviates fingerprints on the bowl. Why? Because no cloud must come between your eyes and the fiery heart of the liquid. Are not the margins on book pages similarly meant to obviate the necessity of fingering the type page? Again: the glass is colorless or at the most only faintly tinged in the bowl, because the connoisseur judges wine

12 / 14

All the virtues of the perfect wine glass are paralleled in typography. There is the long, thin stem that obviates fingerprints on the bowl. Why? Because no cloud must come between your eyes and the fiery heart of the liquid. Are not the margins on book pages similarly meant to obviate the necessity of fingering the type page? Again: the

14 / 16

All the virtues of the perfect wine glass are paralleled in typography. There is the long, thin stem that obviates fingerprints on the bowl. Why? Because no cloud must come between your eyes and the fiery heart of the liquid. Are not the margins on book pages similarly meant to obviate the necessity of fingering the type page? Again: the glass is colorless or at the most only faintly tinged in the bowl, because the connoisseur judges wine partly by its color and is impatient of anything that alters it. There are a thousand mannerisms in typography th

18 / 20

All the virtues of the perfect wine glass are paralleled in typography. There is the long, thin stem that obviates fingerprints on the bowl. Why? Because no cloud must come between your eyes and the fiery heart of the liquid. Are not the margins on book pages similarly meant to obviate the necessity of fingering the type page? Again: the

24 / 26

All the virtues of the perfect wine glass are paralleled in typography. There is the long, thin stem that obviates fingerprints on the bowl. Why? Because no cloud must come between

36 / 39

All the virtues of the perfect wine glass are paralleled in typography. There is the long, thin stem th

LINOTYPE DIDOT ROMAN SMALL CAPS

6 / 8

ALL THE VIRTUES OF THE PERFECT WINE GLASS ARE PARALLELED IN TYPOGRAPHY. THERE IS THE LONG, THIN STEM THAT OBVIATES FINGERPRINTS ON THE BOWL. WHY? BECAUSE NO CLOUD MUST COME BETWEEN YOUR EYES AND THE FIERY HEART OF THE LIQUID. ARE NOT THE MARGINS ON BOOK PAGES SIMILARLY MEANT TO OBVIATE THE NECESSITY OF FINGERING THE TYPE PAGE? AGAIN: THE GLASS IS COLORLESS OR AT THE MOST ONLY FAINTLY TINGED IN THE BOWL, BECAUSE THE CONNOISSEUR JUDGES WINE PARTLY BY ITS COLOR AND IS IMPATIENT OF ANYTHING THAT ALTERS IT. THERE ARE A THOUSAND MANNERISMS IN TYPOGRAPHY THAT ARE AS IMPUDENT AND ARBITRARY AS PUTTING PORT IN TUMBLERS OF RED OR GREEN GLASS! WHEN A GOBLET HAS A BASE THAT LOOKS TOO SMALL FOR SECURITY, IT DOES NOT MATTER HOW CLEVERLY IT IS WEIGHTED; YOU FEEL NERVOUS LEST IT SHOULD TIP OVER. THERE ARE WAYS OF SETTING LINES OF TYPE WHICH MAY WORK WELL ENOUGH, AND YET KEEP THE READER SUBCONSCIOUSLY WORRIED BY THE FEAR OF "DOUBLING" LINES, READING THREE WORDS AS ONE, AND SO FORTH. NOW THE MAN WHO FIRST CHOSE GLA

8 / 10

ALL THE VIRTUES OF THE PERFECT WINE GLASS ARE PARALLELED IN TYPOGRAPHY. THERE IS THE LONG, THIN STEM THAT OBVIATES FINGERPRINTS ON THE BOWL. WHY? BECAUSE NO CLOUD MUST COME BETWEEN YOUR EYES AND THE FIERY HEART OF THE LIQUID. ARE NOT THE MARGINS ON BOOK PAGES SIMILARLY MEANT TO OBVIATE THE NECESSITY OF FINGERING THE TYPE PAGE? AGAIN: THE GLASS IS COLORLESS OR AT THE MOST ONLY FAINTLY TINGED IN THE BOWL, BECAUSE THE CONNOISSEUR JUDGES WINE PARTLY BY ITS COLOR AND IS IMPATIENT OF ANYTHING THAT ALTERS IT. THERE ARE A THOUSAND MANNERISMS IN TYPOGRAPHY THAT ARE AS IMPUDENT AND ARBITRARY AS PUTTING PORT IN TUMB

10 / 12

ALL THE VIRTUES OF THE PERFECT WINE GLASS ARE PARALLELED IN TYPOGRAPHY. THERE IS THE LONG, THIN STEM THAT OBVIATES FINGERPRINTS ON THE BOWL. WHY? BECAUSE NO CLOUD MUST COME BETWEEN YOUR EYES AND THE FIERY HEART OF THE LIQUID. ARE NOT THE MARGINS ON BOOK PAGES SIMILARLY MEANT TO OBVIATE THE NECESSITY OF FINGERING THE TYPE PAGE? AGAIN: THE GLASS IS COLORLESS OR AT THE MOST ONLY FAINTLY TINGED

12 / 14

ALL THE VIRTUES OF THE PERFECT WINE GLASS ARE PARALLELED IN TYPOGRAPHY. THERE IS THE LONG, THIN STEM THAT OBVIATES FINGERPRINTS ON THE BOWL. WHY? BECAUSE NO CLOUD MUST COME BETWEEN YOUR EYES AND THE FIERY HEART OF THE LIQUID. ARE NOT THE MARGINS ON BOOK PAGES SIMILARLY MEANT TO OBVIATE THE NECESSITY OF FINGERING THE TYPE PAGE? AG

14 / 16

ALL THE VIRTUES OF THE PERFECT WINE GLASS ARE PARALLELED IN TYPOGRAPHY. THERE IS THE LONG, THIN STEM THAT OBVIATES FINGERPRINTS ON THE BOWL. WHY? BECAUSE NO CLOUD MUST COME BETWEEN YOUR EYES AND THE FIERY HEART OF THE LIQUID. ARE NOT THE MARGINS ON BOOK PAGES SIMILARLY MEANT TO OBVIATE THE NECESSITY OF FINGERING THE TYPE PAGE? AGAIN: THE GLASS IS COLORLESS OR AT THE MOST ONLY FAINTLY TINGED IN THE BOWL, BECAUSE THE CONNOISSEUR JUDGES WINE PARTLY BY ITS COLOR AND IS IMPATIENT OF ANYTHING

18 / 20

ALL THE VIRTUES OF THE PERFECT WINE GLASS ARE PARALLELED IN TYPOGRAPHY. THERE IS THE LONG, THIN STEM THAT OBVIATES FINGERPRINTS ON THE BOWL. WHY? BECAUSE NO CLOUD MUST COME BETWEEN YOUR EYES AND THE FIERY HEART OF THE LIQUID. ARE NOT THE MARGINS ON BOOK PAGES SIMILARLY MEANT TO OBVIATE THE NECESS

24 / 26

ALL THE VIRTUES OF THE PERFECT WINE GLASS ARE PARALLELED IN TYPOGRAPHY. THERE IS THE LONG, THIN STEM THAT OBVIATES FINGERPRINTS ON THE BOWL. WHY? BECAUSE NO CLOUD

36 / 39

ALL THE VIRTUES OF THE PERFECT WINE GLASS ARE PARALLELED IN TYPOGRAPHY. THERE IS THE LONG, T

Berthold Walbaum Book

Foundry:	*H. Berthold AG*
Supplier:	*Adobe Systems*
Letterform authenticity:	*Excellent*
Digital outline:	*Excellent*
Side bearings:	*Fair*
Kerning:	*Fair*
Hinting:	*Excellent*
Expert editions:	*Yes*
Multiple masters:	*No*
Family completeness:	*Excellent*
Formats:	*Type 1*
Platforms:	*Mac/PC*

ABCDEFGHIJ
KLMNOPQRST
UVWXYZ&
1234567890$£
ABCDEFGHIJKLM
NOPQRSTUVWXYZ
abcdefghijklmn
opqrstuvwxyz
1234567890$&!?
ß(!?,.-:;)"

72 points

ABCDEFGHIJ
KLMNOPQRST
UVWXYZ&
1234567890$£
abcdefghijklm
nopqrstuvwxyz
1234567890$
ß(!?,.-:;)"

Berthold Walbaum Book

6 / 8

All the virtues of the perfect wine glass are paralleled in typography. There is the long, thin stem that obviates fingerprints on the bowl. Why? Because no cloud must come between your eyes and the fiery heart of the liquid. Are not the margins on book pages similarly meant to obviate the necessity of fingering the type page? Again: the glass is colorless or at the most only faintly tinged in the bowl, because the connoisseur judges wine partly by its color and is impatient of anything that alters it. There are a thousand mannerisms in typography that are as impudent and arbitrary as putting port in tumblers of red or green glass! When a goblet has a base that looks too small for security, it does not matter how cleverly it is weighted; you feel nervous lest it should tip over. There are ways of setting lines of type which may work well enough, and yet keep the reader subconsciously worried by the fear of "doubling" lines, reading three words as one, and so forth. Now the man who first chos

8 / 10

All the virtues of the perfect wine glass are paralleled in typography. There is the long, thin stem that obviates fingerprints on the bowl. Why? Because no cloud must come between your eyes and the fiery heart of the liquid. Are not the margins on book pages similarly meant to obviate the necessity of fingering the type page? Again: the glass is colorless or at the most only faintly tinged in the bowl, because the connoisseur judges wine partly by its color and is impatient of anything that alters it. There are a thousand mannerisms in typography that are as impudent and arbitrary as putting port

10 / 12

All the virtues of the perfect wine glass are paralleled in typography. There is the long, thin stem that obviates fingerprints on the bowl. Why? Because no cloud must come between your eyes and the fiery heart of the liquid. Are not the margins on book pages similarly meant to obviate the necessity of fingering the type page? Again: the glass is colorless or at the most only faintly tinged in the bowl, because the conoisseur

12 / 14

All the virtues of the perfect wine glass are paralleled in typography. There is the long, thin stem that obviates fingerprints on the bowl. Why? Because no cloud must come between your eyes and the fiery heart of the liquid. Are not the margins on book pages similarly meant to obviate the necessit

14 / 16

All the virtues of the perfect wine glass are paralleled in typography. There is the long, thin stem that obviates fingerprints on the bowl. Why? Because no cloud must come between your eyes and the fiery heart of the liquid. Are not the margins on book pages similarly meant to obviate the necessity of fingering the type page? Again: the glass is colorless or at the most only faintly tinged in the bowl, because the connoisseur judges wine partly by its color and is impatient of anythin

18 / 20

All the virtues of the perfect wine glass are paralleled in typography. There is the long, thin stem that obviates fingerprints on the bowl. Why? Because no cloud must come between your eyes and the fiery heart of the liquid. Are not the margins on book pages similarly meant to obviate the necessity of

24 / 25

All the virtues of the perfect wine glass are paralleled in typography. There is the long, thin stem that obviates fingerprints on the bowl. Why? Because no cloud must come between your eyes an

36 / 36

All the virtues of the perfect perfect wine glass are paralleled in typography. There is the long, thi

Berthold Walbaum Book Italic

6 / 8

All the virtues of the perfect wine glass are paralleled in typography. There is the long, thin stem that obviates fingerprints on the bowl. Why? Because no cloud must come between your eyes and the fiery heart of the liquid. Are not the margins on book pages similarly meant to obviate the necessity of fingering the type page? Again: the glass is colorless or at the most only faintly tinged in the bowl, because the connoisseur judges wine partly by its color and is impatient of anything that alters it. There are a thousand mannerisms in typography that are as impudent and arbitrary as putting port in tumblers of red or green glass! When a goblet has a base that looks too small for security, it does not matter how cleverly it is weighted; you feel nervous lest it should tip over. There are ways of setting lines of type which may work well enough, and yet keep the reader subconsciously worried by the fear of "doubling" lines, reading three words as one, and so forth. Now the man who first chose glass instead of clay or

8 / 10

All the virtues of the perfect wine glass are paralleled in typography. There is the long, thin stem that obviates fingerprints on the bowl. Why? Because no cloud must come between your eyes and the fiery heart of the liquid. Are not the margins on book pages similarly meant to obviate the necessity of fingering the type page? Again: the glass is colorless or at the most only faintly tinged in the bowl, because the connoisseur judges wine partly by its color and is impatient of anything that alters it. There are a thousand mannerisms in typography that are as impudent and arbitrary as putting port in tumblers of red

10 / 12

All the virtues of the perfect wine glass are paralleled in typography. There is the long, thin stem that obviates fingerprints on the bowl. Why? Because no cloud must come between your eyes and the fiery heart of the liquid. Are not the margins on book pages similarly meant to obviate the necessity of fingering the type page? Again: the glass is colorless or at the most only faintly tinged in the bowl, because the connoisseur judges wine pa

12 / 14

All the virtues of the perfect wine glass are paralleled in typography. There is the long, thin stem that obviates fingerprints on the bowl. Why? Because no cloud must come between your eyes and the fiery heart of the liquid. Are not the margins on book pages similarly meant to obviate the necessity of fin

14 / 16

All the virtues of the perfect wine glass are paralleled in typography. There is the long, thin stem that obviates fingerprints on the bowl. Why? Because no cloud must come between your eyes and the fiery heart of the liquid. Are not the margins on book pages similarly meant to obviate the necessity of fingering the type page? Again: the glass is colorless or at the most only faintly tinged in the bowl, because the connoisseur judges wine partly by its color and is impatient of anything that alters it.

18 / 20

All the virtues of the perfect wine glass are paralleled in typography. There is the long, thin stem that obviates fingerprints on the bowl. Why? Because no cloud must come between your eyes and the fiery heart of the liquid. Are not the margins on book pages similarly meant to obviate the necessity of fin

24 / 25

All the virtues of the perfect wine glass are paralleled in typography. There is the long, thin stem that obviates fingerprints on the bowl. Why? Because no cloud must come between your eyes and the

36 / 36

All the virtues of the perfect wine glass are paralleled in typography. There is the long, th

Berthold Walbaum Book Medium

6 / 8

All the virtues of the perfect wine glass are paralleled in typography. There is the long, thin stem that obviates fingerprints on the bowl. Why? Because no cloud must come between your eyes and the fiery heart of the liquid. Are not the margins on book pages similarly meant to obviate the necessity of fingering the type page? Again: the glass is colorless or at the most only faintly tinged in the bowl, because the connoisseur judges wine partly by its color and is impatient of anything that alters it. There are a thousand mannerisms in typography that are as impudent and arbitrary as putting port in tumblers of red or green glass! When a goblet has a base that looks too small for security, it does not matter how cleverly it is weighted; you feel nervous lest it should tip over. There are ways of setting lines of type which may work well enough, and yet keep the reader subconsciously worried by the fear of "doubling" lines, reading three words

8 / 10

All the virtues of the perfect wine glass are paralleled in typography. There is the long, thin stem that obviates fingerprints on the bowl. Why? Because no cloud must come between your eyes and the fiery heart of the liquid. Are not the margins on book pages similarly meant to obviate the necessity of fingering the type page? Again: the glass is colorless or at the most only faintly tinged in the bowl, because the connoisseur judges wine partly by its color and is impatient of anything that alters it. There are a thousand mannerisms in typography that are as impudent

10 / 12

All the virtues of the perfect wine glass are paralleled in typography. There is the long, thin stem that obviates fingerprints on the bowl. Why? Because no cloud must come between your eyes and the fiery heart of the liquid. Are not the margins on book pages similarly meant to obviate the necessity of fingering the type page? Again: the glass is colorless or at the most only faintly tinged in the bowl, be

12 / 14

All the virtues of the perfect wine glass are paralleled in typography. There is the long, thin stem that obviates fingerprints on the bowl. Why? Because no cloud must come between your eyes and the fiery heart of the liquid. Are not the margins on book pages similarly meant to

14 / 16

All the virtues of the perfect wine glass are paralleled in typography. There is the long, thin stem that obviates fingerprints on the bowl. Why? Because no cloud must come between your eyes and the fiery heart of the liquid. Are not the margins on book pages similarly meant to obviate the necessity of fingering the type page? Again: the glass is colorless or at the most only faintly tinged in the bowl, because the connoisseur judges wine partly by its color

18 / 20

All the virtues of the perfect wine glass are paralleled in typography. There is the long, thin stem that obviates fingerprints on the bowl. Why? Because no cloud must come between your eyes and the fiery heart of the liquid. Are not the margins on book pages similarly meant to ob

24 / 25

All the virtues of the perfect wine glass are paralleled in typography. There is the long, thin stem that obviates fingerprints on the bowl. Why? Because no cloud must come between y

36 / 36

All the virtues of the perfect wine glass are paralleled in typography. There is the l

Berthold Walbaum Book Medium Italic

6 / 8

All the virtues of the perfect wine glass are paralleled in typography. There is the long, thin stem that obviates fingerprints on the bowl. Why? Because no cloud must come between your eyes and the fiery heart of the liquid. Are not the margins on book pages similarly meant to obviate the necessity of fingering the type page? Again: the glass is colorless or at the most only faintly tinged in the bowl, because the connoisseur judges wine partly by its color and is impatient of anything that alters it. There are a thousand mannerisms in typography that are as impudent and arbitrary as putting port in tumblers of red or green glass! When a goblet has a base that looks too small for security, it does not matter how cleverly it is weighted; you feel nervous lest it should tip over. There are ways of setting lines of type which may work well enough, and yet keep the reader subconsciously worried by the fear of "doubling" lines, reading three words

8 / 10

All the virtues of the perfect wine glass are paralleled in typography. There is the long, thin stem that obviates fingerprints on the bowl. Why? Because no cloud must come between your eyes and the fiery heart of the liquid. Are not the margins on book pages similarly meant to obviate the necessity of fingering the type page? Again: the glass is colorless or at the most only faintly tinged in the bowl, because the connoisseur judges wine partly by its color and is impatient of anything that alters it. There are a thousand mannerisms in typography that are as impude

10 / 12

All the virtues of the perfect wine glass are paralleled in typography. There is the long, thin stem that obviates fingerprints on the bowl. Why? Because no cloud must come between your eyes and the fiery heart of the liquid. Are not the margins on book pages similarly meant to obviate the necessity of fingering the type page? Again: the glass is colorless or at the most only faintly tinged in the bowl, be

12 / 14

All the virtues of the perfect wine glass are paralleled in typography. There is the long, thin stem that obviates fingerprints on the bowl. Why? Because no cloud must come between your eyes and the fiery heart of the liquid. Are not the margins on book pages similarly meant to

14 / 16

All the virtues of the perfect wine glass are paralleled in typography. There is the long, thin stem that obviates fingerprints on the bowl. Why? Because no cloud must come between your eyes and the fiery heart of the liquid. Are not the margins on book pages similarly meant to obviate the necessity of fingering the type page? Again: the glass is colorless or at the most only faintly tinged in the bowl, because the connoisseur judges wine partly by its color an

18 / 20

All the virtues of the perfect wine glass are paralleled in typography. There is the long, thin stem that obviates fingerprints on the bowl. Why? Because no cloud must come between your eyes and the fiery heart of the liquid. Are not the margins on book pages similarly meant to ob

24 / 25

All the virtues of the perfect wine glass are paralleled in typography. There is the long, thin stem that obviates fingerprints on the bowl. Why? Because no cloud must come between

36 / 36

All the virtues of the perfect wine glass are paralleled in typography. There is the long, t

Berthold Walbaum Book Bold

6 / 8
All the virtues of the perfect wine glass are paralleled in typography. There is the long, thin stem that obviates fingerprints on the bowl. Why? Because no cloud must come between your eyes and the fiery heart of the liquid. Are not the margins on book pages similarly meant to obviate the necessity of fingering the type page? Again: the glass is colorless or at the most only faintly tinged in the bowl, because the connoisseur judges wine partly by its color and is impatient of anything that alters it. There are a thousand mannerisms in typography that are as impudent and arbitrary as putting port in tumblers of red or green glass! When a goblet has a base that looks too small for security, it does not matter how cleverly it is weighted; you feel nervous lest it should tip over. There are ways of setting lines of type which may work well enough, and yet keep the reader subconsciously worrie

8 / 10
All the virtues of the perfect wine glass are paralleled in typography. There is the long, thin stem that obviates fingerprints on the bowl. Why? Because no cloud must come between your eyes and the fiery heart of the liquid. Are not the margins on book pages similarly meant to obviate the necessity of fingering the type page? Again: the glass is colorless or at the most only faintly tinged in the bowl, because the connoisseur judges wine partly by its color and is impatient of anything that alters it. There are a thousand mannerisms in ty

10 / 12
All the virtues of the perfect wine glass are paralleled in typography. There is the long, thin stem that obviates fingerprints on the bowl. Why? Because no cloud must come between your eyes and the fiery heart of the liquid. Are not the margins on book pages similarly meant to obviate the necessity of fingering the type page? Again: the glass is colorless or at the most only fain

12 / 14
All the virtues of the perfect wine glass are paralleled in typography. There is the long, thin stem that obviates fingerprints on the bowl. Why? Because no cloud must come between your eyes and the fiery heart of the liquid. Are not the margins on book pages simi

14 / 16
All the virtues of the perfect wine glass are paralleled in typography. There is the long, thin stem that obviates fingerprints on the bowl. Why? Because no cloud must come between your eyes and the fiery heart of the liquid. Are not the margins on book pages similarly meant to obviate the necessity of fingering the type page? Again: the glass is colorless or at the most only faintly tinged in the bowl, because the connoisseur judges

18 / 20
All the virtues of the perfect wine glass are paralleled in typography. There is the long, thin stem that obviates fingerprints on the bowl. Why? Because no cloud must come between your eyes and the fiery heart of the liquid. Are not the margins on book pages sim

24 / 25
All the virtues of the perfect wine glass are paralleled in typography. There is the long, thin stem that obviates fingerprints on the bowl. Why? Because no cloud must come b

36 / 36
All the virtues of the perfect wine glass are paralleled in typography. There i

Berthold Walbaum Book Bold Italic

6 / 8

All the virtues of the perfect wine glass are paralleled in typography. There is the long, thin stem that obviates fingerprints on the bowl. Why? Because no cloud must come between your eyes and the fiery heart of the liquid. Are not the margins on book pages similarly meant to obviate the necessity of fingering the type page? Again: the glass is colorless or at the most only faintly tinged in the bowl, because the connoisseur judges wine partly by its color and is impatient of anything that alters it. There are a thousand mannerisms in typography that are as impudent and arbitrary as putting port in tumblers of red or green glass! When a goblet has a base that looks too small for security, it does not matter how cleverly it is weighted; you feel nervous lest it should tip over. There are ways of setting lines of type which may work well enough, and yet keep the reader subconsciously worried by the fear of "doubli

8 / 10

All the virtues of the perfect wine glass are paralleled in typography. There is the long, thin stem that obviates fingerprints on the bowl. Why? Because no cloud must come between your eyes and the fiery heart of the liquid. Are not the margins on book pages similarly meant to obviate the necessity of fingering the type page? Again: the glass is colorless or at the most only faintly tinged in the bowl, because the connoisseur judges wine partly by its color and is impatient of anything that alters it. There are a thousand mannerisms in typography

10 / 12

All the virtues of the perfect wine glass are paralleled in typography. There is the long, thin stem that obviates fingerprints on the bowl. Why? Because no cloud must come between your eyes and the fiery heart of the liquid. Are not the margins on book pages similarly meant to obviate the necessity of fingering the type page? Again: the glass is colorless or at the most only faintly tin

12 / 14

All the virtues of the perfect wine glass are paralleled in typography. There is the long, thin stem that obviates fingerprints on the bowl. Why? Because no cloud must come between your eyes and the fiery heart of the liquid. Are not the margins on book pages similarly m

14 / 16

All the virtues of the perfect wine glass are paralleled in typography. There is the long, thin stem that obviates fingerprints on the bowl. Why? Because no cloud must come between your eyes and the fiery heart of the liquid. Are not the margins on book pages similarly meant to obviate the necessity of fingering the type page? Again: the glass is colorless or at the most only faintly tinged in the bowl, because the connoisseur judges wine partl

18 / 20

All the virtues of the perfect wine glass are paralleled in typography. There is the long, thin stem that obviates fingerprints on the bowl. Why? Because no cloud must come between your eyes and the fiery heart of the liquid. Are not the margins on book pages similarly mea

24 / 25

All the virtues of the perfect wine glass are paralleled in typography. There is the long, thin stem that obviates fingerprints on the bowl. Why? Because no cloud must come

36 / 36

All the virtues of the perfect wine glass are paralleled in typography. There is t

Berthold Walbaum Book Small Caps

6 / 8

All the virtues of the perfect wine glass are paralleled in typography. There is the long, thin stem that obviates fingerprints on the bowl. Why? Because no cloud must come between your eyes and the fiery heart of the liquid. Are not the margins on book pages similarly meant to obviate the necessity of fingering the type page? Again: the glass is colorless or at the most only faintly tinged in the bowl, because the connoisseur judges wine partly by its color and is impatient of anything that alters it. There are a thousand mannerisms in typography that are as impudent and arbitrary as putting port in tumblers of red or green glass! When a goblet has a base that looks too small for security, it does not matter how cleverly it is weighted; you feel nervous lest it should tip over. There are ways of setting lines of type which may work well enough, and yet keep the reader subconsciously worried by the fear of "doubling" lines, reading

8 / 10

All the virtues of the perfect wine glass are paralleled in typography. There is the long, thin stem that obviates fingerprints on the bowl. Why? Because no cloud must come between your eyes and the fiery heart of the liquid. Are not the margins on book pages similarly meant to obviate the necessity of fingering the type page? Again: the glass is colorless or at the most only faintly tinged in the bowl, because the connoisseur judges wine partly by its color and is impatient of anything that alters it. There are a thousand mannerisms in typography that are as

10 / 12

All the virtues of the perfect wine glass are paralleled in typography. There is the long, thin stem that obviates fingerprints on the bowl. Why? Because no cloud must come between your eyes and the fiery heart of the liquid. Are not the margins on book pages similarly meant to obviate the necessity of fingering the type page? Again: the glass is colorless or at the mos

12 / 14

All the virtues of the perfect wine glass are paralleled in typography. There is the long, thin stem that obviates fingerprints on the bowl. Why? Because no cloud must come between your eyes and the fiery heart of the liquid. Are not the margins on book pages

14 / 16

All the virtues of the perfect wine glass are paralleled in typography. There is the long, thin stem that obviates fingerprints on the bowl. Why? Because no cloud must come between your eyes and the fiery heart of the liquid. Are not the margins on book pages similarly meant to obviate the necessity of fingering the type page? Again: the glass is colorless or at the most only faintly tinged in the bowl, because the connoisseu

18 / 20

All the virtues of the perfect wine glass are paralleled in typography. There is the long, thin stem that obviates fingerprints on the bowl. Why? Because no cloud must come between your eyes and the fiery heart of the liquid. Are not the margins on book pag

24 / 25

All the virtues of the perfect wine glass are paralleled in typography. There is the long, thin stem that obviates fingerprints on the bowl. Why? Because no cloud must

36 / 36

All the virtues of the perfect wine glass are paralleled in typography. There

News Gothic

1EaQp

Berthold News Gothic

Foundry:	*H. Berthold AG*
Supplier:	*FontShop*
Letterform authenticity:	*Excellent*
Digital outline:	*Fair*
Side bearings:	*Excellent*
Kerning:	*Fair*
Hinting:	*Excellent*
Expert editions:	*No*
Multiple masters:	*No*
Family completeness:	*Good*
Formats:	*Type 1*
Platforms:	*Mac / PC / UNIX*

Berthold News Gothic

72 points

ABCDEFGHIJKLM
NOPQRSTUVWXYZ&
1234567890$£
abcdefghijklmnop
qrstuvwxyz
ß(!?,.-:;)"

Berthold News Gothic Italic

72 points

*ABCDEFGHIJKLM
NOPQRSTUVWXYZ&
1234567890$£
abcdefghijklmnop
qrstuvwxyz
ß(!?,.-:;)"*

Berthold News Gothic

6 / 8

All the virtues of the perfect wine glass are paralleled in typography. There is the long, thin stem that obviates fingerprints on the bowl. Why? Because no cloud must come between your eyes and the fiery heart of the liquid. Are not the margins on book pages similarly meant to obviate the necessity of fingering the type page? Again: the glass is colorless or at the most only faintly tinged in the bowl, because the connoisseur judges wine partly by its color and is impatient of anything that alters it. There are a thousand mannerisms in typography that are as impudent and arbitrary as putting port in tumblers of red or green glass! When a goblet has a base that looks too small for security, it does not matter how cleverly it is weighted; you feel nervous lest it should tip over. There are ways of setting lines of type which may work well enough, and yet keep the reader subconsciously worried by the fear of "doubling" lines, reading three words as one, and so forth. Now the man who first chose glass instead of clay or metal to hold his wine was a "modernist" in the sense in which I am going to use that term. That is, the first thing he asked of this particular object was not "How should it look?" but "What must it do?" and to that extent all good typography is modernist.

8 / 10

All the virtues of the perfect wine glass are paralleled in typography. There is the long, thin stem that obviates fingerprints on the bowl. Why? Because no cloud must come between your eyes and the fiery heart of the liquid. Are not the margins on book pages similarly meant to obviate the necessity of fingering the type page? Again: the glass is colorless or at the most only faintly tinged in the bowl, because the connoisseur judges wine partly by its color and is impatient of anything that alters it. There are a thousand mannerisms in typography that are as impudent and arbitrary as putting port in tumblers of red or green glass! When a goblet has a base that looks too small for security, it does not matter how cleverly it is weighted; you feel nervous les

10 / 12

All the virtues of the perfect wine glass are paralleled in typography. There is the long, thin stem that obviates fingerprints on the bowl. Why? Because no cloud must come between your eyes and the fiery heart of the liquid. Are not the margins on book pages similarly meant to obviate the necessity of fingering the type page? Again: the glass is colorless or at the most only faintly tinged in the bowl, because the connoisseur judges wine partly by its color and is impatient of anything that alters it. There are a thousand mann

12 / 14

All the virtues of the perfect wine glass are paralleled in typography. There is the long, thin stem that obviates fingerprints on the bowl. Why? Because no cloud must come between your eyes and the fiery heart of the liquid. Are not the margins on book pages similarly meant to obviate the necessity of fingering the type page? Again: the glass is colorless or at the

14 / 16

All the virtues of the perfect wine glass are paralleled in typography. There is the long, thin stem that obviates fingerprints on the bowl. Why? Because no cloud must come between your eyes and the fiery heart of the liquid. Are not the margins on book pages similarly meant to obviate the necessity of fingering the type page? Again: the glass is colorless or at the most only faintly tinged in the bowl, because the connoisseur judges wine partly by its color and is impatient of anything that alters it. There are a thousand mannerisms in typography that are as impudent and arbitrary as putting port in tumblers

18 / 20

All the virtues of the perfect wine glass are paralleled in typography. There is the long, thin stem that obviates fingerprints on the bowl. Why? Because no cloud must come between your eyes and the fiery heart of the liquid. Are not the margins on book pages similarly meant to obviate the necessity of fingering the type page? Again: the glass is colorless or at the most

24 / 25

All the virtues of the perfect wine glass are paralleled in typography. There is the long, thin stem that obviates fingerprints on the bowl. Why? Because no cloud must come between your eyes and the fiery heart of the liquid. Are not the margins o

36 / 36

All the virtues of the perfect wine glass are paralleled in typography. There is the long, thin stem that obviates fi

Berthoold News Gothic Italic

6 / 8

All the virtues of the perfect wine glass are paralleled in typography. There is the long, thin stem that obviates fingerprints on the bowl. Why? Because no cloud must come between your eyes and the fiery heart of the liquid. Are not the margins on book pages similarly meant to obviate the necessity of fingering the type page? Again: the glass is colorless or at the most only faintly tinged in the bowl, because the connoisseur judges wine partly by its color and is impatient of anything that alters it. There are a thousand mannerisms in typography that are as impudent and arbitrary as putting port in tumblers of red or green glass! When a goblet has a base that looks too small for security, it does not matter how cleverly it is weighted; you feel nervous lest it should tip over. There are ways of setting lines of type which may work well enough, and yet keep the reader subconsciously worried by the fear of "doubling" lines, reading three words as one, and so forth. Now the man who first chose glass instead of clay or metal to hold his wine was a "modernist" in the sense in which I am going to use that term. That is, the first thing he asked of this particular object was not "How should it look?" but "What must it do?" and to that extent all good typography is modernist. Wi

8 / 10

All the virtues of the perfect wine glass are paralleled in typography. There is the long, thin stem that obviates fingerprints on the bowl. Why? Because no cloud must come between your eyes and the fiery heart of the liquid. Are not the margins on book pages similarly meant to obviate the necessity of fingering the type page? Again: the glass is colorless or at the most only faintly tinged in the bowl, because the connoisseur judges wine partly by its color and is impatient of anything that alters it. There are a thousand mannerisms in typography that are as impudent and arbitrary as putting port in tumblers of red or green glass! When a goblet has a base that looks too small for security, it does not matter how cleverly it is weighted; you feel nervous lest it

10 / 12

All the virtues of the perfect wine glass are paralleled in typography. There is the long, thin stem that obviates fingerprints on the bowl. Why? Because no cloud must come between your eyes and the fiery heart of the liquid. Are not the margins on book pages similarly meant to obviate the necessity of fingering the type page? Again: the glass is colorless or at the most only faintly tinged in the bowl, because the connoisseur judges wine partly by its color and is impatient of anything that alters it. There are a thou

12 / 14

All the virtues of the perfect wine glass are paralleled in typography. There is the long, thin stem that obviates fingerprints on the bowl. Why? Because no cloud must come between your eyes and the fiery heart of the liquid. Are not the margins on book pages similarly meant to obviate the necessity of fingering the type page? Again: the glass is colorless or at the m

14 / 16

All the virtues of the perfect wine glass are paralleled in typography. There is the long, thin stem that obviates fingerprints on the bowl. Why? Because no cloud must come between your eyes and the fiery heart of the liquid. Are not the margins on book pages similarly meant to obviate the necessity of fingering the type page? Again: the glass is colorless or at the most only faintly tinged in the bowl, because the connoisseur judges wine partly by its color and is impatient of anything that alters it. There are a thousand mannerisms in typography that are as impudent and arbitrary as putting port in tumblers of

18 / 20

All the virtues of the perfect wine glass are paralleled in typography. There is the long, thin stem that obviates fingerprints on the bowl. Why? Because no cloud must come between your eyes and the fiery heart of the liquid. Are not the margins on book pages similarly meant to obviate the necessity of fingering the type page? Again: the glass is colorless or at the most only

24 / 25

All the virtues of the perfect wine glass are paralleled in typography. There is the long, thin stem that obviates fingerprints on the bowl. Why? Because no cloud must come between your eyes and the fiery heart of the liquid. Are not the margins o

36 / 36

All the virtues of the perfect wine glass are paralleled in typography. There is the long, thin stem that obviates fi

Berthold News Gothic Bold

6 / 8

All the virtues of the perfect wine glass are paralleled in typogr aphy. There is the long, thin stem that obviates fingerprints on the bowl. Why? Because no cloud must come between your ey es and the fiery heart of the liquid. Are not the margins on bo ok pages similarly meant to obviate the necessity of fingering the type page? Again: the glass is colorless or at the most only faintly tinged in the bowl, because the connoisseur judges wine partly by its color and is impatient of anything that alters it. Th ere are a thousand mannerisms in typography that are as imp udent and arbitrary as putting port in tumblers of red or green glass! When a goblet has a base that looks too small for securi ty, it does not matter how cleverly it is weighted; you feel ner vous lest it should tip over. There are ways of setting lines of t ype which may work well enough, and yet keep the reader sub consciously worried by the fear of "doubling" lines, reading thr ee words as one, and so forth. Now the man who first chose gla ss instead of clay or metal to hold his wine was a "modernist" in the sense in which I am going to use that term. That is, the first

8 / 10

All the virtues of the perfect wine glass are paral leled in typography. There is the long, thin stem that obviates fingerprints on the bowl. Why? Bec ause no cloud must come between your eyes and the fiery heart of the liquid. Are not the mar gins on book pages similarly meant to obviate the necessity of fingering the type page? Again: the glass is colorless or at the most only faintly tinged in the bowl, because the connoisseur jud ges wine partly by its color and is impatient of anything that alters it. There are a thousand ma nnerisms in typography that are as impudent and arbitrary as putting port in tumblers of red or green glass! When a goblet has a base that loo

10 / 12

All the virtues of the perfect wine gla ss are paralleled in typography. There is the long, thin stem that obviates fing erprints on the bowl. Why? Because no cloud must come between your eyes and the fiery heart of the liquid. Are not the margins on book pages similar ly meant to obviate the necessity of fin gering the type page? Again: the glass is colorless or at the most only faintly tinged in the bowl, because the connoi sseur judges wine partly by its color a

12 / 14

All the virtues of the perfect wi ne glass are paralleled in typogr aphy. There is the long, thin stem that obviates fingerprints on the bowl. Why? Because no cloud mu st come between your eyes and the fiery heart of the liquid. Are not the margins on book pages similarly meant to obviate the necessity of fingering the type

14 / 16

All the virtues of the perfect wine glass are paralleled in typ ography. There is the long, thin stem that obviates fingerpri nts on the bowl. Why? Because no cloud must come betwe en your eyes and the fiery heart of the liquid. Are not the ma rgins on book pages similarly meant to obviate the necessi ty of fingering the type page? Again: the glass is colorless or at the most only faintly tinged in the bowl, because the conn oisseur judges wine partly by its color and is impatient of an ything that alters it. There are a thousand mannerisms in ty

18 / 20

All the virtues of the perfect wine glass are par alleled in typography. There is the long, thin ste m that obviates fingerprints on the bowl. Why? Because no cloud must come between your ey es and the fiery heart of the liquid. Are not the margins on book pages similarly meant to obvi ate the necessity of fingering the type page?

24 / 25

All the virtues of the perfect wine gl ass are paralleled in typography. Th ere is the long, thin stem that obviat es fingerprints on the bowl. Why? Be cause no cloud must come between your eyes and the fiery heart of the l

36 / 36

All the virtues of the perf ect wine glass are parall eled in typography. Ther e is the long, thin stem t

Berthold News Gothic Bold Italic

6 / 0
All the virtues of the perfect wine glass are paralleled in typography. There is the long, thin stem that obviates fingerprints on the bowl. Why? Because no cloud must come between your eyes and the fiery heart of the liquid. Are not the margins on book pages similarly meant to obviate the necessity of fingering the type page? Again: the glass is colorless or at the most only faintly tinged in the bowl, because the connoisseur judges wine partly by its color and is impatient of anything that alters it. There are a thousand mannerisms in typography that are as impudent and arbitrary as putting port in tumblers of red or green glass! When a goblet has a base that looks too small for security, it does not matter how cleverly it is weighted; you feel nervous lest it should tip over. There are ways of setting lines of type which may work well enough, and yet keep the reader subconsciously worried by the fear of "doubling" lines, reading three words as one, and so forth. Now the man who first chose glass instead of clay or metal to hold his wine was a "modernist" in the sense in which I am going to use that term. That is, the first thing he a

8 / 10
All the virtues of the perfect wine glass are paralleled in typography. There is the long, thin stem that obviates fingerprints on the bowl. Why? Because no cloud must come between your eyes and the fiery heart of the liquid. Are not the margins on book pages similarly meant to obviate the necessity of fingering the type page? Again: the glass is colorless or at the most only faintly tinged in the bowl, because the connoisseur judges wine partly by its color and is impatient of anything that alters it. There are a thousand mannerisms in typography that are as impudent and arbitrary as putting port in tumblers of red or green glass! When a goblet has a base that looks too

10 / 12
All the virtues of the perfect wine glass are paralleled in typography. There is the long, thin stem that obviates fingerprints on the bowl. Why? Because no cloud must come between your eyes and the fiery heart of the liquid. Are not the margins on book pages similarly meant to obviate the necessity of fingering the type page? Again: the glass is colorless or at the most only faintly tinged in the bowl, because the connoisseur judges wine partly by its color a

12 / 14
All the virtues of the perfect wine glass are paralleled in typography. There is the long, thin stem that obviates fingerprints on the bowl. Why? Because no cloud must come between your eyes and the fiery heart of the liquid. Are not the margins on book pages similarly meant to obviate the necessity of fingering the type page

14 / 16
All the virtues of the perfect wine glass are paralleled in typography. There is the long, thin stem that obviates fingerprints on the bowl. Why? Because no cloud must come between your eyes and the fiery heart of the liquid. Are not the margins on book pages similarly meant to obviate the necessity of fingering the type page? Again: the glass is colorless or at the most only faintly tinged in the bowl, because the connoisseur judges wine partly by its color and is impatient of anything that alters it. There are a thousand mannerisms in typo

18 / 20
All the virtues of the perfect wine glass are paralleled in typography. There is the long, thin stem that obviates fingerprints on the bowl. Why? Because no cloud must come between your eyes and the fiery heart of the liquid. Are not the margins on book pages similarly meant to obviate the necessity of fingering the type page? Ag

24 / 25
All the virtues of the perfect wine glass are paralleled in typography. There is the long, thin stem that obviates fingerprints on the bowl. Why? Because no cloud must come between your eyes and the fiery heart of the l

36 / 36
All the virtues of the perfect wine glass are paralleled in typography. There is the long, thin stem th

Berthold News Gothic Condensed

6/8

All the virtues of the perfect wine glass are paralleled in typography. There is the long, thin stem that obviates fingerprints on the bowl. Why? Because no cloud must come between your eyes and the fiery heart of the liquid. Are not the margins on book pages similarly meant to obviate the necessity of fingering the type page? Again: the glass is colorless or at the most only faintly tinged in the bowl, because the connoisseur judges wine partly by its color and is impatient of anything that alters it. There are a thousand mannerisms in typography that are as impudent and arbitrary as putting port in tumblers of red or green glass! When a goblet has a base that looks too small for security, it does not matter how cleverly it is weighted; you feel nervous lest it should tip over. There are ways of setting lines of type which may work well enough, and yet keep the reader subconsciously worried by the fear of "doubling" lines, reading three words as one, and so forth. Now the man who first chose glass instead of clay or metal to hold his wine was a "modernist" in the sense in which I am going to use that term. That is, the first thing he asked of this particular object was not "How should it look?" but "What must it do?" and to that extent all good typography is modernist. Wine is so strange and potent a thing that it has been used in the central ritual of religion in one place and time, and attacked by a virago with a hatchet in another. There is only one other thing in the world that is capable of stirring and altering men's minds to the same extent, and that is the coherent

8/10

All the virtues of the perfect wine glass are paralleled in typography. There is the long, thin stem that obviates fingerprints on the bowl. Why? Because no cloud must come between your eyes and the fiery heart of the liquid. Are not the margins on book pages similarly meant to obviate the necessity of fingering the type page? Again: the glass is colorless or at the most only faintly tinged in the bowl, because the connoisseur judges wine partly by its color and is impatient of anything that alters it. There are a thousand mannerisms in typography that are as impudent and arbitrary as putting port in tumblers of red or green glass! When a goblet has a base that looks too small for security, it does not matter how cleverly it is weighted; you feel nervous lest it should tip over. There are ways of setting lines of type which may work well enough, and yet keep the reader subconsciously worried by the fear of "doubling" lines, reading thr

10/12

All the virtues of the perfect wine glass are paralleled in typography. There is the long, thin stem that obviates fingerprints on the bowl. Why? Because no cloud must come between your eyes and the fiery heart of the liquid. Are not the margins on book pages similarly meant to obviate the necessity of fingering the type page? Again: the glass is colorless or at the most only faintly tinged in the bowl, because the connoisseur judges wine partly by its color and is impatient of anything that alters it. There are a thousand mannerisms in typography that are as impudent and arbitrary as putting port in tumblers of red or green glass! When a gob

12/14

All the virtues of the perfect wine glass are paralleled in typography. There is the long, thin stem that obviates fingerprints on the bowl. Why? Because no cloud must come between your eyes and the fiery heart of the liquid. Are not the margins on book pages similarly meant to obviate the necessity of fingering the type page? Again: the glass is colorless or at the most only faintly tinged in the bowl, because the connoisseur judges wine partly by its

14/16

All the virtues of the perfect wine glass are paralleled in typography. There is the long, thin stem that obviates fingerprints on the bowl. Why? Because no cloud must come between your eyes and the fiery heart of the liquid. Are not the margins on book pages similarly meant to obviate the necessity of fingering the type page? Again: the glass is colorless or at the most only faintly tinged in the bowl, because the connoisseur judges wine partly by its color and is impatient of anything that alters it. There are a thousand mannerisms in typography that are as impudent and arbitrary as putting port in tumblers of red or green glass! When a goblet has a base that looks too small for security, it does not matter how cleverly it is weighted; you feel ner

18/20

All the virtues of the perfect wine glass are paralleled in typography. There is the long, thin stem that obviates fingerprints on the bowl. Why? Because no cloud must come between your eyes and the fiery heart of the liquid. Are not the margins on book pages similarly meant to obviate the necessity of fingering the type page? Again: the glass is colorless or at the most only faintly tinged in the bowl, because the connoisseur judges wine partly by its color and is

24/25

All the virtues of the perfect wine glass are paralleled in typography. There is the long, thin stem that obviates fingerprints on the bowl. Why? Because no cloud must come between your eyes and the fiery heart of the liquid. Are not the margins on book pages similarly meant to obviate the necessity

36/36

All the virtues of the perfect wine glass are paralleled in typography. There is the long, thin stem that obviates fingerprints on the bowl. W

Futura

Berthold Futura

Foundry:	*H. Berthold AG*
Supplier:	*FontShop*
Letterform authenticity:	*Excellent*
Digital outline:	*Fair*
Side bearings:	*Excellent*
Kerning:	*Good*
Hinting:	*Excellent*
Expert editions:	*No*
Multiple masters:	*No*
Family completeness:	*Excellent*
Formats:	*Type 1*
Platforms:	*Mac / PC / UNIX*

Berthold Futura

72 points

ABCDEFGHIJKLM
NOPQRSTUVWXY
Z$£&1234567890
abcdefghijklm
nopqrstuvwxyz
ß(!?,.-:;)"

Berthold Futura Book Oblique

72 points

ABCDEFGHIJKLM
NOPQRSTUVWXY
Z$£&1234567890
abcdefghijklmn
opqrstuvwxyz
ß(!?,.-:;)"

Berthold Futura Light

6 / 7

All the virtues of the perfect wine glass are paralleled in typography. There is the long, thin stem that obviates fingerprints on the bowl. Why? Because no cloud must come between your eyes and the fiery heart of the liquid. Are not the margins on book pages similarly meant to obviate the necessity of fingering the type page? Again: the glass is colorless or at the most only faintly tinged in the bowl, because the connoisseur judges wine partly by its color and is impatient of anything that alters it. There are a thousand mannerisms in typography that are as impudent and arbitrary as putting port in tumblers of red or green glass! When a goblet has a base that looks too small for security, it does not matter how cleverly it is weighted; you feel nervous lest it should tip over. There are ways of setting lines of type which may work well enough, and yet keep the reader subconsciously worried by the fear of "doubling" lines, reading three words as one, and so forth. Now the man who first chose glass instead of clay or metal to hold his wine was a "modernist" in the sense in which I am going to use that term. That is, the first thing he asked of this particular object was not "How should it look?" but "What must it do?" and to that extent all good typography is modernist. Wine is so strange and potent a thing that it has been used in the central ritual of religion

8 / 9

All the virtues of the perfect wine glass are paralleled in typography. There is the long, thin stem that obviates fingerprints on the bowl. Why? Because no cloud must come between your eyes and the fiery heart of the liquid. Are not the margins on book pages similarly meant to obviate the necessity of fingering the type page? Again: the glass is colorless or at the most only faintly tinged in the bowl, because the connoisseur judges wine partly by its color and is impatient of anything that alters it. There are a thousand mannerisms in typography that are as impudent and arbitrary as putting port in tumblers of red or green glass! When a goblet has a base that looks too small for security, it does not matter how cleverly it is weighted; you feel nervous lest it should tip over. There are

10 / 11

All the virtues of the perfect wine glass are paralleled in typography. There is the long, thin stem that obviates fingerprints on the bowl. Why? Because no cloud must come between your eyes and the fiery heart of the liquid. Are not the margins on book pages similarly meant to obviate the necessity of fingering the type page? Again: the glass is colorless or at the most only faintly tinged in the bowl, because the connoisseur judges wine partly by its color and is impatient of anything that alters it. There are a

12 / 13

All the virtues of the perfect wine glass are paralleled in typography. There is the long, thin stem that obviates fingerprints on the bowl. Why? Because no cloud must come between your eyes and the fiery heart of the liquid. Are not the margins on book pages similarly meant to obviate the necessity of fingering the type page? Again: the glass is colorless or at the most onl

14 / 15

All the virtues of the perfect wine glass are paralleled in typography. There is the long, thin stem that obviates fingerprints on the bowl. Why? Because no cloud must come between your eyes and the fiery heart of the liquid. Are not the margins on book pages similarly meant to obviate the necessity of fingering the type page? Again: the glass is colorless or at the most only faintly tinged in the bowl, because the connoisseur judges wine partly by its color and is impatient of anything that alters it. There are a thousand mannerisms in typography that are as impudent and arbitrary as putting port in tumblers o

18 / 19

All the virtues of the perfect wine glass are paralleled in typography. There is the long, thin stem that obviates fingerprints on the bowl. Why? Because no cloud must come between your eyes and the fiery heart of the liquid. Are not the margins on book pages similarly meant to obviate the necessity of fingering the type page? Again: the glass is colorless or at the most only faintly tinged in the

24 / 24

All the virtues of the perfect wine glass are paralleled in typography. There is the long, thin stem that obviates fingerprints on the bowl. Why? Because no cloud must come between your eyes and the fiery heart of the liquid. Are not th

36 / 36

All the virtues of the perfect wine glass are paralleled in typography. There is the long, thin stem that obviat

Berthold Futura Light Oblique

6 / 7

All the virtues of the perfect wine glass are paralleled in typography. There is the long, thin stem that obviates fingerprints on the bowl. Why? Because no cloud must come between your eyes and the fiery heart of the liquid. Are not the margins on book pages similarly meant to obviate the necessity of fingering the type page? Again: the glass is colorless or at the most only faintly tinged in the bowl, because the connoisseur judges wine partly by its color and is impatient of anything that alters it. There are a thousand mannerisms in typography that are as impudent and arbitrary as putting port in tumblers of red or green glass! When a goblet has a base that looks too small for security, it does not matter how cleverly it is weighted; you feel nervous lest it should tip over. There are ways of setting lines of type which may work well enough, and yet keep the reader subconsciously worried by the fear of "doubling" lines, reading three words as one, and so forth. Now the man who first chose glass instead of clay or metal to hold his wine was a "modernist" in the sense in which I am going to use that term. That is, the first thing he asked of this particular object was not "How should it look?" but "What must it do?" and to that extent all good typography is modernist. Wine is so strange and potent a thing that it has been used in the central ritual of religion in one place and time, and attacked by a virago with a hatchet in another. There

8 / 9

All the virtues of the perfect wine glass are paralleled in typography. There is the long, thin stem that obviates fingerprints on the bowl. Why? Because no cloud must come between your eyes and the fiery heart of the liquid. Are not the margins on book pages similarly meant to obviate the necessity of fingering the type page? Again: the glass is colorless or at the most only faintly tinged in the bowl, because the connoisseur judges wine partly by its color and is impatient of anything that alters it. There are a thousand mannerisms in typography that are as impudent and arbitrary as putting port in tumblers of red or green glass! When a goblet has a base that looks too small for security, it does not matter how cleverly it is weighted; you feel nervous lest it should tip over. There are ways of setting lines of type which may work well enough, and y

10 / 11

All the virtues of the perfect wine glass are paralleled in typography. There is the long, thin stem that obviates fingerprints on the bowl. Why? Because no cloud must come between your eyes and the fiery heart of the liquid. Are not the margins on book pages similarly meant to obviate the necessity of fingering the type page? Again: the glass is colorless or at the most only faintly tinged in the bowl, because the connoisseur judges wine partly by its color and is impatient of anything that alters it. There are a thousand mannerisms in typography that are

12 / 13

All the virtues of the perfect wine glass are paralleled in typography. There is the long, thin stem that obviates fingerprints on the bowl. Why? Because no cloud must come between your eyes and the fiery heart of the liquid. Are not the margins on book pages similarly meant to obviate the necessity of fingering the type page? Again: the glass is colorless or at the most only faintly tinged in the bowl, bec

14 / 15

All the virtues of the perfect wine glass are paralleled in typography. There is the long, thin stem that obviates fingerprints on the bowl. Why? Because no cloud must come between your eyes and the fiery heart of the liquid. Are not the margins on book pages similarly meant to obviate the necessity of fingering the type page? Again: the glass is colorless or at the most only faintly tinged in the bowl, because the connoisseur judges wine partly by its color and is impatient of anything that alters it. There are a thousand mannerisms in typography that are as impudent and arbitrary as putting port in tumblers of red or green glass! When a goblet has a base

18 / 19

All the virtues of the perfect wine glass are paralleled in typography. There is the long, thin stem that obviates fingerprints on the bowl. Why? Because no cloud must come between your eyes and the fiery heart of the liquid. Are not the margins on book pages similarly meant to obviate the necessity of fingering the type page? Again: the glass is colorless or at the most only faintly tinged in the bowl, because the connoisseur

24 / 24

All the virtues of the perfect wine glass are paralleled in typography. There is the long, thin stem that obviates fingerprints on the bowl. Why? Because no cloud must come between your eyes and the fiery heart of the liquid. Are not the margin

36 / 36

All the virtues of the perfect wine glass are paralleled in typography. There is the long, thin stem that obviates fi

Berthold Futura Book

6 / 7

All the virtues of the perfect wine glass are paralleled in typography. There is the long, thin stem that obviates fingerprints on the bowl. Why? Because no cloud must come between your eyes and the fiery heart of the liquid. Are not the margins on book pages similarly meant to obviate the necessity of fingering the type page? Again: the glass is colorless or at the most only faintly tinged in the bowl, because the connoisseur judges wine partly by its color and is impatient of anything that alters it. There are a thousand mannerisms in typography that are as impudent and arbitrary as putting port in tumblers of red or green glass! When a goblet has a base that looks too small for security, it does not matter how cleverly it is weighted; you feel nervous lest it should tip over. There are ways of setting lines of type which may work well enough, and yet keep the reader subconsciously worried by the fear of "doubling" lines, reading three words as one, and so forth. Now the man who first chose glass instead of clay or metal to hold his wine was a "modernist" in the sense in which I am going to use that term. That is, the first thing he asked of this particular object was not "How should it look?" but "What must it do?" and to that extent all good typography is modernist. Wine is so strange and potent a thing that it has been used in the central ritual of religion in one place and time, and attacked by

8 / 9

All the virtues of the perfect wine glass are paralleled in typography. There is the long, thin stem that obviates fingerprints on the bowl. Why? Because no cloud must come between your eyes and the fiery heart of the liquid. Are not the margins on book pages similarly meant to obviate the necessity of fingering the type page? Again: the glass is colorless or at the most only faintly tinged in the bowl, because the connoisseur judges wine partly by its color and is impatient of anything that alters it. There are a thousand mannerisms in typography that are as impudent and arbitrary as putting port in tumblers of red or green glass! When a goblet has a base that looks too small for security, it does not matter how cleverly it is weighted; you feel nervous lest it should tip over. There are ways of setting lines of type which

10 / 11

All the virtues of the perfect wine glass are paralleled in typography. There is the long, thin stem that obviates fingerprints on the bowl. Why? Because no cloud must come between your eyes and the fiery heart of the liquid. Are not the margins on book pages similarly meant to obviate the necessity of fingering the type page? Again: the glass is colorless or at the most only faintly tinged in the bowl, because the connoisseur judges wine partly by its color and is impatient of anything that alters it. There are a thousand mannerisms in typo

12 / 13

All the virtues of the perfect wine glass are paralleled in typography. There is the long, thin stem that obviates fingerprints on the bowl. Why? Because no cloud must come between your eyes and the fiery heart of the liquid. Are not the margins on book pages similarly meant to obviate the necessity of fingering the type page? Again: the glass is colorless or at the most only faintly tinged in the

14 / 15

All the virtues of the perfect wine glass are paralleled in typography. There is the long, thin stem that obviates fingerprints on the bowl. Why? Because no cloud must come between your eyes and the fiery heart of the liquid. Are not the margins on book pages similarly meant to obviate the necessity of fingering the type page? Again: the glass is colorless or at the most only faintly tinged in the bowl, because the connoisseur judges wine partly by its color and is impatient of anything that alters it. There are a thousand mannerisms in typography that are as impudent and arbitrary as putting port in tumblers of red or green glass! When a

18 / 19

All the virtues of the perfect wine glass are paralleled in typography. There is the long, thin stem that obviates fingerprints on the bowl. Why? Because no cloud must come between your eyes and the fiery heart of the liquid. Are not the margins on book pages similarly meant to obviate the necessity of fingering the type page? Again: the glass is colorless or at the most only faintly tinged in the bowl, because the co

24 / 24

All the virtues of the perfect wine glass are paralleled in typography. There is the long, thin stem that obviates fingerprints on the bowl. Why? Because no cloud must come between your eyes and the fiery heart of the liquid. Are not the

36 / 36

All the virtues of the perfect wine glass are paralleled in typography. There is the long, thin stem that obvi

Berthold Futura Book Oblique

6 / 7

All the virtues of the perfect wine glass are paralleled in typography. There is the long, thin stem that obviates fingerprints on the bowl. Why? Because no cloud must come between your eyes and the fiery heart of the liquid. Are not the margins on book pages similarly meant to obviate the necessity of fingering the type page? Again: the glass is colorless or at the most only faintly tinged in the bowl, because the connoisseur judges wine partly by its color and is impatient of anything that alters it. There are a thousand mannerisms in typography that are as impudent and arbitrary as putting port in tumblers of red or green glass! When a goblet has a base that looks too small for security, it does not matter how cleverly it is weighted; you feel nervous lest it should tip over. There are ways of setting lines of type which may work well enough, and yet keep the reader subconsciously worried by the fear of "doubling" lines, reading three words as one, and so forth. Now the man who first chose glass instead of clay or metal to hold his wine was a "modernist" in the sense in which I am going to use that term. That is, the first thing he asked of this particular object was not "How should it look?" but "What must it do?" and to that extent all good typography is modernist. Wine is so strange and potent a thing that it has been used in the central ritual of religion in one place and time, and attacked by a virago with a hatchet in another. There is only

8 / 9

All the virtues of the perfect wine glass are paralleled in typography. There is the long, thin stem that obviates fingerprints on the bowl. Why? Because no cloud must come between your eyes and the fiery heart of the liquid. Are not the margins on book pages similarly meant to obviate the necessity of fingering the type page? Again: the glass is colorless or at the most only faintly tinged in the bowl, because the connoisseur judges wine partly by its color and is impatient of anything that alters it. There are a thousand mannerisms in typography that are as impudent and arbitrary as putting port in tumblers of red or green glass! When a goblet has a base that looks too small for security, it does not matter how cleverly it is weighted; you feel nervous lest it should tip over. There are ways of setting lines of type which may work well eno

10 / 11

All the virtues of the perfect wine glass are paralleled in typography. There is the long, thin stem that obviates fingerprints on the bowl. Why? Because no cloud must come between your eyes and the fiery heart of the liquid. Are not the margins on book pages similarly meant to obviate the necessity of fingering the type page? Again: the glass is colorless or at the most only faintly tinged in the bowl, because the connoisseur judges wine partly by its color and is impatient of anything that alters it. There are a thousand mannerisms in typography that

12 / 13

All the virtues of the perfect wine glass are paralleled in typography. There is the long, thin stem that obviates fingerprints on the bowl. Why? Because no cloud must come between your eyes and the fiery heart of the liquid. Are not the margins on book pages similarly meant to obviate the necessity of fingering the type page? Again: the glass is colorless or at the most only faintly tinged in the bowl,

14 / 15

All the virtues of the perfect wine glass are paralleled in typography. There is the long, thin stem that obviates fingerprints on the bowl. Why? Because no cloud must come between your eyes and the fiery heart of the liquid. Are not the margins on book pages similarly meant to obviate the necessity of fingering the type page? Again: the glass is colorless or at the most only faintly tinged in the bowl, because the connoisseur judges wine partly by its color and is impatient of anything that alters it. There are a thousand mannerisms in typography that are as impudent and arbitrary as putting port in tumblers of red or green glass! When a goblet has

18 / 19

All the virtues of the perfect wine glass are paralleled in typography. There is the long, thin stem that obviates fingerprints on the bowl. Why? Because no cloud must come between your eyes and the fiery heart of the liquid. Are not the margins on book pages similarly meant to obviate the necessity of fingering the type page? Again: the glass is colorless or at the most only faintly tinged in the bowl, because the

24 / 24

All the virtues of the perfect wine glass are paralleled in typography. There is the long, thin stem that obviates fingerprints on the bowl. Why? Because no cloud must come between your eyes and the fiery heart of the liquid. Are not the margi

36 / 36

All the virtues of the perfect wine glass are paralleled in typography. There is the long, thin stem that obviate

Berthold Futura Medium

6 / 7

All the virtues of the perfect wine glass are paralleled in typography. There is the long, thin stem that obviates fingerprints on the bowl. Why? Because no cloud must come between your eyes and the fiery heart of the liquid. Are not the margins on book pages similarly meant to obviate the necessity of fingering the type page? Again: the glass is colorless or at the most only faintly tinged in the bowl, because the connoisseur judges wine partly by its color and is impatient of anything that alters it. There are a thousand mannerisms in typography that are as impudent and arbitrary as putting port in tumblers of red or green glass! When a goblet has a base that looks too small for security, it does not matter how cleverly it is weighted; you feel nervous lest it should tip over. There are ways of setting lines of type which may work well enough, and yet keep the reader subconsciously worried by the fear of "doubling" lines, reading three words as one, and so forth. Now the man who first chose glass instead of clay or metal to hold his wine was a "modernist" in the sense in which I am going to use that term. That is, the first thing he asked of this particular object was not "How should it look?" but "What must it do?" and to that extent all good typography is modernist. Wine is so strange and potent a thing that it has been used in the central ritual of religion in one place and tim

8 / 9

All the virtues of the perfect wine glass are paralleled in typography. There is the long, thin stem that obviates fingerprints on the bowl. Why? Because no cloud must come between your eyes and the fiery heart of the liquid. Are not the margins on book pages similarly meant to obviate the necessity of fingering the type page? Again: the glass is colorless or at the most only faintly tinged in the bowl, because the connoisseur judges wine partly by its color and is impatient of anything that alters it. There are a thousand mannerisms in typography that are as impudent and arbitrary as putting port in tumblers of red or green glass! When a goblet has a base that looks too small for security, it does not matter how cleverly it is weighted; you feel nervous lest it should tip over. There are ways of settin

10 / 11

All the virtues of the perfect wine glass are paralleled in typography. There is the long, thin stem that obviates fingerprints on the bowl. Why? Because no cloud must come between your eyes and the fiery heart of the liquid. Are not the margins on book pages similarly meant to obviate the necessity of fingering the type page? Again: the glass is colorless or at the most only faintly tinged in the bowl, because the connoisseur judges wine partly by its color and is impatient of anything that alters it. There are a thousand manne

12 / 13

All the virtues of the perfect wine glass are paralleled in typography. There is the long, thin stem that obviates fingerprints on the bowl. Why? Because no cloud must come between your eyes and the fiery heart of the liquid. Are not the margins on book pages similarly meant to obviate the necessity of fingering the type page? Again: the glass is colorless or at the most only fa

14 / 15

All the virtues of the perfect wine glass are paralleled in typography. There is the long, thin stem that obviates fingerprints on the bowl. Why? Because no cloud must come between your eyes and the fiery heart of the liquid. Are not the margins on book pages similarly meant to obviate the necessity of fingering the type page? Again: the glass is colorless or at the most only faintly tinged in the bowl, because the connoisseur judges wine partly by its color and is impatient of anything that alters it. There are a thousand mannerisms in typography that are as impudent and arbitrary as putting port in tumblers of red or green

18 / 19

All the virtues of the perfect wine glass are paralleled in typography. There is the long, thin stem that obviates fingerprints on the bowl. Why? Because no cloud must come between your eyes and the fiery heart of the liquid. Are not the margins on book pages similarly meant to obviate the necessity of fingering the type page? Again: the glass is colorless or at the most only faintly tinged in the bow

24 / 24

All the virtues of the perfect wine glass are paralleled in typography. There is the long, thin stem that obviates fingerprints on the bowl. Why? Because no cloud must come between your eyes and the fiery heart of the liquid. Are n

36 / 36

All the virtues of the perfect wine glass are paralleled in typography. There is the long, thin stem that ob

Berthold Futura Medium Oblique

6 / 7

All the virtues of the perfect wine glass are paralleled in typography. There is the long, thin stem that obviates fingerprints on the bowl. Why? Because no cloud must come between your eyes and the fiery heart of the liquid. Are not the margins on book pages similarly meant to obviate the necessity of fingering the type page? Again: the glass is colorless or at the most only faintly tinged in the bowl, because the connoisseur judges wine partly by its color and is impatient of anything that alters it. There are a thousand mannerisms in typography that are as impudent and arbitrary as putting port in tumblers of red or green glass! When a goblet has a base that looks too small for security, it does not matter how cleverly it is weighted; you feel nervous lest it should tip over. There are ways of setting lines of type which may work well enough, and yet keep the reader subconsciously worried by the fear of "doubling" lines, reading three words as one, and so forth. Now the man who first chose glass instead of clay or metal to hold his wine was a "modernist" in the sense in which I am going to use that term. That is, the first thing he asked of this particular object was not "How should it look?" but "What must it do?" and to that extent all good typography is modernist. Wine is so strange and potent a thing that it has been used in the central ritual of religion in one place and time, an

8 / 9

All the virtues of the perfect wine glass are paralleled in typography. There is the long, thin stem that obviates fingerprints on the bowl. Why? Because no cloud must come between your eyes and the fiery heart of the liquid. Are not the margins on book pages similarly meant to obviate the necessity of fingering the type page? Again: the glass is colorless or at the most only faintly tinged in the bowl, because the connoisseur judges wine partly by its color and is impatient of anything that alters it. There are a thousand mannerisms in typography that are as impudent and arbitrary as putting port in tumblers of red or green glass! When a goblet has a base that looks too small for security, it does not matter how cleverly it is weighted; you feel nervous lest it should tip over. There are ways of setting li

10 / 11

All the virtues of the perfect wine glass are paralleled in typography. There is the long, thin stem that obviates fingerprints on the bowl. Why? Because no cloud must come between your eyes and the fiery heart of the liquid. Are not the margins on book pages similarly meant to obviate the necessity of fingering the type page? Again: the glass is colorless or at the most only faintly tinged in the bowl, because the connoisseur judges wine partly by its color and is impatient of anything that alters it. There are a thousand manne

12 / 13

All the virtues of the perfect wine glass are paralleled in typography. There is the long, thin stem that obviates fingerprints on the bowl. Why? Because no cloud must come between your eyes and the fiery heart of the liquid. Are not the margins on book pages similarly meant to obviate the necessity of fingering the type page? Again: the glass is colorless or at the most only faintly

14 / 15

All the virtues of the perfect wine glass are paralleled in typography. There is the long, thin stem that obviates fingerprints on the bowl. Why? Because no cloud must come between your eyes and the fiery heart of the liquid. Are not the margins on book pages similarly meant to obviate the necessity of fingering the type page? Again: the glass is colorless or at the most only faintly tinged in the bowl, because the connoisseur judges wine partly by its color and is impatient of anything that alters it. There are a thousand mannerisms in typography that are as impudent and arbitrary as putting port in tumblers of red or green g

18 / 19

All the virtues of the perfect wine glass are paralleled in typography. There is the long, thin stem that obviates fingerprints on the bowl. Why? Because no cloud must come between your eyes and the fiery heart of the liquid. Are not the margins on book pages similarly meant to obviate the necessity of fingering the type page? Again: the glass is colorless or at the most only faintly tinged in the bowl

24 / 24

All the virtues of the perfect wine glass are paralleled in typography. There is the long, thin stem that obviates fingerprints on the bowl. Why? Because no cloud must come between your eyes and the fiery heart of the liquid. Are not th

36 / 36

All the virtues of the perfect wine glass are paralleled in typography. There is the long, thin stem that ob

Berthold Futura Demi Bold

6 / 7

All the virtues of the perfect wine glass are paralleled in typography. There is the long, thin stem that obviates fingerprints on the bowl. Why? Because no cloud must come between your eyes and the fiery heart of the liquid. Are not the margins on book pages similarly meant to obviate the necessity of fingering the type page? Again: the glass is colorless or at the most only faintly tinged in the bowl, because the connoisseur judges wine partly by its color and is impatient of anything that alters it. There are a thousand mannerisms in typography that are as impudent and arbitrary as putting port in tumblers of red or green glass! When a goblet has a base that looks too small for security, it does not matter how cleverly it is weighted; you feel nervous lest it should tip over. There are ways of setting lines of type which may work well enough, and yet keep the reader subconsciously worried by the fear of "doubling" lines, reading three words as one, and so forth. Now the man who first chose glass instead of clay or metal to hold his wine was a "modernist" in the sense in which I am going to use that term. That is, the first thing he asked of this particular object was not "How should it look?" but "What must it do?" and to that extent all good typograp

8 / 9

All the virtues of the perfect wine glass are paralleled in typography. There is the long, thin stem that obviates fingerprints on the bowl. Why? Because no cloud must come between your eyes and the fiery heart of the liquid. Are not the margins on book pages similarly meant to obviate the necessity of fingering the type page? Again: the glass is colorless or at the most only faintly tinged in the bowl, because the connoisseur judges wine partly by its color and is impatient of anything that alters it. There are a thousand mannerisms in typography that are as impudent and arbitrary as putting port in tumblers of red or green glass! When a goblet has a base that looks too small for security, it does not matter how cleverly it is weigh

10 / 11

All the virtues of the perfect wine glass are paralleled in typography. There is the long, thin stem that obviates fingerprints on the bowl. Why? Because no cloud must come between your eyes and the fiery heart of the liquid. Are not the margins on book pages similarly meant to obviate the necessity of fingering the type page? Again: the glass is colorless or at the most only faintly tinged in the bowl, because the connoisseur judges wine partly by its color and is impatient of anythi

12 / 13

All the virtues of the perfect wine glass are paralleled in typography. There is the long, thin stem that obviates fingerprints on the bowl. Why? Because no cloud must come between your eyes and the fiery heart of the liquid. Are not the margins on book pages similarly meant to obviate the necessity of fingering the type page? Again: the glass

14 / 15

All the virtues of the perfect wine glass are paralleled in typography. There is the long, thin stem that obviates fingerprints on the bowl. Why? Because no cloud must come between your eyes and the fiery heart of the liquid. Are not the margins on book pages similarly meant to obviate the necessity of fingering the type page? Again: the glass is colorless or at the most only faintly tinged in the bowl, because the connoisseur judges wine partly by its color and is impatient of anything that alters it. There are a thousand mannerisms in typography that are as impu

18 / 19

All the virtues of the perfect wine glass are paralleled in typography. There is the long, thin stem that obviates fingerprints on the bowl. Why? Because no cloud must come between your eyes and the fiery heart of the liquid. Are not the margins on book pages similarly meant to obviate the necessity of fingering the type page? Again: the glass is colorless or at the most

24 / 24

All the virtues of the perfect wine glass are paralleled in typography. There is the long, thin stem that obviates fingerprints on the bowl. Why? Because no cloud must come between your eyes and the fiery heart

36 / 36

All the virtues of the perfect wine glass are paralleled in typography. There is the long, thin stem

Berthold Futura Demi Bold Oblique

6 / 7

All the virtues of the perfect wine glass are paralleled in typography. There is the long, thin stem that obviates fingerprints on the bowl. Why? Because no cloud must come between your eyes and the fiery heart of the liquid. Are not the margins on book pages similarly meant to obviate the necessity of fingering the type page? Again: the glass is colorless or at the most only faintly tinged in the bowl, because the connoisseur judges wine partly by its color and is impatient of anything that alters it. There are a thousand mannerisms in typography that are as impudent and arbitrary as putting port in tumblers of red or green glass! When a goblet has a base that looks too small for security, it does not matter how cleverly it is weighted; you feel nervous lest it should tip over. There are ways of setting lines of type which may work well enough, and yet keep the reader subconsciously worried by the fear of "doubling" lines, reading three words as one, and so forth. Now the man who first chose glass instead of clay or metal to hold his wine was a "modernist" in the sense in which I am going to use that term. That is, the first thing he asked of this particular object was not "How should it look?" but "What must it do?" and to that extent all good typography is modernist. Wine is so strange and pote

8 / 9

All the virtues of the perfect wine glass are paralleled in typography. There is the long, thin stem that obviates fingerprints on the bowl. Why? Because no cloud must come between your eyes and the fiery heart of the liquid. Are not the margins on book pages similarly meant to obviate the necessity of fingering the type page? Again: the glass is colorless or at the most only faintly tinged in the bowl, because the connoisseur judges wine partly by its color and is impatient of anything that alters it. There are a thousand mannerisms in typography that are as impudent and arbitrary as putting port in tumblers of red or green glass! When a goblet has a base that looks too small for security, it does not matter how cleverly it is weighted; you feel nervous lest

10 / 11

All the virtues of the perfect wine glass are paralleled in typography. There is the long, thin stem that obviates fingerprints on the bowl. Why? Because no cloud must come between your eyes and the fiery heart of the liquid. Are not the margins on book pages similarly meant to obviate the necessity of fingering the type page? Again: the glass is colorless or at the most only faintly tinged in the bowl, because the connoisseur judges wine partly by its color and is impatient of anything that alters

12 / 13

All the virtues of the perfect wine glass are paralleled in typography. There is the long, thin stem that obviates fingerprints on the bowl. Why? Because no cloud must come between your eyes and the fiery heart of the liquid. Are not the margins on book pages similarly meant to obviate the necessity of fingering the type page? Again: the glass is colorless or at th

14 / 15

All the virtues of the perfect wine glass are paralleled in typography. There is the long, thin stem that obviates fingerprints on the bowl. Why? Because no cloud must come between your eyes and the fiery heart of the liquid. Are not the margins on book pages similarly meant to obviate the necessity of fingering the type page? Again: the glass is colorless or at the most only faintly tinged in the bowl, because the connoisseur judges wine partly by its color and is impatient of anything that alters it. There are a thousand mannerisms in typography that are as impudent and arbitrary as

18 / 19

All the virtues of the perfect wine glass are paralleled in typography. There is the long, thin stem that obviates fingerprints on the bowl. Why? Because no cloud must come between your eyes and the fiery heart of the liquid. Are not the margins on book pages similarly meant to obviate the necessity of fingering the type page? Again: the glass is colorless or at the most only faint

24 / 24

All the virtues of the perfect wine glass are paralleled in typography. There is the long, thin stem that obviates fingerprints on the bowl. Why? Because no cloud must come between your eyes and the fiery heart of th

36 / 36

All the virtues of the perfect wine glass are paralleled in typography. There is the long, thin stem that

Berthold Futura Bold

6 / 7

All the virtues of the perfect wine glass are paralleled in typography. There is the long, thin stem that obviates fingerprints on the bowl. Why? Because no cloud must come between your eyes and the fiery heart of the liquid. Are not the margins on book pages similarly meant to obviate the necessity of fingering the type page? Again: the glass is colorless or at the most only faintly tinged in the bowl, because the connoisseur judges wine partly by its color and is impatient of anything that alters it. There are a thousand mannerisms in typography that are as impudent and arbitrary as putting port in tumblers of red or green glass! When a goblet has a base that looks too small for security, it does not matter how cleverly it is weighted; you feel nervous lest it should tip over. There are ways of setting lines of type which may work well enough, and yet keep the reader subconsciously worried by the fear of "doubling" lines, reading three words as one, and so forth. Now the man who first chose glass instead of clay or metal to hold his wine was a "modernist" in the sense in which I am going to use that ter

8 / 9

All the virtues of the perfect wine glass are paralleled in typography. There is the long, thin stem that obviates fingerprints on the bowl. Why? Because no cloud must come between your eyes and the fiery heart of the liquid. Are not the margins on book pages similarly meant to obviate the necessity of fingering the type page? Again: the glass is colorless or at the most only faintly tinged in the bowl, because the connoisseur judges wine partly by its color and is impatient of anything that alters it. There are a thousand mannerisms in typography that are as impudent and arbitrary as putting port in tumblers of red or green glass! Whe

10 / 11

All the virtues of the perfect wine glass are paralleled in typography. There is the long, thin stem that obviates fingerprints on the bowl. Why? Because no cloud must come between your eyes and the fiery heart of the liquid. Are not the margins on book pages similarly meant to obviate the necessity of fingering the type page? Again: the glass is colorless or at the most only faintly tinged in the bowl, because the connoisse

12 / 13

All the virtues of the perfect wine glass are paralleled in typography. There is the long, thin stem that obviates fingerprints on the bowl. Why? Because no cloud must come between your eyes and the fiery heart of the liquid. Are not the margins on book pages similarly meant to obviate the necessity of fingeri

14 / 15

All the virtues of the perfect wine glass are paralleled in typography. There is the long, thin stem that obviates fingerprints on the bowl. Why? Because no cloud must come between your eyes and the fiery heart of the liquid. Are not the margins on book pages similarly meant to obviate the necessity of fingering the type page? Again: the glass is colorless or at the most only faintly tinged in the bowl, because the connoisseur judges wine partly by its color and is impatient of anything that alters it. There

18 / 19

All the virtues of the perfect wine glass are paralleled in typography. There is the long, thin stem that obviates fingerprints on the bowl. Why? Because no cloud must come between your eyes and the fiery heart of the liquid. Are not the margins on book pages similarly meant to obviate the necessity of fingering the type pag

24 / 24

All the virtues of the perfect wine glass are paralleled in typography. There is the long, thin stem that obviates fingerprints on the bowl. Why? Because no cloud must come between you

36 / 36

All the virtues of the perfect wine glass are paralleled in typography. There is the

Berthold Futura Bold Oblique

6 / 7

All the virtues of the perfect wine glass are paralleled in typography. There is the long, thin stem that obviates fingerprints on the bowl. Why? Because no cloud must come between your eyes and the fiery heart of the liquid. Are not the margins on book pages similarly meant to obviate the necessity of fingering the type page? Again: the glass is colorless or at the most only faintly tinged in the bowl, because the connoisseur judges wine partly by its color and is impatient of anything that alters it. There are a thousand mannerisms in typography that are as impudent and arbitrary as putting port in tumblers of red or green glass! When a goblet has a base that looks too small for security, it does not matter how cleverly it is weighted; you feel nervous lest it should tip over. There are ways of setting lines of type which may work well enough, and yet keep the reader subconsciously worried by the fear of "doubling" lines, reading three words as one, and so forth. Now the man who first chose glass instead of clay or metal to hold his wine was a "modernist" in the sense in which I am going to use that

8 / 9

All the virtues of the perfect wine glass are paralleled in typography. There is the long, thin stem that obviates fingerprints on the bowl. Why? Because no cloud must come between your eyes and the fiery heart of the liquid. Are not the margins on book pages similarly meant to obviate the necessity of fingering the type page? Again: the glass is colorless or at the most only faintly tinged in the bowl, because the connoisseur judges wine partly by its color and is impatient of anything that alters it. There are a thousand mannerisms in typography that are as impudent and arbitrary as putting port in tumblers of red or green glass! When a goblet has a base that looks t

10 / 11

All the virtues of the perfect wine glass are paralleled in typography. There is the long, thin stem that obviates fingerprints on the bowl. Why? Because no cloud must come between your eyes and the fiery heart of the liquid. Are not the margins on book pages similarly meant to obviate the necessity of fingering the type page? Again: the glass is colorless or at the most only faintly tinged in the bowl, because the connoisseur judges

12 / 13

All the virtues of the perfect wine glass are paralleled in typography. There is the long, thin stem that obviates fingerprints on the bowl. Why? Because no cloud must come between your eyes and the fiery heart of the liquid. Are not the margins on book pages similarly meant to obviate the necessity of fingerin

14 / 15

All the virtues of the perfect wine glass are paralleled in typography. There is the long, thin stem that obviates fingerprints on the bowl. Why? Because no cloud must come between your eyes and the fiery heart of the liquid. Are not the margins on book pages similarly meant to obviate the necessity of fingering the type page? Again: the glass is colorless or at the most only faintly tinged in the bowl, because the connoisseur judges wine partly by its color and is impatient of anything that alters it. There

18 / 19

All the virtues of the perfect wine glass are paralleled in typography. There is the long, thin stem that obviates fingerprints on the bowl. Why? Because no cloud must come between your eyes and the fiery heart of the liquid. Are not the margins on book pages similarly meant to obviate the necessity of fingering the type

24 / 24

All the virtues of the perfect wine glass are paralleled in typography. There is the long, thin stem that obviates fingerprints on the bowl. Why? Because no cloud must come between you

36 / 36

All the virtues of the perfect wine glass are paralleled in typography. There is the long,

Berthold Futura Condensed Light

6 / 7

All the virtues of the perfect wine glass are paralleled in typography. There is the long, thin stem that obviates fingerprints on the bowl. Why? Because no cloud must come between your eyes and the fiery heart of the liquid. Are not the margins on book pages similarly meant to obviate the necessity of fingering the type page? Again: the glass is colorless or at the most only faintly tinged in the bowl, because the connoisseur judges wine partly by its color and is impatient of anything that alters it. There are a thousand mannerisms in typography that are as impudent and arbitrary as putting port in tumblers of red or green glass! When a goblet has a base that looks too small for security, it does not matter how cleverly it is weighted; you feel nervous lest it should tip over. There are ways of setting lines of type which may work well enough, and yet keep the reader subconsciously worried by the fear of "doubling" lines, reading three words as one, and so forth. Now the man who first chose glass instead of clay or metal to hold his wine was a "modernist" in the sense in which I am going to use that term. That is, the first thing he asked of this particular object was not "How should it look?" but "What must it do?" and to that extent all good typography is modernist. Wine is so strange and potent a thing that it has been used in the central ritual of religion in one place and time, and attacked by a virago with a hatchet in another. There is only one other thing in the world that is capable of stirring and altering men's minds to the same extent, and that is the coherent expression of thought. That is man's chief miracle, unique to no man. There is no "explanation" whatever of the fact that I can make arbitrary sounds which will lead a total stranger to think my own thought. It is sheer magic that I should be able to hold a one-sided conversation by means of black marks on paper with an unknown person half-way across the world. Talking, broadcasting, writing and printing are all quite literally forms of thought tr

8 / 9

All the virtues of the perfect wine glass are paralleled in typography. There is the long, thin stem that obviates fingerprints on the bowl. Why? Because no cloud must come between your eyes and the fiery heart of the liquid. Are not the margins on book pages similarly meant to obviate the necessity of fingering the type page? Again: the glass is colorless or at the most only faintly tinged in the bowl, because the connoisseur judges wine partly by its color and is impatient of anything that alters it. There are a thousand mannerisms in typography that are as impudent and arbitrary as putting port in tumblers of red or green glass! When a goblet has a base that looks too small for security, it does not matter how cleverly it is weighted; you feel nervous lest it should tip over. There are ways of setting lines of type which may work well enough, and yet keep the reader subconsciously worried by the fear of "doubling" lines, reading three words as one, and so forth. Now the man who first chose glass instead of clay or metal to hold his wine was a "modernist" in the sense in which I am going to use that term. That is, the first thing he asked of this particular object was not

10 / 11

All the virtues of the perfect wine glass are paralleled in typography. There is the long, thin stem that obviates fingerprints on the bowl. Why? Because no cloud must come between your eyes and the fiery heart of the liquid. Are not the margins on book pages similarly meant to obviate the necessity of fingering the type page? Again: the glass is colorless or at the most only faintly tinged in the bowl, because the connoisseur judges wine partly by its color and is impatient of anything that alters it. There are a thousand mannerisms in typography that are as impudent and arbitrary as putting port in tumblers of red or green glass! When a goblet has a base that looks too small for security, it does not matter how cleverly it is weighted; you feel nervous lest it should tip

12 / 13

All the virtues of the perfect wine glass are paralleled in typography. There is the long, thin stem that obviates fingerprints on the bowl. Why? Because no cloud must come between your eyes and the fiery heart of the liquid. Are not the margins on book pages similarly meant to obviate the necessity of fingering the type page? Again: the glass is colorless or at the most only faintly tinged in the bowl, because the connoisseur judges wine partly by its color and is impatient of anything that alters it. There are a thousand mannerisms in typography that are as impu

14 / 15

All the virtues of the perfect wine glass are paralleled in typography. There is the long, thin stem that obviates fingerprints on the bowl. Why? Because no cloud must come between your eyes and the fiery heart of the liquid. Are not the margins on book pages similarly meant to obviate the necessity of fingering the type page? Again: the glass is colorless or at the most only faintly tinged in the bowl, because the connoisseur judges wine partly by its color and is impatient of anything that alters it. There are a thousand mannerisms in typography that are as impudent and arbitrary as putting port in tumblers of red or green glass! When a goblet has a base that looks too small for security, it does not matter how cleverly it is weighted; you feel nervous lest it should tip over. There are ways of setting lines of type which may work well enough, and yet keep the reader subconsciously worried by the fear of "dou

18 / 19

All the virtues of the perfect wine glass are paralleled in typography. There is the long, thin stem that obviates fingerprints on the bowl. Why? Because no cloud must come between your eyes and the fiery heart of the liquid. Are not the margins on book pages similarly meant to obviate the necessity of fingering the type page? Again: the glass is colorless or at the most only faintly tinged in the bowl, because the connoisseur judges wine partly by its color and is impatient of anything that alters it. There are a thousand mannerisms intipography that are as impudent and arbitrary as putt

24 / 24

All the virtues of the perfect wine glass are paralleled in typography. There is the long, thin stem that obviates fingerprints on the bowl. Why? Because no cloud must come between your eyes and the fiery heart of the liquid. Are not the margins on book pages similarly meant to obviate the necessity of fingering the type page? Again: the

36 / 36

All the virtues of the perfect wine glass s are paralleled in typography. There is the long, thin stem that obviates fing erprints on the bowl. Why? Because n

Berthold Futura Condensed Medium

6 / 7

All the virtues of the perfect wine glass are paralleled in typography. There is the long, thin stem that obviates fingerprints on the bowl. Why? Because no cloud must come between your eyes and the fiery heart of the liquid. Are not the margins on book pages similarly meant to obviate the necessity of fingering the type page? Again: the glass is colorless or at the most only faintly tinged in the bowl, because the connoisseur judges wine partly by its color and is impatient of anything that alters it. There are a thousand mannerisms in typography that are as impudent and arbitrary as putting port in tumblers of red or green glass! When a goblet has a base that looks too small for security, it does not matter how cleverly it is weighted; you feel nervous lest it should tip over. There are ways of setting lines of type which may work well enough, and yet keep the reader subconsciously worried by the fear of "doubling" lines, reading three words as one, and so forth. Now the man who first chose glass instead of clay or metal to hold his wine was a "modernist" in the sense in which I am going to use that term. That is, the first thing he asked of this particular object was not "How should it look?" but "What must it do?" and to that extent all good typography is modernist. Wine is so strange and potent a thing that it has been used in the central ritual of religion in one place and time, and attacked by a virago with a hatchet in another. There is only one other thing in the world that is capable of stirring and altering men's minds to the same extent, and that is the coherent expression of thought. That is man's chief miracle, unique to man. There is no "explanation" whatever of the fact that I can make arbitrary sounds which will lead a total stranger to think my own thought. It is sheer magic that I should be able to hold

8 / 9

All the virtues of the perfect wine glass are paralleled in typography. There is the long, thin stem that obviates fingerprints on the bowl. Why? Because no cloud must come between your eyes and the fiery heart of the liquid. Are not the margins on book pages similarly meant to obviate the necessity of fingering the type page? Again: the glass is colorless or at the most only faintly tinged in the bowl, because the connoisseur judges wine partly by its color and is impatient of anything that alters it. There are a thousand mannerisms in typography that are as impudent and arbitrary as putting port in tumblers of red or green glass! When a goblet has a base that looks too small for security, it does not matter how cleverly it is weighted; you feel nervous lest it should tip over. There are ways of setting lines of type which may work well enough, and yet keep the reader subconsciously worried by the fear of "doubling" lines, reading three words as one, and so forth. Now the man who first chose glass instead of clay or metal to hold his wine was a "moder

10 / 11

All the virtues of the perfect wine glass are paralleled in typography. There is the long, thin stem that obviates fingerprints on the bowl. Why? Because no cloud must come between your eyes and the fiery heart of the liquid. Are not the margins on book pages similarly meant to obviate the necessity of fingering the type page? Again: the glass is colorless or at the most only faintly tinged in the bowl, because the connoisseur judges wine partly by its color and is impatient of anything that alters it. There are a thousand mannerisms in typography that are as impudent and arbitrary as putting port in tumblers of red or green glass! When a goblet has a base that looks too small for security, it

12 / 13

All the virtues of the perfect wine glass are paralleled in typography. There is the long, thin stem that obviates fingerprints on the bowl. Why? Because no cloud must come between your eyes and the fiery heart of the liquid. Are not the margins on book pages similarly meant to obviate the necessity of fingering the type page? Again: the glass is colorless or at the most only faintly tinged in the bowl, because the connoisseur judges wine partly by its color and is impatient of anything that alters it. The

14 / 15

All the virtues of the perfect wine glass are paralleled in typography. There is the long, thin stem that obviates fingerprints on the bowl. Why? Because no cloud must come between your eyes and the fiery heart of the liquid. Are not the margins on book pages similarly meant to obviate the necessity of fingering the type page? Again: the glass is colorless or at the most only faintly tinged in the bowl, because the connoisseur judges wine partly by its color and is impatient of anything that alters it. There are a thousand mannerisms in typography that are as impudent and arbitrary as putting port in tumblers of red or green glass! When a goblet has a base that looks too small for security, it does not matter how cleverly it is weighted; you feel nervous lest it should tip over. There are ways of setting lines of type whic

18 / 19

All the virtues of the perfect wine glass are paralleled in typography. There is the long, thin stem that obviates fingerprints on the bowl. Why? Because no cloud must come between your eyes and the fiery heart of the liquid. Are not the margins on book pages similarly meant to obviate the necessity of fingering the type page? Again: the glass is colorless or at the most only faintly tinged in the bowl, because the connoisseur judges wine partly by its color and is impatient of anything that alters it. There are a thousand manneri

24 / 24

All the virtues of the perfect wine glass are paralleled in typography. There is the long, thin stem that obviates fingerprints on the bowl. Why? Because no cloud must come between your eyes and the fiery heart of the liquid. Are not the margins on book pages similarly meant to obviate the necessity of f

36 / 36

All the virtues of the perfect wine glass are paralleled in typography. There is the long, thin stem that obviates fingerprints on the bowl

Berthold Futura Condensed Bold

6 / 7

All the virtues of the perfect wine glass are paralleled in typography. There is the long, thin stem that obviates fingerprints on the bowl. Why? Because no cloud must come between your eyes and the fiery heart of the liquid. Are not the margins on book pages similarly meant to obviate the necessity of fingering the type page? Again: the glass is colorless or at the most only faintly tinged in the bowl, because the connoisseur judges wine partly by its color and is impatient of anything that alters it. There are a thousand mannerisms in typography that are as impudent and arbitrary as putting port in tumblers of red or green glass! When a goblet has a base that looks too small for security, it does not matter how cleverly it is weighted; you feel nervous lest it should tip over. There are ways of setting lines of type which may work well enough, and yet keep the reader subconsciously worried by the fear of "doubling" lines, reading three words as one, and so forth. Now the man who first chose glass instead of clay or metal to hold his wine was a "modernist" in the sense in which I am going to use that term. That is, the first thing he asked of this particular object was not "How should it look?" but "What must it do?" and to that extent all good typography is modernist. Wine is so strange and potent a thing that it has been used in the central ritual of religion in one place and time, and attacked by a virago with a hatchet in another. There is only one other thing in the world that is capable of stirring and altering men's minds to the same extent, and that is the coherent expression of thou

8 / 9

All the virtues of the perfect wine glass are paralleled in typography. There is the long, thin stem that obviates fingerprints on the bowl. Why? Because no cloud must come between your eyes and the fiery heart of the liquid. Are not the margins on book pages similarly meant to obviate the necessity of fingering the type page? Again: the glass is colorless or at the most only faintly tinged in the bowl, because the connoisseur judges wine partly by its color and is impatient of anything that alters it. There are a thousand mannerisms in typography that are as impudent and arbitrary as putting port in tumblers of red or green glass! When a goblet has a base that looks too small for security, it does not matter how cleverly it is weighted; you feel nervous lest it should tip over. There are ways of setting lines of type which may work well enough, and yet keep the reader subconsciously worried by the fear of "doubling" li

10 / 11

All the virtues of the perfect wine glass are paralleled in typography. There is the long, thin stem that obviates fingerprints on the bowl. Why? Because no cloud must come between your eyes and the fiery heart of the liquid. Are not the margins on book pages similarly meant to obviate the necessity of fingering the type page? Again: the glass is colorless or at the most only faintly tinged in the bowl, because the connoisseur judges wine partly by its color and is impatient of anything that alters it. There are a thousand mannerisms in typography that are as impudent and arbitrary as putting port in tu

12 / 13

All the virtues of the perfect wine glass are paralleled in typography. There is the long, thin stem that obviates fingerprints on the bowl. Why? Because no cloud must come between your eyes and the fiery heart of the liquid. Are not the margins on book pages similarly meant to obviate the necessity of fingering the type page? Again: the glass is colorless or at the most only faintly tinged in the bowl, because the connoisseur judges wine pa

14 / 15

All the virtues of the perfect wine glass are paralleled in typography. There is the long, thin stem that obviates fingerprints on the bowl. Why? Because no cloud must come between your eyes and the fiery heart of the liquid. Are not the margins on book pages similarly meant to obviate the necessity of fingering the type page? Again: the glass is colorless or at the most only faintly tinged in the bowl, because the connoisseur judges wine partly by its color and is impatient of anything that alters it. There are a thousand mannerisms in typography that are as impudent and arbitrary as putting port in tumblers of red or green glass! When a goblet has a base that looks too small for security, it does not matter how cle

18 / 19

All the virtues of the perfect wine glass are paralleled in typography. There is the long, thin stem that obviates fingerprints on the bowl. Why? Because no cloud must come between your eyes and the fiery heart of the liquid. Are not the margins on book pages similarly meant to obviate the necessity of fingering the type page? Again: the glass is colorless or at the most only faintly tinged in the bowl, because the connoisseur judges wine partly by its color and is

24 / 24

All the virtues of the perfect wine glass are paralleled in typography. There is the long, thin stem that obviates fingerprints on the bowl. Why? Because no cloud must come between your eyes and the fiery heart of the liquid. Are not the margins on book pages si

36 / 36

All the virtues of the perfect wine glass are paralleled in typography. There is the long, thin stem that obviates finger

Gill Sans

eagMa

Monotype Gill Sans

Foundry:	Monotype Typography
Supplier:	Monotype Typography
Letterform authenticity:	Excellent
Digital outline:	Good
Side bearings:	Good
Kerning:	Fair
Hinting:	Excellent
Expert editions:	No
Multiple masters:	No
Family completeness:	Excellent
Formats:	Type 1 / partial TrueType
Platforms:	Mac / PC

Monotype, the foundry that has originally released this classically-proportioned sans serif has done a good job in translating the typeface into the digital environment.

Monotype Gill Sans

72 points

ABCDEFGHIJKL
MNOPQRST
UVWXYZ$£&
1234567890
abcdefghijklmno
pqrstuvwxyz
ß(!?,.-:;)''

Monotype Gill Sans Italic

72 points

ABCDEFGHIJKLM
NOPQRSTUVWXY
Z$£&1234567890
abcdefghijklmnopqr
stuvwxyzß(!?,.-:;)"

Monotype Gill Sans Light

6 / 7

All the virtues of the perfect wine glass are paralleled in typogr aphy. There is the long, thin stem that obviates fingerprints on the bowl. Why? Because no cloud must come between your ey es and the fiery heart of the liquid. Are not the margins on bo ok pages similarly meant to obviate the necessity of fingering the type page? Again: the glass is colorless or at the most only faintly tinged in the bowl, because the connoisseur judges wine partly by its color and is impatient of anything that alters it. The re are a thousand mannerisms in typography that are as impu dent and arbitrary as putting port in tumblers of red or green gl ass! When a goblet has a base that looks too small for security, it does not matter how cleverly it is weighted; you feel nervous lest it should tip over. There are ways of setting lines of type which may work well enough, and yet keep the reader subcons ciously worried by the fear of "doubling" lines, reading three words as one, and so forth. Now the man who first chose glass instead of clay or metal to hold his wine was a "modernist" in the sense in which I am going to use that term. That is, the first thing he asked of this particular object was not "How should it look?" but "What must it do?" and to that extent all good typo graphy is modernist. Wine is so strange and potent a thing that

8 / 9

All the virtues of the perfect wine glass are paral leled in typography. There is the long, thin stem that obviates fingerprints on the bowl. Why? Bec ause no cloud must come between your eyes and the fiery heart of the liquid. Are not the mar gins on book pages similarly meant to obviate the necessity of fingering the type page? Again: the glass is colorless or at the most only faintly ti nged in the bowl, because the connoisseur judg es wine partly by its color and is impatient of an ything that alters it. There are a thousand manne risms in typography that are as impudent and ar bitrary as putting port in tumblers of red or gre en glass! When a goblet has a base that looks too small for security, it does not matter how cle verly it is weighted; you feel nervous lest it shoul

10 / 11

All the virtues of the perfect wine glass are paralleled in typography. There is the long, thin stem that obviates fingerp rints on the bowl. Why? Because no clo ud must come between your eyes and the fiery heart of the liquid. Are not the margins on book pages similarly meant to obviate the necessity of fingering the type page? Again: the glass is colorless or at the most only faintly tinged in the bowl, because the connoisseur judges wine partly by its color and is impatient of anything that alters it. There are a th

12 / 13

All the virtues of the perfect wine glass are paralleled in typography. There is the long, thin stem that obviates fingerprints on the bowl. Why? Because no cloud must co me between your eyes and the fie ry heart of the liquid. Are not the margins on book pages similarly meant to obviate the necessity of fingering the type page? Again: the glass is colorless or at the most on

14 / 15

All the virtues of the perfect wine glass are paralleled in typo graphy. There is the long, thin stem that obviates fingerprints on the bowl. Why? Because no cloud must come between your eyes and the fiery heart of the liquid. Are not the margi ns on book pages similarly meant to obviate the necessity of fingering the type page? Again: the glass is colorless or at the most only faintly tinged in the bowl, because the connoisseur judges wine partly by its color and is impatient of anything th at alters it. There are a thousand mannerisms in typography that are as impudent and arbitrary as putting port in tumbler

18 / 19

All the virtues of the perfect wine glass are paral leled in typography. There is the long, thin stem that obviates fingerprints on the bowl. Why? Bec ause no cloud must come between your eyes an d the fiery heart of the liquid. Are not the margi ns on book pages similarly meant to obviate the necessity of fingering the type page? Again: the g lass is colorless or at the most only faintly tinged

24 / 25

All the virtues of the perfect wine gla ss are paralleled in typography. There is the long, thin stem that obviates fin gerprints on the bowl. Why? Because no cloud must come between your e yes and the fiery heart of the liquid.

36 / 36

All the virtues of the perf ect wine glass are parallel ed in typography. There is the long, thin stem that o

Monotype Gill Sans Light Italic

6 / 7

All the virtues of the perfect wine glass are paralleled in typography. There is the long, thin stem that obviates fingerprints on the bowl. Why? Because no cloud must come between your eyes and the fiery heart of the liquid. Are not the margins on book pages similarly meant to obviate the necessity of fingering the type page? Again: the glass is colorless or at the most only faintly tinged in the bowl, because the connoisseur judges wine partly by its color and is impatient of anything that alters it. There are a thousand mannerisms in typography that are as impudent and arbitrary as putting port in tumblers of red or green glass! When a goblet has a base that looks too small for security, it does not matter how cleverly it is weighted; you feel nervous lest it should tip over. There are ways of setting lines of type which may work well enough, and yet keep the reader subconsciously worried by the fear of "doubling" lines, reading three words as one, and so forth. Now the man who first chose glass instead of clay or metal to hold his wine was a "modernist" in the sense in which I am going to use that term. That is, the first thing he asked of this particular object was not "How should it look?" but "What must it do?" and to that extent all good typography is modernist. Wine is so strange and potent a thing that it has been used in the central ritual of religion in one place and

8 / 9

All the virtues of the perfect wine glass are paralleled in typography. There is the long, thin stem that obviates fingerprints on the bowl. Why? Because no cloud must come between your eyes and the fiery heart of the liquid. Are not the margins on book pages similarly meant to obviate the necessity of fingering the type page? Again: the glass is colorless or at the most only faintly tinged in the bowl, because the connoisseur judges wine partly by its color and is impatient of anything that alters it. There are a thousand mannerisms in typography that are as impudent and arbitrary as putting port in tumblers of red or green glass! When a goblet has a base that looks too small for security, it does not matter how cleverly it is weighted; you feel nervous lest it should tip over. There are ways of setting lines of

10 / 11

All the virtues of the perfect wine glass are paralleled in typography. There is the long, thin stem that obviates fingerprints on the bowl. Why? Because no cloud must come between your eyes and the fiery heart of the liquid. Are not the margins on book pages similarly meant to obviate the necessity of fingering the type page? Again: the glass is colorless or at the most only faintly tinged in the bowl, because the connoisseur judges wine partly by its color and is impatient of anything that alters it. There are a thousand mannerisms in typography

12 / 13

All the virtues of the perfect wine glass are paralleled in typography. There is the long, thin stem that obviates fingerprints on the bowl. Why? Because no cloud must come between your eyes and the fiery heart of the liquid. Are not the margins on book pages similarly meant to obviate the necessity of fingering the type page? Again: the glass is colorless or at the most only faintly tinged in the

14 / 15

All the virtues of the perfect wine glass are paralleled in typography. There is the long, thin stem that obviates fingerprints on the bowl. Why? Because no cloud must come between your eyes and the fiery heart of the liquid. Are not the margins on book pages similarly meant to obviate the necessity of fingering the type page? Again: the glass is colorless or at the most only faintly tinged in the bowl, because the connoisseur judges wine partly by its color and is impatient of anything that alters it. There are a thousand mannerisms in typography that are as impudent and arbitrary as putting port in tumblers of red or green glass! When

18 / 19

All the virtues of the perfect wine glass are paralleled in typography. There is the long, thin stem that obviates fingerprints on the bowl. Why? Because no cloud must come between your eyes and the fiery heart of the liquid. Are not the margins on book pages similarly meant to obviate the necessity of fingering the type page? Again: the glass is colorless or at the most only faintly tinged in the bowl, because

24 / 25

All the virtues of the perfect wine glass are paralleled in typography. There is the long, thin stem that obviates fingerprints on the bowl. Why? Because no cloud must come between your eyes and the fiery heart of the liquid. Are not the margi

36 / 36

All the virtues of the perfect wine glass are paralleled in typography. There is the long, thin stem that obviate

Monotype Gill Sans

6 / 7

All the virtues of the perfect wine glass are paralleled in typography. There is the long, thin stem that obviates fingerprints on the bowl. Why? Because no cloud must come between your eyes and the fiery heart of the liquid. Are not the margins on book pages similarly meant to obviate the necessity of fingering the type page? Again: the glass is colorless or at the most only faintly tinged in the bowl, because the connoisseur judges wine partly by its color and is impatient of anything that alters it. There are a thousand mannerisms in typography that are as impudent and arbitrary as putting port in tumblers of red or green glass! When a goblet has a base that looks too small for security, it does not matter how cleverly it is weighted; you feel nervous lest it should tip over. There are ways of setting lines of type which may work well enough, and yet keep the reader subconsciously worried by the fear of "doubling" lines, reading three words as one, and so forth. Now the man who first chose glass instead of clay or metal to hold his wine was a "modernist" in the sense in which I am going to use that term. That is, the first thing he asked of this particular object was not "How should it look?" but "What must it do?" and to that extent all good typography is modernist. Wi

8 / 9

All the virtues of the perfect wine glass are paralleled in typography. There is the long, thin stem that obviates fingerprints on the bowl. Why? Because no cloud must come between your eyes and the fiery heart of the liquid. Are not the margins on book pages similarly meant to obviate the necessity of fingering the type page? Again: the glass is colorless or at the most only faintly tinged in the bowl, because the connoisseur judges wine partly by its color and is impatient of anything that alters it. There are a thousand mannerisms in typography that are as impudent and arbitrary as putting port in tumblers of red or green glass! When a goblet has a base that looks too small for security, it does not matter how cleverly it is weighted; you feel

10 / 11

All the virtues of the perfect wine glass are paralleled in typography. There is the long, thin stem that obviates fingerprints on the bowl. Why? Because no cloud must come between your eyes and the fiery heart of the liquid. Are not the margins on book pages similarly meant to obviate the necessity of fingering the type page? Again: the glass is colorless or at the most only faintly tinged in the bowl, because the connoisseur judges wine partly by its color and is impatient of anything that alters

12 / 13

All the virtues of the perfect wine glass are paralleled in typography. There is the long, thin stem that obviates fingerprints on the bowl. Why? Because no cloud must come between your eyes and the fiery heart of the liquid. Are not the margins on book pages similarly meant to obviate the necessity of fingering the type page? Again: the glass is colorless or at

14 / 15

All the virtues of the perfect wine glass are paralleled in typography. There is the long, thin stem that obviates fingerprints on the bowl. Why? Because no cloud must come between your eyes and the fiery heart of the liquid. Are not the margins on book pages similarly meant to obviate the necessity of fingering the type page? Again: the glass is colorless or at the most only faintly tinged in the bowl, because the connoisseur judges wine partly by its color and is impatient of anything that alters it. There are a thousand mannerisms in typography that are as impudent and arbitrary as putting

18 / 19

All the virtues of the perfect wine glass are paralleled in typography. There is the long, thin stem that obviates fingerprints on the bowl. Why? Because no cloud must come between your eyes and the fiery heart of the liquid. Are not the margins on book pages similarly meant to obviate the necessity of fingering the type page? Again: the glass is colorless or at the most only fa

24 / 25

All the virtues of the perfect wine glass are paralleled in typography. There is the long, thin stem that obviates fingerprints on the bowl. Why? Because no cloud must come between your eyes and the fiery heart of the li

36 / 36

All the virtues of the perfect wine glass are paralleled in typography. There is the long, thin stem th

Monotype Gill Sans Italic

6 / 7

All the virtues of the perfect wine glass are paralleled in typography. There is the long, thin stem that obviates fingerprints on the bowl. Why? Because no cloud must come between your eyes and the fiery heart of the liquid. Are not the margins on book pages similarly meant to obviate the necessity of fingering the type page? Again: the glass is colorless or at the most only faintly tinged in the bowl, because the connoisseur judges wine partly by its color and is impatient of anything that alters it. There are a thousand mannerisms in typography that are as impudent and arbitrary as putting port in tumblers of red or green glass! When a goblet has a base that looks too small for security, it does not matter how cleverly it is weighted; you feel nervous lest it should tip over. There are ways of setting lines of type which may work well enough, and yet keep the reader subconsciously worried by the fear of "doubling" lines, reading three words as one, and so forth. Now the man who first chose glass instead of clay or metal to hold his wine was a "modernist" in the sense in which I am going to use that term. That is, the first thing he asked of this particular object was not "How should it look?" but "What must it do?" and to that extent all good typography is modernist. Wine is so strange and potent a thing that it has been used in the central ritual of religion in one

8 / 9

All the virtues of the perfect wine glass are paralleled in typography. There is the long, thin stem that obviates fingerprints on the bowl. Why? Because no cloud must come between your eyes and the fiery heart of the liquid. Are not the margins on book pages similarly meant to obviate the necessity of fingering the type page? Again: the glass is colorless or at the most only faintly tinged in the bowl, because the connoisseur judges wine partly by its color and is impatient of anything that alters it. There are a thousand mannerisms in typography that are as impudent and arbitrary as putting port in tumblers of red or green glass! When a goblet has a base that looks too small for security, it does not matter how cleverly it is weighted; you feel nervous lest it should tip over. There are ways of setting lin

10 / 11

All the virtues of the perfect wine glass are paralleled in typography. There is the long, thin stem that obviates fingerprints on the bowl. Why? Because no cloud must come between your eyes and the fiery heart of the liquid. Are not the margins on book pages similarly meant to obviate the necessity of fingering the type page? Again: the glass is colorless or at the most only faintly tinged in the bowl, because the connoisseur judges wine partly by its color and is impatient of anything that alters it. There are a thousand mannerisms in

12 / 13

All the virtues of the perfect wine glass are paralleled in typography. There is the long, thin stem that obviates fingerprints on the bowl. Why? Because no cloud must come between en your eyes and the fiery heart of the liquid. Are not the margins on book pages similarly meant to obviate the necessity of fingering the type page? Again: the glass is colorless or at the most only faintly tinged

14 / 15

All the virtues of the perfect wine glass are paralleled in typography. There is the long, thin stem that obviates fingerprints on the bowl. Why? Because no cloud must come between your eyes and the fiery heart of the liquid. Are not the margins on book pages similarly meant to obviate the necessity of fingering the type page? Again: the glass is colorless or at the most only faintly tinged in the bowl, because the connoisseur judges wine partly by its color and is impatient of anything that alters it. There are a thousand mannerisms in typography that are as impudent and arbitrary as putting port in tumblers of red or green gla

18 / 19

All the virtues of the perfect wine glass are paralleled in typography. There is the long, thin stem that obviates fingerprints on the bowl. Why? Because no cloud must come between your eyes and the fiery heart of the liquid. Are not the margins on book pages similarly meant to obviate the necessity of fingering the type page? Again: the glass is colorless or at the most only faintly tinged in the bowl, beca

24 / 25

All the virtues of the perfect wine glass are paralleled in typography. There is the long, thin stem that obviates fingerprints on the bowl. Why? Because no cloud must come between your eyes and the fiery heart of the liquid. Are not the mar

36 / 36

All the virtues of the perfect wine glass are paralleled in typography. There is the long, thin stem that obviate

Monotype Gill Sans Bold

6/7

All the virtues of the perfect wine glass are paralleled in typography. There is the long, thin stem that obviates fingerprints on the bowl. Why? Because no cloud must come between your eyes and the fiery heart of the liquid. Are not the margins on book pages similarly meant to obviate the necessity of fingering the ty pe page? Again: the glass is colorless or at the most only faintly tinged in the bowl, because the connoisse ur judges wine partly by its color and is impatient of anything that alters it. There are a thousand manneri sms in typography that are as impudent and arbitrary as putting port in tumblers of red or green glass! Wh en a goblet has a base that looks too small for securi ty, it does not matter how cleverly it is weighted; you feel nervous lest it should tip over. There are ways of setting lines of type which may work well enough, and yet keep the reader subconsciously worried by the fe ar of "doubling" lines, reading three words as one, and so forth. Now the man who first chose glass inste ad of clay or metal to hold his wine was a "moderni st" in the sense in which I am going to use that term.

8/9

All the virtues of the perfect wine glass are paralleled in typography. There is the long, thin stem that obviates fingerprints on the bowl. Why? Because no cloud mu st come between your eyes and the fiery heart of the liquid. Are not the margins on book pages similarly meant to obviate the necessity of fingering the type page? Again: the glass is colorless or at the mo st only faintly tinged in the bowl, because the connoisseur judges wine partly by its color and is impatient of anything that al ters it. There are a thousand mannerisms in typography that are as impudent and arbitrary as putting port in tumblers of red or green glass! When a goblet has a

10/11

All the virtues of the perfect wine glass are paralleled in typograp hy. There is the long, thin stem th at obviates fingerprints on the bo wl. Why? Because no cloud must come between your eyes and the fiery heart of the liquid. Are not t he margins on book pages similar ly meant to obviate the necessity of fingering the type page? Again: the glass is colorless or at the mo st only faintly tinged in the bowl, because the connoisseur judges w

12/13

All the virtues of the perfec t wine glass are paralleled in typography. There is the lon g, thin stem that obviates fi ngerprints on the bowl. Wh y? Because no cloud must c ome between your eyes and the fiery heart of the liquid. Are not the margins on boo k pages similarly meant to o bviate the necessity of finge

14/15

All the virtues of the perfect wine glass are parallel ed in typography. There is the long, thin stem that o bviates fingerprints on the bowl. Why? Because no cloud must come between your eyes and the fiery heart of the liquid. Are not the margins on book pa ges similarly meant to obviate the necessity of fing ering the type page? Again: the glass is colorless or at the most only faintly tinged in the bowl, because the connoisseur judges wine partly by its color and is impatient of anything that alters it. There are a th

18/19

All the virtues of the perfect wine glass a re paralleled in typography. There is the l ong, thin stem that obviates fingerprints on the bowl. Why? Because no cloud must come between your eyes and the fiery he art of the liquid. Are not the margins on b ook pages similarly meant to obviate the necessity of fingering the type page? Aga

24/25

All the virtues of the perfect wi ne glass are paralleled in typogr aphy. There is the long, thin ste m that obviates fingerprints on the bowl. Why? Because no clo ud must come between your ey

36/36

All the virtues of the p erfect wine glass are p aralleled in typograph y. There is the long, thi

180

Helvetica

2ak

Berthold Helvetica

Foundry:	*H. Berthold AG*
Supplier:	*FontShop*
Letterform authenticity:	*Excellent*
Digital outline:	*Fair*
Side bearings:	*Excellent*
Kerning:	*Good*
Hinting:	*Excellent*
Expert editions:	*No*
Multiple masters:	*No*
Family completeness:	*Excellent*
Formats:	*Type 1*
Platforms:	*Mac / PC / UNIX*

Berthold Helvetica

72 points

ABCDEFGHIJK
LMNOPQRS
TUVWXYZ$£&
1234567890
abcdefghijklmn
opqrstuvwxyz
ß(!?,.-:;)"

Berthold Helvetica Italic

72 points

ABCDEFGHIJK
LMNOPQRS
TUVWXYZ$£&
1234567890
abcdefghijklmn
opqrstuvwxyz
ß(!?,.-:;)"

Berthold Helvetica Light

6 / 8

All the virtues of the perfect wine glass are paralleled in typography. There is the long, thin stem that obviates fingerprints on the bowl. Why? Because no cloud must come between your eyes and the fiery heart of the liquid. Are not the margins on book pages similarly meant to obviate the necessity of fingering the type page? Again: the glass is colorless or at the most only faintly tinged in the bowl, because the connoisseur judges wine partly by its color and is impatient of anything that alters it. There are a thousand mannerisms in typography that are as impudent and arbitrary as putting port in tumblers of red or green glass! When a goblet has a base that looks too small for security, it does not matter how cleverly it is weighted; you feel nervous lest it should tip over. There are ways of setting lines of type which may work well enough, and yet keep the reader subconsciously worried by the fear of "doubling" lines, reading three words as one, and so forth. Now the man who first chose glass instead of clay or metal to hold his wine was a "modernist" in the sense in which I am going to use that term.

8 / 10

All the virtues of the perfect wine glass are paralleled in typography. There is the long, thin stem that obviates fingerprints on the bowl. Why? Because no cloud must come between your eyes and the fiery heart of the liquid. Are not the margins on book pages similarly meant to obviate the necessity of fingering the type page? Again: the glass is colorless or at the most only faintly tinged in the bowl, because the connoisseur judges wine partly by its color and is impatient of anything that alters it. There are a thousand mannerisms in typography that are as impudent and arbitrary as putting port in tumblers of red or green glass! When a goblet has a base

10 / 12

All the virtues of the perfect wine glass are paralleled in typography. There is the long, thin stem that obviates finger prints on the bowl. Why? Because no cloud must come between your eyes and the fiery heart of the liquid. Are not the margins on book pages similarly meant to obviate the necessity of fingering the type page? Again: the glass is colorless or at the most only faintly tinged in the bowl, because the connoisseur judges wine partly by its color an

12 / 14

All the virtues of the perfect wine glass are paralleled in typography. There is the long, thin stem that obviates fingerprints on the bowl. Why? Because no cloud must come between your eyes and the fiery heart of the liquid. Are not the margins on book pages similarly meant to obviate the necessity of fingering the type pag

14 / 16

All the virtues of the perfect wine glass are paralleled in typography. There is the long, thin stem that obviates fingerprints on the bowl. Why? Because no cloud must come between your eyes and the fiery heart of the liquid. Are not the margins on book pages similarly meant to obviate the necessity of fingering the type page? Again: the glass is colorless or at the most only faintly tinged in the bowl, because the connoisseur judges wine partly by its color and is impatient of anything that alters it. There are a thousand mann

18 / 20

All the virtues of the perfect wine glass are paralleled in typography. There is the long, thin stem that obviates fingerprints on the bowl. Why? Because no cloud must come between your eyes and the fiery heart of the liquid. Are not the margins on book pages similarly meant to obviate the necessity of fingering the type page? Aga

24 / 25

All the virtues of the perfect wine glass are paralleled in typography. There is the long, thin stem that obviates fingerprints on the bowl. Why? Because no cloud must come between your eyes and the fiery heart of the li

36 / 36

All the virtues of the perfect wine glass are paralleled in typography. There is the long, thin stem th

Berthold Helvetica Light Italic

6 / 8

All the virtues of the perfect wine glass are paralleled in typography. There is the long, thin stem that obviates fingerprints on the bowl. Why? Because no cloud must come between your eyes and the fiery heart of the liquid. Are not the margins on book pages similarly meant to obviate the necessity of fingering the type page? Again: the glass is colorless or at the most only faintly tinged in the bowl, because the connoisseur judges wine partly by its color and is impatient of anything that alters it. There are a thousand mannerisms in typography that are as impudent and arbitrary as putting port in tumblers of red or green glass! When a goblet has a base that looks too small for security, it does not matter how cleverly it is weighted; you feel nervous lest it should tip over. There are ways of setting lines of type which may work well enough, and yet keep the reader subconsciously worried by the fear of "doubling" lines, reading three words as one, and so forth. Now the man who first chose glass instead of clay or metal to hold his wine was a "modernist" in the sense in which I am going to us

8 / 10

All the virtues of the perfect wine glass are paralleled in typography. There is the long, thin stem that obviates fingerprints on the bowl. Why? Because no cloud must come between your eyes and the fiery heart of the liquid. Are not the margins on book pages similarly meant to obviate the necessity of fingering the type page? Again: the glass is colorless or at the most only faintly tinged in the bowl, because the connoisseur judges wine partly by its color and is impatient of anything that alters it. There are a thousand mannerisms in typography that are as impudent and arbitrary as putting port in tumblers of red or green glass! When a goblet

10 / 12

All the virtues of the perfect wine glass are paralleled in typography. There is the long, thin stem that obviates fingerprints on the bowl. Why? Because no cloud must come between your eyes and the fiery heart of the liquid. Are not the margins on book pages similarly meant to obviate the necessity of fingering the type page? Again: the glass is colorless or at the most only faintly tinged in the bowl, because the connoisseur judges wine partly by its c

12 / 14

All the virtues of the perfect wine glass are paralleled in typography. There is the long, thin stem that obviates fingerprints on the bowl. Why? Because no cloud must come between your eyes and the fiery heart of the liquid. Are not the margins on book pages similarly meant to obviate the necessity of fingering the

14 / 16

All the virtues of the perfect wine glass are paralleled in typography. There is the long, thin stem that obviates fingerprints on the bowl. Why? Because no cloud must come between your eyes and the fiery heart of the liquid. Are not the margins on book pages similarly meant to obviate the necessity of fingering the type page? Again: the glass is colorless or at the most only faintly tinged in the bowl, because the connoisseur judges wine partly by its color and is impatient of anything that alters it. There are a thousand m

18 / 20

All the virtues of the perfect wine glass are paralleled in typography. There is the long, thin stem that obviates fingerprints on the bowl. Why? Because no cloud must come between your eyes and the fiery heart of the liquid. Are not the margins on book pages similarly meant to obviate the necessity of fingering the type page?

24 / 25

All the virtues of the perfect wine glass are paralleled in typography. There is the long, thin stem that obviates fingerprints on the bowl. Why? Because no cloud must come between your eyes and the fiery heart of t

36 / 36

All the virtues of the perfect wine glass are paralleled in typography. There is the long, thin stem t

Berthold Helvetica

6 / 8

All the virtues of the perfect wine glass are paralleled in typography. There is the long, thin stem that obviates fingerprints on the bowl. Why? Because no cloud must come between your eyes and the fiery heart of the liquid. Are not the margins on book pages similarly meant to obviate the necessity of fingering the type page? Again: the glass is colorless or at the most only faintly tinged in the bowl, because the connoisseur judges wine partly by its color and is impatient of anything that alters it. There are a thousand mannerisms in typography that are as impudent and arbitrary as putting port in tumblers of red or green glass! When a goblet has a base that looks too small for security, it does not matter how cleverly it is weighted; you feel nervous lest it should tip over. There are ways of setting lines of type which may work well enough, and yet keep the reader subconsciously worried by the fear of "doubling" lines, reading three words as one, and so forth. Now the man who first chose glass instead of clay or metal to hold his wine was a"mod

8 / 10

All the virtues of the perfect wine glass are paralleled in typography. There is the long, thin stem that obviates fingerprints on the bowl. Why? Because no cloud must come between your eyes and the fiery heart of the liquid. Are not the margins on book pages similarly meant to obviate the necessity of fingering the type page? Again: the glass is colorless or at the most only faintly tinged in the bowl, because the connoisseur judges wine partly by its color and is impatient of anything that alters it. There are a thousand mannerisms in typography that are as impudent and arbitrary as putting port in tumblers of red or green

10 / 12

All the virtues of the perfect wine glass are paralleled in typography. There is the long, thin stem that obviates fingerprints on the bowl. Why? Because no cloud must come between your eyes and the fiery heart of the liquid. Are not the margins on book pages similarly meant to obviate the necessity of fingering the type page? Again: the glass is colorless or at the most only faintly tinged in the bowl, because the connoisseur judges

12 / 14

All the virtues of the perfect wine glass are paralleled in typography. There is the long, thin stem that obviates fingerprints on the bowl. Why? Because no cloud must come between your eyes and the fiery heart of the liquid. Are not the margins on book pages similarly meant to obviate the necessity of fingeri

11 / 16

All the virtues of the perfect wine glass are paralleled In typography. There is the long, thin stem that obviates fingerprints on the bowl. Why? Because no cloud must come between your eyes and the fiery heart of the liquid. Are not the margins on book pages similarly meant to obviate the necessity of fingering the type page? Again: the glass is colorless or at the most only faintly tinged in the bowl, because the connoisseur judges wine partly by its color and is impatient of anything that alt

18 / 20

All the virtues of the perfect wine glass are paralleled in typography. There is the long, thin stem that obviates fingerprints on the bowl. Why? Because no cloud must come between your eyes and the fiery heart of the liquid. Are not the margins on book pages similarly meant to obviate the necessity of fingerin

24 / 25

All the virtues of the perfect wine glass are paralleled in typography. There is the long, thin stem that obviates fingerprints on the bowl. Why? Because no cloud must come between your eyes and the fie

36 / 36

All the virtues of the perfect wine glass are paralleled in typography. There is the long, thin ste

Berthold Helvetica Italic

6 / 8

All the virtues of the perfect wine glass are paralleled in typo graphy. There is the long, thin stem that obviates fingerprints on the bowl. Why? Because no cloud must come between yo ur eyes and the fiery heart of the liquid. Are not the margins on book pages similarly meant to obviate the necessity of fin gering the type page? Again: the glass is colorless or at the most only faintly tinged in the bowl, because the connoisse ur judges wine partly by its color and is impatient of anything that alters it. There are a thousand mannerisms in typograp hy that are as impudent and arbitrary as putting port in tumbl ers of red or green glass! When a goblet has a base that loo ks too small for security, it does not matter how cleverly it is weighted; you feel nervous lest it should tip over. There are ways of setting lines of type which may work well enough, and yet keep the reader subconsciously worried by the fear of "doubling" lines, reading three words as one, and so forth. Now the man who first chose glass instead of clay or metal to hold his wine was a "modernist" in the sense in which I am

8 / 10

All the virtues of the perfect wine glass are pa ralleled in typography. There is the long, thin st em that obviates fingerprints on the bowl. Wh y? Because no cloud must come between yo ur eyes and the fiery heart of the liquid. Are not the margins on book pages similarly mea nt to obviate the necessity of fingering the ty pe page? Again: the glass is colorless or at the most only faintly tinged in the bowl, becau se the connoisseur judges wine partly by its c olor and is impatient of anything that alters it. There are a thousand mannerisms in typograp hy that are as impudent and arbitrary as putti ng port in tumblers of red or green glass! Whe

10 / 12

All the virtues of the perfect wine gla ss are paralleled in typography. There is the long, thin stem that obviates fin gerprints on the bowl. Why? Because no cloud must come between your eyes and the fiery heart of the liquid. Are not the margins on book pages si milarly meant to obviate the necessi ty of fingering the type page? Again: the glass is colorless or at the most only faintly tinged in the bowl, becau se the connoisseur judges wine partl

12 / 14

All the virtues of the perfect wi ne glass are paralleled in typog raphy. There is the long, thin st em that obviates fingerprints o n the bowl. Why? Because no cl oud must come between your e yes and the fiery heart of the liq uid. Are not the margins on boo k pages similarly meant to obvi ate the necessity of fingering th

14 / 16

All the virtues of the perfect wine glass are paralleled in typography. There is the long, thin stem that obviates fing erprints on the bowl. Why? Because no cloud must come between your eyes and the fiery heart of the liquid. Are not the margins on book pages similarly meant to obvia te the necessity of fingering the type page? Again: the gl ass is colorless or at the most only faintly tinged in the bo wl, because the connoisseur judges wine partly by its col or and is impatient of anything that alters it. There are a th

18 / 20

All the virtues of the perfect wine glass are pa ralleled in typography. There is the long, thin st em that obviates fingerprints on the bowl. Wh y? Because no cloud must come between yo ur eyes and the fiery heart of the liquid. Are no t the margins on book pages similarly meant to obviate the necessity of fingering the type

24 / 25

All the virtues of the perfect wine gl ass are paralleled in typography. Th ere is the long, thin stem that obviat es fingerprints on the bowl. Why? B ecause no cloud must come betwe en your eyes and the fiery heart of th

36 / 36

All the virtues of the per fect wine glass are para lleled in typography. The re is the long, thin stem t

Berthold Helvetica Medium

6 / 8

All the virtues of the perfect wine glass are paralleled in typography. There is the long, thin stem that obviates finger prints on the bowl. Why? Because no cloud must come between your eyes and the fiery heart of the liquid. Are not the margins on book pages similarly meant to obviate the necessity of fingering the type page? Again: the glass is colorless or at the most only faintly tinged in the bowl, because the connoisseur judges wine partly by its color and is impatient of anything that alters it. There are a thousand mannerisms in typography that are as impudent and arbitrary as putting port in tumblers of red or green glass! When a goblet has a base that looks too small for security, it does not matter how cleverly it is weighted; you feel nervous lest it should tip over. There are ways of setting lines of type which may work well enough, and yet keep the reader subconsciously worried by the fear of "doubling" lines, reading three words as one, and so forth. Now the man who first chose glass instead of clay or metal to hold his wine

8 / 10

All the virtues of the perfect wine glass are paralleled in typography. There is the long, thin stem that obviates fingerprints on the bowl. Why? Because no cloud must come between your eyes and the fiery heart of the liquid. Are not the margins on book pages similarly meant to obviate the necessity of fingering the type page? Again: the glass is colorless or at the most only faintly tinged in the bowl, because the connoisseur judges wine partly by its color and is impatient of anything that alters it. There are a thousand mannerisms in typography that are as impudent and arbitrary as putting port in tumblers of red

10 / 12

All the virtues of the perfect wine glass are paralleled in typography. There is the long, thin stem that obviates fingerprints on the bowl. Why? Because no cloud must come between your eyes and the fiery heart of the liquid. Are not the margins on book pages similarly meant to obviate the necessity of fingering the type page? Again: the glass is colorless or at the most only faintly tinged in the bowl, because the connoisse

12 / 14

All the virtues of the perfect wine glass are paralleled in typography. There is the long, thin stem that obviates fingerprints on the bowl. Why? Because no cloud must come between your eyes and the fiery heart of the liquid. Are not the margins on book pages similarly meant to obviate the necessit

14 / 16

All the virtues of the perfect wine glass are paralleled in typography. There is the long, thin stem that obviates fingerprints on the bowl. Why? Because no cloud must come between your eyes and the fiery heart of the liquid. Are not the margins on book pages similarly meant to obviate the necessity of fingering the type page? Again: the glass is colorless or at the most only faintly tinged in the bowl, because the connoisseur judges wine partly by its color and is impatient of anything that

18 / 20

All the virtues of the perfect wine glass are paralleled in typography. There is the long, thin stem that obviates fingerprints on the bowl. Why? Because no cloud must come between your eyes and the fiery heart of the liquid. Are not the margins on book pages similarly meant to obviate the necessity of fin

24 / 25

All the virtues of the perfect wine glass are paralleled in typography. There is the long, thin stem that obviates fingerprints on the bowl. Why? Because no cloud must come between your eyes and t

36 / 36

All the virtues of the perfect wine glass are paralleled in typography. There is the long, thin

Berthold Helvetica Medium Italic

6 / 8

All the virtues of the perfect wine glass are paralleled in typography. There is the long, thin stem that obviates fingerprints on the bowl. Why? Because no cloud must come between your eyes and the fiery heart of the liquid. Are not the margins on book pages similarly meant to obviate the necessity of fingering the type page? Again: the glass is colorless or at the most only faintly tinged in the bowl, because the connoisseur judges wine partly by its color and is impatient of anything that alters it. There are a thousand mannerisms in typography that are as impudent and arbitrary as putting port in tumblers of red or green glass! When a goblet has a base that looks too small for security, it does not matter how cleverly it is weighted; you feel nervous lest it should tip over. There are ways of setting lines of type which may work well enough, and yet keep the reader subconsciously worried by the fear of "doubling" lines, reading three words as one, and so forth. Now the man who first chose glass instead of clay or metal to hold his wine was a "m

8 / 10

All the virtues of the perfect wine glass are paralleled in typography. There is the long, thin stem that obviates fingerprints on the bowl. Why? Because no cloud must come between your eyes and the fiery heart of the liquid. Are not the margins on book pages similarly meant to obviate the necessity of fingering the type page? Again: the glass is colorless or at the most only faintly tinged in the bowl, because the connoisseur judges wine partly by its color and is impatient of anything that alters it. There are a thousand mannerisms in typography that are as impudent and arbitrary as putting port in tumblers of red or

10 / 12

All the virtues of the perfect wine glass are paralleled in typography. There is the long, thin stem that obviates fingerprints on the bowl. Why? Because no cloud must come between your eyes and the fiery heart of the liquid. Are not the margins on book pages similarly meant to obviate the necessity of fingering the type page? Again: the glass is colorless or at the most only faintly tinged in the bowl, because the connoisseur

12 / 14

All the virtues of the perfect wine glass are paralleled in typography. There is the long, thin stem that obviates fingerprints on the bowl. Why? Because no cloud must come between your eyes and the fiery heart of the liquid. Are not the margins on book pages similarly meant to obviate the necessity of fi

14 / 16

All the virtues of the perfect wine glass are paralleled in typography. There is the long, thin stem that obviates fingerprints on the bowl. Why? Because no cloud must come between your eyes and the fiery heart of the liquid. Are not the margins on book pages similarly meant to obviate the necessity of fingering the type page? Again: the glass is colorless or at the most only faintly tinged in the bowl, because the connoisseur judges wine partly by its color and is impatient of anything that alters

18 / 20

All the virtues of the perfect wine glass are paralleled in typography. There is the long, thin stem that obviates fingerprints on the bowl. Why? Because no cloud must come between your eyes and the fiery heart of the liquid. Are not the margins on book pages similarly meant to obviate the necessity of fin

24 / 25

All the virtues of the perfect wine glass are paralleled in typography. There is the long, thin stem that obviates fingerprints on the bowl. Why? Because no cloud must come me between your eyes and the fie

36 / 36

All the virtues of the perfect wine glass are paralleled in typography. There is the long, thin s

Berthold Helvetica Demi Bold

6 / 8

All the virtues of the perfect wine glass are paralleled in typography. There is the long, thin stem that obviates fingerprints on the bowl. Why? Because no cloud must come between your eyes and the fiery heart of the liquid. Are not the margins on book pages similarly meant to obviate the necessity of fingering the type page? Again: the glass is colorless or at the most only faintly tinged in the bowl, because the connoisseur judges wine partly by its color and is impatient of anything that alters it. There are a thousand mannerisms in typography that are as impudent and arbitrary as putting port in tumblers of red or green glass! When a goblet has a base that looks too small for security, it does not matter how cleverly it is weighted; you feel nervous lest it should tip over. There are ways of setting lines of type which may work well enough, and yet keep the reader subconsciously worried by the fear of "doubling" lines, reading three words as one, and so forth.

8 / 10

All the virtues of the perfect wine glass are paralleled in typography. There is the long, thin stem that obviates fingerprints on the bowl. Why? Because no cloud must come between your eyes and the fiery heart of the liquid. Are not the margins on book pages similarly meant to obviate the necessity of fingering the type page? Again: the glass is colorless or at the most only faintly tinged in the bowl, because the connoisseur judges wine partly by its color and is impatient of anything that alters it. There are a thousand mannerisms in typography that are as impudent and a

10 / 12

All the virtues of the perfect wine glass are paralleled in typography. There is the long, thin stem that obviates fingerprints on the bowl. Why? Because no cloud must come between your eyes and the fiery heart of the liquid. Are not the margins on book pages similarly meant to obviate the necessity of fingering the type page? Again: the glass is colorless or at the most only faintly tinged in the bowl,

12 / 14

All the virtues of the perfect wine glass are paralleled in typography. There is the long, thin stem that obviates fingerprints on the bowl. Why? Because no cloud must come between your eyes and the fiery heart of the liquid. Are not the margins on book pages similarly meant to

14 / 16

All the virtues of the perfect wine glass are paralleled in typography. There is the long, thin stem that obviates fingerprints on the bowl. Why? Because no cloud must come between your eyes and the fiery heart of the liquid. Are not the margins on book pages similarly meant to obviate the necessity of fingering the type page? Again: the glass is colorless or at the most only faintly tinged in the bowl, because the connoisseur judges wine partly by its col

18 / 20

All the virtues of the perfect wine glass are paralleled in typography. There is the long, thin stem that obviates fingerprints on the bowl. Why? Because no cloud must come between your eyes and the fiery heart of the liquid. Are not the margins on book pages similarly meant to obviate

24 / 25

All the virtues of the perfect wine glass are paralleled in typography. There is the long, thin stem that obviates fingerprints on the bowl. Why? Because no cloud must come between your e

36 / 36

All the virtues of the perfect wine glass are paralleled in typography. There is the lon

Berthold Helvetica Demi Bold Italic

6 / 8

All the virtues of the perfect wine glass are paralleled in typography. There is the long, thin stem that obviates fingerprints on the bowl. Why? Because no cloud must come between your eyes and the fiery heart of the liquid. Are not the margins on book pages similarly meant to obviate the necessity of fingering the type page? Again: the glass is colorless or at the most only faintly tinged in the bowl, because the connoisseur judges wine partly by its color and is impatient of anything that alters it. There are a thousand mannerisms in typography that are as impudent and arbitrary as putting port in tumblers of red or green glass! When a goblet has a base that looks too small for security, it does not matter how cleverly it is weighted; you feel nervous lest it should tip over. There are ways of setting lines of type which may work well enough, and yet keep the reader subconsciously worried by the fear of "doubling" lines, reading three words as one, and so forth. Now

8 / 10

All the virtues of the perfect wine glass are paralleled in typography. There is the long, thin stem that obviates fingerprints on the bowl. Why? Because no cloud must come between your eyes and the fiery heart of the liquid. Are not the margins on book pages similarly meant to obviate the necessity of fingering the type page? Again: the glass is colorless or at the most only faintly tinged in the bowl, because the connoisseur judges wine partly by its color and is impatient of anything that alters it. There are a thousand mannerisms in typography that are as impudent and ar

10 / 12

All the virtues of the perfect wine glass are paralleled in typography. There is the long, thin stem that obviates fingerprints on the bowl. Why? Because no cloud must come between your eyes and the fiery heart of the liquid. Are not the margins on book pages similarly meant to obviate the necessity of fingering the type page? Again: the glass is colorless or at the most only faintly tinged in the bo

12 / 14

All the virtues of the perfect wine glass are paralleled in typography. There is the long, thin stem that obviates fingerprints on the bowl. Why? Because no cloud must come between your eyes and the fiery heart of the liquid. Are not the margins on book pages similarly meant to

14 / 16

All the virtues of the perfect wine glass are paralleled in typography. There is the long, thin stem that obviates fingerprints on the bowl. Why? Because no cloud must come between your eyes and the fiery heart of the liquid. Are not the margins on book pages similarly meant to obviate the necessity of fingering the type page? Again: the glass is colorless or at the most only faintly tinged in the bowl, because the connoisseur judges wine partly by its color

18 / 20

All the virtues of the perfect wine glass are paralleled in typography. There is the long, thin stem that obviates fingerprints on the bowl. Why? Because no cloud must come between your eyes and the fiery heart of the liquid. Are not the margins on book pages similarly meant to obviat

24 / 25

All the virtues of the perfect wine glass are paralleled in typography. There is the long, thin stem that obviates fingerprints on the bowl. Why? Because no cloud must come between your ey

36 / 36

All the virtues of the perfect wine glass are paralleled in typography. There is the lon

Berthold Helvetica Bold

6 / 8
All the virtues of the perfect wine glass are paralleled in typography. There is the long, thin stem that obviates fingerprints on the bowl. Why? Because no cloud must come between your eyes and the fiery heart of the liquid. Are not the margins on book pages similarly meant to obviate the necessity of fingering the type page? Again: the glass is colorless or at the most only faintly tinged in the bowl, because the connoisseur judges wine partly by its color and is impatient of anything that alters it. There are a thousand mannerisms in typography that are as impudent and arbitrary as putting port in tumblers of red or green glass! When a goblet has a base that looks too small for security, it does not matter how cleverly it is weighted; you feel nervous lest it should tip over. There are ways of setting lines of type which may work well enough, and yet keep the reader subconsciously worried by the fear of "doubling" lines, reading three wor

8 / 10
All the virtues of the perfect wine glass are paralleled in typography. There is the long, thin stem that obviates fingerprints on the bowl. Why? Because no cloud must come between your eyes and the fiery heart of the liquid. Are not the margins on book pages similarly meant to obviate the necessity of fingering the type page? Again: the glass is colorless or at the most only faintly tinged in the bowl, because the connoisseur judges wine partly by its color and is impatient of anything that alters it. There are a thousand mannerisms in typography that a

10 / 12
All the virtues of the perfect wine glass are paralleled in typography. There is the long, thin stem that obviates fingerprints on the bowl. Why? Because no cloud must come between your eyes and the fiery heart of the liquid. Are not the margins on book pages similarly meant to obviate the necessity of fingering the type page? Again: the glass is colorless or at the most only faintly ting

12 / 14
All the virtues of the perfect wine glass are paralleled in typography. There is the long, thin stem that obviates fingerprints on the bowl. Why? Because no cloud must come between your eyes and the fiery heart of the liquid. Are not the margins on book pages similarly

14 / 16
All the virtues of the perfect wine glass are paralleled in typography. There is the long, thin stem that obviates fingerprints on the bowl. Why? Because no cloud must come between your eyes and the fiery heart of the liquid. Are not the margins on book pages similarly meant to obviate the necessity of fingering the type page? Again: the glass is colorless or at the most only faintly tinged in the bowl, because the connoisseur judges wine partl

18 / 20
All the virtues of the perfect wine glass are paralleled in typography. There is the long, thin stem that obviates fingerprints on the bowl. Why? Because no cloud must come between your eyes and the fiery heart of the liquid. Are not the margins on book pages similarly meant

24 / 25
All the virtues of the perfect wine glass are paralleled in typography. There is the long, thin stem that obviates fingerprints on the bowl. Why? Because no cloud must come between

36 / 36
All the virtues of the perfect wine glass are paralleled in typography. There is t

Berthold Helvetica Bold Italic

6 / 8

All the virtues of the perfect wine glass are parallel ed in typography. There is the long, thin stem that obviates fingerprints on the bowl. Why? Because no cloud must come between your eyes and the fiery heart of the liquid. Are not the margins on book pag es similarly meant to obviate the necessity of finger ing the type page? Again: the glass is colorless or at the most only faintly tinged in the bowl, because the connoisseur judges wine partly by its color and is impatient of anything that alters it. There are a th ousand mannerisms in typography that are as impu dent and arbitrary as putting port in tumblers of red or green glass! When a goblet has a base that looks too small for security, it does not matter how clever ly it is weighted; you feel nervous lest it should tip over. There are ways of setting lines of type which may work well enough, and yet keep the reader sub consciously worried by the fear of "doubling" lines,

8 / 10

All the virtues of the perfect wine glass are paralleled in typography. There is the long, thin stem that obviates finger prints on the bowl. Why? Because no cl oud must come between your eyes and the fiery heart of the liquid. Are not the margins on book pages similarly meant to obviate the necessity of fingering the type page? Again: the glass is colorle ss or at the most only faintly tinged in t he bowl, because the connoisseur judg es wine partly by its color and is impat ient of anything that alters it. There are a thousand mannerisms in typography

10 / 12

All the virtues of the perfect wi ne glass are paralleled in typog raphy. There is the long, thin st em that obviates fingerprints on the bowl. Why? Because no clo ud must come between your ey es and the fiery heart of the liqu id. Are not the margins on book pages similarly meant to obvia te the necessity of fingering the type page? Again: the glass is c olorless or at the most only faint

12 / 14

All the virtues of the perfe ct wine glass are parallele d in typography. There is th e long, thin stem that obvi ates fingerprints on the bo wl. Why? Because no cloud must come between your eyes and the fiery heart of the liquid. Are not the marg ins on book pages similarl

14 / 16

All the virtues of the perfect wine glass are paral leled in typography. There is the long, thin stem that obviates fingerprints on the bowl. Why? Bec ause no cloud must come between your eyes and the fiery heart of the liquid. Are not the marg ins on book pages similarly meant to obviate the necessity of fingering the type page? Again: the glass is colorless or at the most only faintly ting ed in the bowl, because the connoisseur judges

18 / 20

All the virtues of the perfect wine glass are paralleled in typography. There is t he long, thin stem that obviates finger prints on the bowl. Why? Because no cl oud must come between your eyes an d the fiery heart of the liquid. Are not th e margins on book pages similarly me

24 / 25

All the virtues of the perfect wine glass are paralleled in typography. There is the long, thin stem that obviates fing erprints on the bowl. Why? B ecause no cloud must come

36 / 36

All the virtues of th e perfect wine glas s are paralleled in t ypography. There is

Berthold Helvetica Condensed Light

6 / 8

All the virtues of the perfect wine glass are paralleled in typography. There is the long, thin stem that obviates fingerprints on the bowl. Why? Because no cloud must come between your eyes and the fiery heart of the liquid. Are not the margins on book pages similarly meant to obviate the necessity of fingering the type page? Again: the glass is colorless or at the most only faintly tinged in the bowl, because the connoisseur judges wine partly by its color and is impatient of anything that alters it. There are a thousand mannerisms in typography that are as impudent and arbitrary as putting port in tumblers of red or green glass! When a goblet has a base that looks too small for security, it does not matter how cleverly it is weighted; you feel nervous lest it should tip over. There are ways of setting lines of type which may work well enough, and yet keep the reader subconsciously worried by the fear of "doubling" lines, reading three words as one, and so forth. Now the man who first chose glass instead of clay or metal to hold his wine was a "modernist" in the sense in which I am going to use that term. That is, the first thing he asked of this particular object was not "How should it look?" but "What must it do?" and to that extent all good typography is modernist. Wine is so strange and potent a thing that it has been used in the central ritual of

8 / 10

All the virtues of the perfect wine glass are paralleled in typography. There is the long, thin stem that obviates fingerprints on the bowl. Why? Because no cloud must come between your eyes and the fiery heart of the liquid. Are not the margins on book pages similarly meant to obviate the necessity of fingering the type page? Again: the glass is colorless or at the most only faintly tinged in the bowl, because the connoisseur judges wine partly by its color and is impatient of anything that alters it. There are a thousand mannerisms in typography that are as impudent and arbitrary as putting port in tumblers of red or green glass! When a goblet has a base that looks too small for security, it does not matter how cleverly it is weighted; you feel nervous lest it should tip over. There are ways of

10 / 12

All the virtues of the perfect wine glass are paralleled in typography. There is the long, thin stem that obviates fingerprints on the bowl. Why? Because no cloud must come between your eyes and the fiery heart of the liquid. Are not the margins on book pages similarly meant to obviate the necessity of fingering the type page? Again: the glass is colorless or at the most only faintly tinged in the bowl, because the connoisseur judges wine partly by its color and is impatient of anything that alters it. There are a thousand mannerisms in typograp

12 / 14

All the virtues of the perfect wine glass are paralleled in typography. There is the long, thin stem that obviates fingerprints on the bowl. Why? Because no cloud must come between your eyes and the fiery heart of the liquid. Are not the margins on book pages similarly meant to obviate the necessity of fingering the type page? Again: the glass is colorless or at the most only faintly ting

14 / 16

All the virtues of the perfect wine glass are paralleled in typography. There is the long, thin stem that obviates fingerprints on the bowl. Why? Because no cloud must come between your eyes and the fiery heart of the liquid. Are not the margins on book pages similarly meant to obviate the necessity of fingering the type page? Again: the glass is colorless or at the most only faintly tinged in the bowl, because the connoisseur judges wine partly by its color and is impatient of anything that alters it. There are a thousand mannerisms in typography that are as impudent and arbitrary as putting port in tumblers of red or green glass!

18 / 20

All the virtues of the perfect wine glass are paralleled in typography. There is the long, thin stem that obviates fingerprints on the bowl. Why? Because no cloud must come between your eyes and the fiery heart of the liquid. Are not the margins on book pages similarly meant to obviate the necessity of fingering the type page? Again: the glass is colorless or at the most only faintly tinged in the

24 / 25

All the virtues of the perfect wine glass are paralleled in typography. There is the long, thin stem that obviates fingerprints on the bowl. Why? Because no cloud must come between your eyes and the fiery heart of the liquid. Are not the margins on book pages

36 / 36

All the virtues of the perfect wine glass are paralleled in typography. There is the long, thin stem that obviates fingerprint

Berthold Helvetica Condensed Light Italic

6 / 8

All the virtues of the perfect wine glass are paralleled in typography. There is the long, thin stem that obviates fingerprints on the bowl. Why? Because no cloud must come between your eyes and the fiery heart of the liquid. Are not the margins on book pages similarly meant to obviate the necessity of fingering the type page? Again: the glass is colorless or at the most only faintly tinged in the bowl, because the connoisseur judges wine partly by its color and is impatient of anything that alters it. There are a thousand mannerisms in typography that are as impudent and arbitrary as putting port in tumblers of red or green glass! When a goblet has a base that looks too small for security, it does not matter how cleverly it is weighted; you feel nervous lest it should tip over. There are ways of setting lines of type which may work well enough, and yet keep the reader subconsciously worried by the fear of "doubling" lines, reading three words as one, and so forth. Now the man who first chose glass instead of clay or metal to hold by his wine was a "modernist" in the sense in which I am going to use that term. That is, the first thing he asked of this particular object was not "How should it look?" but "What must it do?" and to that extent all good typography is modernist. Wine is so strange and potent a thing that it has been

8 / 10

All the virtues of the perfect wine glass are paralleled in typography. There is the long, thin stem that obviates fingerprints on the bowl. Why? Because no cloud must come between your eyes and the fiery heart of the liquid. Are not the margins on book pages similarly meant to obviate the necessity of fingering the type page? Again: the glass is colorless or at the most only faintly tinged in the bowl, because the connoisseur judges wine partly by its color and is impatient of anything that alters it. There are a thousand mannerisms in typography that are as impudent and arbitrary as putting port in tumblers of red or green glass! When a goblet has a base that looks too small for security, it does not matter how cleverly it is weighted; you feel nervous lest it should tip over. The

10 / 12

All the virtues of the perfect wine glass are paralleled in typography. There is the long, thin stem that obviates fingerprints on the bowl. Why? Because no cloud must come between your eyes and the fiery heart of the liquid. Are not the margins on book pages similarly meant to obviate the necessity of fingering the type page? Again: the glass is colorless or at the most only faintly tinged in the bowl, because the connoisseur judges wine partly by its color and is impatient of anything that alters it. There are a thousand mannerisms in typogr

12 / 14

All the virtues of the perfect wine glass are paralleled in typography. There is the long, thin stem that obviates fingerprints on the bowl. Why? Because no cloud must come between your eyes and the fiery heart of the liquid. Are not the margins on book pages similarly meant to obviate the necessity of fingering the type page? Again: the glass is colorless or at the most only faint

14 / 16

All the virtues of the perfect wine glass are paralleled in typography. There is the long, thin stem that obviates fingerprints on the bowl. Why? Because no cloud must come between your eyes and the fiery heart of the liquid. Are not the margins on book pages similarly meant to obviate the necessity of fingering the type page? Again: the glass is colorless or at the most only faintly tinged in the bowl, because the connoisseur judges wine partly by its color and is impatient of anything that alters it. There are a thousand mannerisms in typography that are as impudent and arbitrary as putting port in tumblers of red or green

18 / 20

All the virtues of the perfect wine glass are paralleled in typography. There is the long, thin stem that obviates fingerprints on the bowl. Why? Because no cloud must come between your eyes and the fiery heart of the liquid. Are not the margins on book pages similarly meant to obviate the necessity of fingering the type page? Again: the glass is colorless or at the most only faintly tinged in

24 / 25

All the virtues of the perfect wine glass are paralleled in typography. There is the long, thin stem that obviates fingerprints on the bowl. Why? Because no cloud must come between your eyes and the fiery heart of the liquid. Are not the margins on book pag

36 / 36

All the virtues of the perfect wine glass are paralleled in typography. There is the long, thin stem that obviates finger

Berthold Helvetica Condensed Medium

6 / 8

All the virtues of the perfect wine glass are paralleled in typography. There is the long, thin stem that obviates fingerprints on the bowl. Why? Because no cloud must come between your eyes and the fiery heart of the liquid. Are not the margins on book pages similarly meant to obviate the necessity of fingering the type page? Again: the glass is colorless or at the most only faintly tinged in the bowl, because the connoisseur judges wine partly by its color and is impatient of anything that alters it. There are a thousand mannerisms in typography that are as impudent and arbitrary as putting port in tumblers of red or green glass! When a goblet has a base that looks too small for security, it does not matter how cleverly it is weighted; you feel nervous lest it should tip over. There are ways of setting lines of type which may work well enough, and yet keep the reader subconsciously worried by the fear of "doubling" lines, reading three words as one, and so forth. Now the man who first chose glass instead of clay or metal to hold his wine was a "modernist" in the sense in which I am going to use that term. That is, the first thing he asked of this particular object was not "How should it look?" but "What must it do?" and to that extent all good typography is modernist. Wine is so strange and potent a thing that it has been used in the central ritual of religion in one place and time, and attacked by a virago with a hatchet in another. There is only one other thing in the world that is capable of stirring and altering men's minds to the same extent, and that is the coher

8 / 10

All the virtues of the perfect wine glass are paralleled in typography. There is the long, thin stem that obviates fingerprints on the bowl. Why? Because no cloud must come between your eyes and the fiery heart of the liquid. Are not the margins on book pages similarly meant to obviate the necessity of fingering the type page? Again: the glass is colorless or at the most only faintly tinged in the bowl, because the connoisseur judges wine partly by its color and is impatient of anything that alters it. There are a thousand mannerisms in typography that are as impudent and arbitrary as putting port in tumblers of red or green glass! When a goblet has a base that looks too small for security, it does not matter how cleverly it is weighted; you feel nervous lest it should tip over. There are ways of setting lines of type which may work well enough, and yet keep the reader subconsciously worried by the fear of "doubling" lines, readi

10 / 12

All the virtues of the perfect wine glass are paralleled in typography. There is the long, thin stem that obviates fingerprints on the bowl. Why? Because no cloud must come between your eyes and the fiery heart of the liquid. Are not the margins on book pages similarly meant to obviate the necessity of fingering the type page? Again: the glass is colorless or at the most only faintly tinged in the bowl, because the connoisseur judges wine partly by its color and is impatient of anything that alters it. There are a thousand mannerisms in typography that are as impudent and arbitrary as putting port in tumblers of red or green glass! When a gobl

12 / 14

All the virtues of the perfect wine glass are paralleled in typography. There is the long, thin stem that obviates fingerprints on the bowl. Why? Because no cloud must come between your eyes and the fiery heart of the liquid. Are not the margins on book pages similarly meant to obviate the necessity of fingering the type page? Again: the glass is colorless or at the most only faintly tinged in the bowl, because the connoisseur judges wine partly by its col

14 / 16

All the virtues of the perfect wine glass are paralleled in typography. There is the long, thin stem that obviates fingerprints on the bowl. Why? Because no cloud must come between your eyes and the fiery heart of the liquid. Are not the margins on book pages similarly meant to obviate the necessity of fingering the type page? Again: the glass is colorless or at the most only faintly tinged in the bowl, because the connoisseur judges wine partly by its color and is impatient of anything that alters it. There are a thousand mannerisms in typography that are as impudent and arbitrary as putting port in tumblers of red or green glass! When a goblet has a base that looks too small for security, it does not matter how cleverly it is weighted; you

18 / 20

All the virtues of the perfect wine glass are paralleled in typography. There is the long, thin stem that obviates fingerprints on the bowl. Why? Because no cloud must come between your eyes and the fiery heart of the liquid. Are not the margins on book pages similarly meant to obviate the necessity of fingering the type page? Again: the glass is colorless or at the most only faintly tinged in the bowl, because the connoisseur judges wine partly by its color and is

24 / 25

All the virtues of the perfect wine glass are paralleled in typography. There is the long, thin stem that obviates fingerprints on the bowl. Why? Because no cloud must come between your eyes and the fiery heart of the liquid. Are not the margins on book pages similarly meant to obviate the necessity of finge

36 / 36

All the virtues of the perfect wine glass are paralleled in typography. There is the long, thin stem that obviates fingerprints on the bowl

Univers

2kQa

Berthold Univers

Foundry:	*H. Berthold AG*
Supplier:	*FontShop*
Letterform authenticity:	*Excellent*
Digital outline:	*Fair*
Side bearings:	*Excellent*
Kerning:	*Good*
Hinting:	*Excellent*
Expert editions:	*No*
Multiple masters:	*No*
Family completeness:	*Excellent*
Formats:	*Type 1*
Platforms:	*Mac / PC / UNIX*

Berthold Univers 55 Regular

72 points

ABCDEFGHIJK
LMNOPQRS
TUVWXYZ$£&
1234567890
abcdefghijklmn
opqrstuvwxyz
ß(!?,.-:;)"

Berthold Univers 56 Italic

72 points

ABCDEFGHIJK
LMNOPQRS
TUVWXYZ$£&
1234567890
abcdefghijklmn
opqrstuvwxyz
ß(!?,.-:;)"

Berthold Univers 45 Light

6 / 8

All the virtues of the perfect wine glass are paralleled in typogr aphy. There is the long, thin stem that obviates fingerprints on the bowl. Why? Because no cloud must come between your eyes and the fiery heart of the liquid. Are not the margins on book pages similarly meant to obviate the necessity of fingeri ng the type page? Again: the glass is colorless or at the most only faintly tinged in the bowl, because the connoisseur judges wine partly by its color and is impatient of anything that alters it. There are a thousand mannerisms in typography that are as impudent and arbitrary as putting port in tumblers of red or gre en glass! When a goblet has a base that looks too small for sec urity, it does not matter how cleverly it is weighted; you feel ne rvous lest it should tip over. There are ways of setting lines of type which may work well enough, and yet keep the reader su bconsciously worried by the fear of "doubling" lines, reading th ree words as one, and so forth. Now the man who first chose g lass instead of clay or metal to hold his wine was a "moderni st" in the sense in which I am going to use that term. That is, th

8 / 10

All the virtues of the perfect wine glass are parall eled in typography. There is the long, thin stem that obviates fingerprints on the bowl. Why? Because no cloud must come between your ey es and the fiery heart of the liquid. Are not the margins on book pages similarly meant to obvia te the necessity of fingering the type page? Aga in: the glass is colorless or at the most only faint ly tinged in the bowl, because the connoisseur j udges wine partly by its color and is impatient of anything that alters it. There are a thousand man nerisms in typography that are as impudent and arbitrary as putting port in tumblers of red or gre en glass! When a goblet has a base that looks to

10 / 12

All the virtues of the perfect wine glass are paralleled in typography. There is the long, thin stem that obviates finger prints on the bowl. Why? Because no cl oud must come between your eyes an d the fiery heart of the liquid. Are not the margins on book pages similarly meant to obviate the necessity of fingering the type page? Again: the glass is colorless or at the most only faintly tinged in the bowl, because the connoisseur judges wine partly by its color and is impatient

12 / 14

All the virtues of the perfect wine glass are paralleled in typograp hy. There is the long, thin stem th at obviates fingerprints on the bo wl. Why? Because no cloud must come between your eyes and th e fiery heart of the liquid. Are not t he margins on book pages simila rly meant to obviate the necessit y of fingering the type page? Agai

14 / 16

All the virtues of the perfect wine glass are paralleled in typo graphy. There is the long, thin stem that obviates fingerprint s on the bowl. Why? Because no cloud must come between your eyes and the fiery heart of the liquid. Are not the margi ns on book pages similarly meant to obviate the necessity of fingering the type page? Again: the glass is colorless or at th e most only faintly tinged in the bowl, because the connoiss eur judges wine partly by its color and is impatient of anythi ng that alters it. There are a thousand mannerisms in typogra

18 / 20

All the virtues of the perfect wine glass are parall eled in typography. There is the long, thin stem th at obviates fingerprints on the bowl. Why? Bec ause no cloud must come between your eyes and the fiery heart of the liquid. Are not the marg ins on book pages similarly meant to obviate the necessity of fingering the type page? Again: the

24 / 25

All the virtues of the perfect wine gla ss are paralleled in typography. There is the long, thin stem that obviates fi ngerprints on the bowl. Why? Becau se no cloud must come between yo ur eyes and the fiery heart of the liqui

36 / 36

All the virtues of the perf ect wine glass are parall eled in typography. There is the long, thin stem tha

Berthold Univers 46 Light Italic

6 / 8

All the virtues of the perfect wine glass are paralleled in typography. There is the long, thin stem that obviates fingerprints on the bowl. Why? Because no cloud must come between your eyes and the fiery heart of the liquid. Are not the margins on book pages similarly meant to obviate the necessity of fingering the type page? Again: the glass is colorless or at the most only faintly tinged in the bowl, because the connoisseur judges wine partly by its color and is impatient of anything that alters it. There are a thousand mannerisms in typography that are as impudent and arbitrary as putting port in tumblers of red or green glass! When a goblet has a base that looks too small for security, it does not matter how cleverly it is weighted; you feel nervous lest it should tip over. There are ways of setting lines of type which may work well enough, and yet keep the reader subconsciously worried by the fear of "doubling" lines, reading three words as one, and so forth. Now the man who first chose glass instead of clay or metal to hold his wine was a "modernist" in the sense in which I am going to

8 / 10

All the virtues of the perfect wine glass are paralleled in typography. There is the long, thin stem that obviates fingerprints on the bowl. Why? Because no cloud must come between your eyes and the fiery heart of the liquid. Are not the margins on book pages similarly meant to obviate the necessity of fingering the type page? Again: the glass is colorless or at the most only faintly tinged in the bowl, because the connoisseur judges wine partly by its color and is impatient of anything that alters it. There are a thousand mannerisms in typography that are as impudent and arbitrary as putting port in tumblers of red or green glass! When a goblet has a base that lo

10 / 12

All the virtues of the perfect wine glass are paralleled in typography. There is the long, thin stem that obviates finger prints on the bowl. Why? Because no cloud must come between your eyes and the fiery heart of the liquid. Are not the margins on book pages similarly meant to obviate the necessity of fingering the type page? Again: the glass is colorless or at the most only faintly tinged in the bowl, because the connoisseur judges wine partly by its color and is

12 / 14

All the virtues of the perfect wine glass are paralleled in typography. There is the long, thin stem that obviates fingerprints on the bowl. Why? Because no cloud must come between your eyes and the fiery heart of the liquid. Are not the margins on book pages similarly meant to obviate the necessity of fingering the typ

14 / 16

All the virtues of the perfect wine glass are paralleled in typography. There is the long, thin stem that obviates fingerprints on the bowl. Why? Because no cloud must come between your eyes and the fiery heart of the liquid. Are not the margins on book pages similarly meant to obviate the necessity of fingering the type page? Again: the glass is colorless or at the most only faintly tinged in the bowl, because the connoisseur judges wine partly by its color and is impatient of anything that alters it. There are a thousand mannerisms

18 / 20

All the virtues of the perfect wine glass are paralleled in typography. There is the long, thin stem that obviates fingerprints on the bowl. Why? Because no cloud must come between your eyes and the fiery heart of the liquid. Are not the margins on book pages similarly meant to obviate the necessity of fingering the type page? Again:

24 / 25

All the virtues of the perfect wine glass are paralleled in typography. There is the long, thin stem that obviates fingerprints on the bowl. Why? Because no cloud must come between your eyes and the fiery heart of the li

36 / 36

All the virtues of the perfect wine glass are paralleled in typography. There is the long, thin stem t

Berthold Univers 55 Regular

6 / 8

All the virtues of the perfect wine glass are paralleled in typography. There is the long, thin stem that obviates fingerprints on the bowl. Why? Because no cloud must come between your eyes and the fiery heart of the liquid. Are not the margins on book pages similarly meant to obviate the necessity of fingering the type page? Again: the glass is colorless or at the most only faintly tinged in the bowl, because the connoisseur judges wine partly by its color and is impatient of anything that alters it. There are a thousand mannerisms in typography that are as impudent and arbitrary as putting port in tumblers of red or green glass! When a goblet has a base that looks too small for security, it does not matter how cleverly it is weighted; you feel nervous lest it should tip over. There are ways of setting lines of type which may work well enough, and yet keep the reader subconsciously worried by the fear of "doubling" lines, reading three words as one, and so forth. Now the man who first chose glass instead of clay or metal to hold his wine was a "modernist" in

8 / 10

All the virtues of the perfect wine glass are paralleled in typography. There is the long, thin stem that obviates fingerprints on the bowl. Why? Because no cloud must come between your eyes and the fiery heart of the liquid. Are not the margins on book pages similarly meant to obviate the necessity of fingering the type page? Again: the glass is colorless or at the most only faintly tinged in the bowl, because the connoisseur judges wine partly by its color and is impatient of anything that alters it. There are a thousand mannerisms in typography that are as impudent and arbitrary as putting port in tumblers of red or green glass! When a

10 / 12

All the virtues of the perfect wine glass are paralleled in typography. There is the long, thin stem that obviates fingerprints on the bowl. Why? Because no cloud must come between your eyes and the fiery heart of the liquid. Are not the margins on book pages similarly meant to obviate the necessity of fingering the type page? Again: the glass is colorless or at the most only faintly tinged in the bowl, because the connoisseur judges wine part

12 / 14

All the virtues of the perfect wine glass are paralleled in typography. There is the long, thin stem that obviates fingerprints on the bowl. Why? Because no cloud must come between your eyes and the fiery heart of the liquid. Are not the margins on book pages similarly meant to obviate the necessity of fingering th

14 / 16

All the virtues of the perfect wine glass are paralleled in typography. There is the long, thin stem that obviates fingerprints on the bowl. Why? Because no cloud must come between your eyes and the fiery heart of the liquid. Are not the margins on book pages similarly meant to obviate the necessity of fingering the type page? Again: the glass is colorless or at the most only faintly tinged in the bowl, because the connoisseur judges wine partly by its color and is impatient of anything that alters it. There are a thou

18 / 20

All the virtues of the perfect wine glass are paralleled in typography. There is the long, thin stem that obviates fingerprints on the bowl. Why? Because no cloud must come between your eyes and the fiery heart of the liquid. Are not the margins on book pages similarly meant to obviate the necessity of fingering the ty

24 / 25

All the virtues of the perfect wine glass are paralleled in typography. There is the long, thin stem that obviates fingerprints on the bowl. Why? Because no cloud must come between your eyes and the fiery he

36 / 36

All the virtues of the perfect wine glass are paralleled in typography. There is the long, thin ste

6 / 8

All the virtues of the perfect wine glass are paralleled in typography. There is the long, thin stem that obviates fingerprints on the bowl. Why? Because no cloud must come between your eyes and the fiery heart of the liquid. Are not the margins on book pages similarly meant to obviate the necessity of fingering the type page? Again: the glass is colorless or at the most only faintly tinged in the bowl, because the connoisseur judges wine partly by its color and is impatient of anything that alters it. There are a thousand mannerisms in typography that are as impudent and arbitrary as putting port in tumblers of red or green glass! When a goblet has a base that looks too small for security, it does not matter how cleverly it is weighted; you feel nervous lest it should tip over. There are ways of setting lines of type which may work well enough, and yet keep the reader subconsciously worried by the fear of "doubling" lines, reading three words as one, and so forth. Now the man who first chose glass instead of clay or metal to hold his wine was a "modernist" in the sense in which I am going to

8 / 10

All the virtues of the perfect wine glass are paralleled in typography. There is the long, thin stem that obviates fingerprints on the bowl. Why? Because no cloud must come between your eyes and the fiery heart of the liquid. Are not the margins on book pages similarly meant to obviate the necessity of fingering the type page? Again: the glass is colorless or at the most only faintly tinged in the bowl, because the connoisseur judges wine partly by its color and is impatient of anything that alters it. There are a thousand mannerisms in typography that are as impudent and arbitrary as putting port in tumblers of red or green glass! When a goblet has a base that lo

10 / 12

All the virtues of the perfect wine glass are paralleled in typography. There is the long, thin stem that obviates fingerprints on the bowl. Why? Because no cloud must come between your eyes and the fiery heart of the liquid. Are not the margins on book pages similarly meant to obviate the necessity of fingering the type page? Again: the glass is colorless or at the most only faintly tinged in the bowl, because the connoisseur judges wine partly by its color an

12 / 14

All the virtues of the perfect wine glass are paralleled in typography. There is the long, thin stem that obviates fingerprints on the bowl. Why? Because no cloud must come between your eyes and the fiery heart of the liquid. Are not the margins on book pages similarly meant to obviate the necessity of fingering the typ

14 / 16

All the virtues of the perfect wine glass are paralleled in typography. There is the long, thin stem that obviates fingerprints on the bowl. Why? Because no cloud must come between your eyes and the fiery heart of the liquid. Are not the margins on book pages similarly meant to obviate the necessity of fingering the type page? Again: the glass is colorless or at the most only faintly tinged in the bowl, because the connoisseur judges wine partly by its color and is impatient of anything that alters it. There are a thousand manneri

18 / 20

All the virtues of the perfect wine glass are paralleled in typography. There is the long, thin stem that obviates fingerprints on the bowl. Why? Because no cloud must come between your eyes and the fiery heart of the liquid. Are not the margins on book pages similarly meant to obviate the necessity of fingering the type page? Again:

24 / 25

All the virtues of the perfect wine glass are paralleled in typography. There is the long, thin stem that obviates fingerprints on the bowl. Why? Because no cloud must come between your eyes and the fiery heart of

36 / 36

All the virtues of the perfect wine glass are paralleled in typography. There is the long, thin stem t

Berthold Univers 65 Bold

6/8

All the virtues of the perfect wine glass are paralleled in typography. There is the long, thin stem that obviates fingerprints on the bowl. Why? Because no cloud must come between your eyes and the fiery heart of the liquid. Are not the margins on book pages similarly meant to obviate the necessity of fingering the type page? Again: the glass is colorless or at the most only faintly tinged in the bowl, because the connoisseur judges wine partly by its color and is impatient of anything that alters it. There are a thousand mannerisms in typography that are as impudent and arbitrary as putting port in tumblers of red or green glass! When a goblet has a base that looks too small for security, it does not matter how cleverly it is weighted; you feel nervous lest it should tip over. There are ways of setting lines of type which may work well enough, and yet keep the reader subconsciously worried by the fear of "doubling" lines, reading three words as one, and so forth. Now the man who first chose glass

8/10

All the virtues of the perfect wine glass are paralleled in typography. There is the long, thin stem that obviates fingerprints on the bowl. Why? Because no cloud must come between your eyes and the fiery heart of the liquid. Are not the margins on book pages similarly meant to obviate the necessity of fingering the type page? Again: the glass is colorless or at the most only faintly tinged in the bowl, because the connoisseur judges wine partly by its color and is impatient of anything that alters it. There are a thousand mannerisms in typography that are as impudent and arbitrary as putting port in tu

10/12

All the virtues of the perfect wine glass are paralleled in typography. There is the long, thin stem that obviates fingerprints on the bowl. Why? Because no cloud must come between your eyes and the fiery heart of the liquid. Are not the margins on book pages similarly meant to obviate the necessity of fingering the type page? Again: the glass is colorless or at the most only faintly tinged in the bowl, because the

12/14

All the virtues of the perfect wine glass are paralleled in typography. There is the long, thin stem that obviates fingerprints on the bowl. Why? Because no cloud must come between your eyes and the fiery heart of the liquid. Are not the margins on book pages similarly meant to obviate the neces

11/16

All the virtues of the perfect wine glass are paralleled in typography. There is the long, thin stem that obviates fingerprints on the bowl. Why? Because no cloud must come between your eyes and the fiery heart of the liquid. Are not the margins on book pages similarly meant to obviate the necessity of fingering the type page? Again: the glass is colorless or at the most only faintly tinged in the bowl, because the connoisseur judges wine partly by its color and is impatient of a

18/20

All the virtues of the perfect wine glass are paralleled in typography. There is the long, thin stem that obviates fingerprints on the bowl. Why? Because no cloud must come between your eyes and the fiery heart of the liquid. Are not the margins on book pages similarly meant to obviate the necessity

24/25

All the virtues of the perfect wine glass are paralleled in typography. There is the long, thin stem that obviates fingerprints on the bowl. Why? Because no cloud must come between your eyes and

36/36

All the virtues of the perfect wine glass are paralleled in typography. There is the long, t

Berthold Univers 66 Bold Italic

6 / 8

All the virtues of the perfect wine glass are paralleled in typography. There is the long, thin stem that obviates fingerprints on the bowl. Why? Because no cloud must come between your eyes and the fiery heart of the liquid. Are not the margins on book pages similarly meant to obviate the necessity of fingering the type page? Again: the glass is colorless or at the most only faintly tinged in the bowl, because the connoisseur judges wine partly by its color and is impatient of anything that alters it. There are a thousand mannerisms in typography that are as impudent and arbitrary as putting port in tumblers of red or green glass! When a goblet has a base that looks too small for security, it does not matter how cleverly it is weighted; you feel nervous lest it should tip over. There are ways of setting lines of type which may work well enough, and yet keep the reader subconsciously worried by the fear of "doubling" lines, reading three words as one, and so forth. Now the man who first chose glass

8 / 10

All the virtues of the perfect wine glass are paralleled in typography. There is the long, thin stem that obviates fingerprints on the bowl. Why? Because no cloud must come between your eyes and the fiery heart of the liquid. Are not the margins on book pages similarly meant to obviate the necessity of fingering the type page? Again: the glass is colorless or at the most only faintly tinged in the bowl, because the connoisseur judges wine partly by its color and is impatient of anything that alters it. There are a thousand mannerisms in typography that are as impudent and arbitrary as putting port

10 / 12

All the virtues of the perfect wine glass are paralleled in typography. There is the long, thin stem that obviates fingerprints on the bowl. Why? Because no cloud must come between your eyes and the fiery heart of the liquid. Are not the margins on book pages similarly meant to obviate the necessity of fingering the type page? Again: the glass is colorless or at the most only faintly tinged in the bowl, because the co

12 / 14

All the virtues of the perfect wine glass are paralleled in typography. There is the long, thin stem that obviates fingerprints on the bowl. Why? Because no cloud must come between your eyes and the fiery heart of the liquid. Are not the margins on book pages similarly meant to obviate the neces

14 / 10

All the virtues of the perfect wine glass are paralleled in typography. There is the long, thin stem that obviates fingerprints on the bowl. Why? Because no cloud must come between your eyes and the fiery heart of the liquid. Are not the margins on book pages similarly meant to obviate the necessity of fingering the type page? Again: the glass is colorless or at the most only faintly tinged in the bowl, because the connoisseur judges wine partly by its color and is impatient of anyt

18 / 20

All the virtues of the perfect wine glass are paralleled in typography. There is the long, thin stem that obviates fingerprints on the bowl. Why? Because no cloud must come between your eyes and the fiery heart of the liquid. Are not the margins on book pages similarly meant to obviate the necessity of

24 / 25

All the virtues of the perfect wine glass are paralleled in typography. There is the long, thin stem that obviates fingerprints on the bowl. Why? Because no cloud must come between your eyes an

36 / 36

All the virtues of the perfect wine glass are paralleled in typography. There is the long, thin s

Berthold Univers 75 Black

6 / 8

All the virtues of the perfect wine glass are paralleled in typography. There is the long, thin stem that obviates fingerprints on the bowl. Why? Because no cloud must come between your eyes and the fiery heart of the liquid. Are not the margins on book pages similarly meant to obviate the necessity of fingering the type page? Again: the glass is colorless or at the most only faintly tinged in the bowl, because the connoisseur judges wine partly by its color and is impatient of anything that alters it. There are a thousand mannerisms in typography that are as impudent and arbitrary as putting port in tumblers of red or green glass! When a goblet has a base that looks too small for security, it does not matter how cleverly it is weighted; you feel nervous lest it should tip over. There are ways of setting lines of type which may work well enough, and yet keep the reader subconsciously worried by the fear of "doubling" lines,

8 / 10

All the virtues of the perfect wine glass are paralleled in typography. There is the long, thin stem that obviates fingerprints on the bowl. Why? Because no cloud must come between your eyes and the fiery heart of the liquid. Are not the margins on book pages similarly meant to obviate the necessity of fingering the type page? Again: the glass is colorless or at the most only faintly tinged in the bowl, because the connoisseur judges wine partly by its color and is impatient of anything that alters it. There are a thousand mannerisms in typography that are

10 / 12

All the virtues of the perfect wine glass are paralleled in typography. There is the long, thin stem that obviates fingerprints on the bowl. Why? Because no cloud must come between your eyes and the fiery heart of the liquid. Are not the margins on book pages similarly meant to obviate the necessity of fingering the type page? Again: the glass is colorless or at the most only faintly tinge

12 / 14

All the virtues of the perfect wine glass are paralleled in typography. There is the long, thin stem that obviates fingerprints on the bowl. Why? Because no cloud must come between your eyes and the fiery heart of the liquid. Are not the margins on book pages similarly m

14 / 16

All the virtues of the perfect wine glass are paralleled in typography. There is the long, thin stem that obviates fingerprints on the bowl. Why? Because no cloud must come between your eyes and the fiery heart of the liquid. Are not the margins on book pages similarly meant to obviate the necessity of fingering the type page? Again: the glass is colorless or at the most only faintly tinged in the bowl, because the connoisseur judges wine

18 / 20

All the virtues of the perfect wine glass are paralleled in typography. There is the long, thin stem that obviates fingerprints on the bowl. Why? Because no cloud must come between your eyes and the fiery heart of the liquid. Are not the margins on book pages similarly meant to o

24 / 25

All the virtues of the perfect wine glass are paralleled in typography. There is the long, thin stem that obviates fingerprints on the bowl. Why? Because no cloud must come between

36 / 36

All the virtues of the perfect wine glass are paralleled in typography. There is the l

Berthold Univers 76 Black Italic

6 / 8

All the virtues of the perfect wine glass are paralleled in typography. There is the long, thin stem that obviates fingerprints on the bowl. Why? Because no cloud must come between your eyes and the fiery heart of the liquid. Are not the margins on book pages similarly meant to obviate the necessity of fingering the type page? Again: the glass is colorless or at the most only faintly tinged in the bowl, because the connoisseur judges wine partly by its color and is impatient of anything that alters it. There are a thousand mannerisms in typography that are as impudent and arbitrary as putting port in tumblers of red or green glass! When a goblet has a base that looks too small for security, it does not matter how cleverly it is weighted; you feel nervous lest it should tip over. There are ways of setting lines of type which may work well enough, and yet keep the reader subconsciously worried by the fear of "doubling" lines, reading thre

8 / 10

All the virtues of the perfect wine glass are paralleled in typography. There is the long, thin stem that obviates fingerprints on the bowl. Why? Because no cloud must come between your eyes and the fiery heart of the liquid. Are not the margins on book pages similarly meant to obviate the necessity of fingering the type page? Again: the glass is colorless or at the most only faintly tinged in the bowl, because the connoisseur judges wine partly by its color and is impatient of anything that alters it. There are a thousand mannerisms in typography that are as

10 / 12

All the virtues of the perfect wine glass are paralleled in typography. There is the long, thin stem that obviates fingerprints on the bowl. Why? Because no cloud must come between your eyes and the fiery heart of the liquid. Are not the margins on book pages similarly meant to obviate the necessity of fingering the type page? Again: the glass is colorless or at the most only faintly tinged in the

12 / 14

All the virtues of the perfect wine glass are paralleled in typography. There is the long, thin stem that obviates fingerprints on the bowl. Why? Because no cloud must come between your eyes and the fiery heart of the liquid. Are not the margins on book pages similarly meant

14 / 16

All the virtues of the perfect wine glass are paralleled in typography. There is the long, thin stem that obviates fingerprints on the bowl. Why? Because no cloud must come between your eyes and the fiery heart of the liquid. Are not the margins on book pages similarly meant to obviate the necessity of fingering the type page? Again: the glass is colorless or at the most only faintly tinged in the bowl, because the connoisseur judges wine partly by its

18 / 20

All the virtues of the perfect wine glass are paralleled in typography. There is the long, thin stem that obviates fingerprints on the bowl. Why? Because no cloud must come between your eyes and the fiery heart of the liquid. Are not the margins on book pages similarly meant to obvi

24 / 25

All the virtues of the perfect wine glass are paralleled in typography. There is the long, thin stem that obviates fingerprints on the bowl. Why? Because no cloud must come between

36 / 36

All the virtues of the perfect wine glass are paralleled in typography. There is the l

Berthold Univers 47 Condensed Light

6 / 8

All the virtues of the perfect wine glass are paralleled in typography. There is the long, thin stem that obviates fingerprints on the bowl. Why? Because no cloud must come between your eyes and the fiery heart of the liquid. Are not the margins on book pages similarly meant to obviate the necessity of fingering the type page? Again: the glass is colorless or at the most only faintly tinged in the bowl, because the connoisseur judges wine partly by its color and is impatient of anything that alters it. There are a thousand mannerisms in typography that are as impudent and arbitrary as putting port in tumblers of red or green glass! When a goblet has a base that looks too small for security, it does not matter how cleverly it is weighted; you feel nervous lest it should tip over. There are ways of setting lines of type which may work well enough, and yet keep the reader subconsciously worried by the fear of "doubling" lines, reading three words as one, and so forth. Now the man who first chose glass instead of clay or metal to hold his wine was a "modernist" in the sense in which I am going to use that term. That is, the first thing he asked of this particular object was not "How should it look?" but "What must it do?" and to that extent all good typography is modernist. Wine is so strange and potent a thing that it has been used in the central ritual of religion in one place and time, and attacked by a virago with a hatchet in another. There is only one other thing in the world that is capable of stirring and altering men's minds to the same extent, and that is the coherent expression of thought. That is man

8 / 10

All the virtues of the perfect wine glass are paralleled in typography. There is the long, thin stem that obviates fingerprints on the bowl. Why? Because no cloud must come between your eyes and the fiery heart of the liquid. Are not the margins on book pages similarly meant to obviate the necessity of fingering the type page? Again: the glass is colorless or at the most only faintly tinged in the bowl, because the connoisseur judges wine partly by its color and is impatient of anything that alters it. There are a thousand mannerisms in typography that are as impudent and arbitrary as putting port in tumblers of red or green glass! When a goblet has a base that looks too small for security, it does not matter how cleverly it is weighted; you feel nervous lest it should tip over. There are ways of setting lines of type which may work well enough, and yet keep the reader subconsciously worried by the fear of "doubling" lines, reading three words as one, and so forth. Now th

10 / 12

All the virtues of the perfect wine glass are paralleled in typography. There is the long, thin stem that obviates fingerprints on the bowl. Why? Because no cloud must come between your eyes and the fiery heart of the liquid. Are not the margins on book pages similarly meant to obviate the necessity of fingering the type page? Again: the glass is colorless or at the most only faintly tinged in the bowl, because the connoisseur judges wine partly by its color and is impatient of anything that alters it. There are a thousand mannerisms in typography that are as impudent and arbitrary as putting port in tumblers of red or green glass! When a goblet has a base that looks too

12 / 14

All the virtues of the perfect wine glass are paralleled in typography. There is the long, thin stem that obviates fingerprints on the bowl. Why? Because no cloud must come between your eyes and the fiery heart of the liquid. Are not the margins on book pages similarly meant to obviate the necessity of fingering the type page? Again: the glass is colorless or at the most only faintly tinged in the bowl, because the connoisseur judges wine partly by its color and is impatient of

14 / 16

All the virtues of the perfect wine glass are paralleled in typography. There is the long, thin stem that obviates fingerprints on the bowl. Why? Because no cloud must come between your eyes and the fiery heart of the liquid. Are not the margins on book pages similarly meant to obviate the necessity of fingering the type page? Again: the glass is colorless or at the most only faintly tinged in the bowl, because the connoisseur judges wine partly by its color and is impatient of anything that alters it. There are a thousand mannerisms in typography that are as impudent and arbitrary as putting port in tumblers of red or green glass! When a goblet has a base that looks too small for security, it does not matter how cleverly it is weighted; you feel nervous lest it should tip over.

18 / 20

All the virtues of the perfect wine glass are paralleled in typography. There is the long, thin stem that obviates fingerprints on the bowl. Why? Because no cloud must come between your eyes and the fiery heart of the liquid. Are not the margins on book pages similarly meant to obviate the necessity of fingering the type page? Again: the glass is colorless or at the most only faintly tinged in the bowl, because the connoisseur judges wine partly by its color and is impatient of anything

24 / 25

All the virtues of the perfect wine glass are paralleled in typography. There is the long, thin stem that obviates fingerprints on the bowl. Why? Because no cloud must come between your eyes and the fiery heart of the liquid. Are not the margins on book pages similarly meant to obviate the necessity of fingering the t

36 / 36

All the virtues of the perfect wine glass are paralleled in typography. There is the long, thin stem that obviates fingerprints on the bowl. Why?

Berthold Univers 48 Condensed Light Italic

6 / 8

All the virtues of the perfect wine glass are paralleled in typography. There is the long, thin stem that obviates fingerprints on the bowl. Why? Because no cloud must come between your eyes and the fiery heart of the liquid. Are not the margins on book pages similarly meant to obviate the necessity of fingering the type page? Again: the glass is colorless or at the most only faintly tinged in the bowl, because the connoisseur judges wine partly by its color and is impatient of anything that alters it. There are a thousand mannerisms in typography that are as impudent and arbitrary as putting port in tumblers of red or green glass! When a goblet has a base that looks too small for security, it does not matter how cleverly it is weighted; you feel nervous lest it should tip over. There are ways of setting lines of type which may work well enough, and yet keep the reader subconsciously worried by the fear of "doubling" lines, reading three words as one, and so forth. Now the man who first chose glass instead of clay or metal to hold his wine was a "modernist" in the sense in which I am going to use that term. That is, the first thing he asked of this particular object was not "How should it look?" but "What must it do?" and to that extent all good typography is modernist. Wine is so strange and potent a thing that it has been used in the central ritual of religion in one place and time, and attacked by a virago with a hatchet in another. There is only one other thing in the world that is capable of stirring and altering men's minds to the same extent, and that is the coherent expre

8 / 10

All the virtues of the perfect wine glass are paralleled in typography. There is the long, thin stem that obviates fingerprints on the bowl. Why? Because no cloud must come between your eyes and the fiery heart of the liquid. Are not the margins on book pages similarly meant to obviate the necessity of fingering the type page? Again: the glass is colorless or at the most only faintly tinged in the bowl, because the connoisseur judges wine partly by its color and is impatient of anything that alters it. There are a thousand mannerisms in typography that are as impudent and arbitrary as putting port in tumblers of red or green glass! When a goblet has a base that looks too small for security, it does not matter how cleverly it is weighted; you feel nervous lest it should tip over. There are ways of setting lines of type which may work well enough, and yet keep the reader subconsciously worried by the fear of "doubling" lines, reading three words as one,

10 / 12

All the virtues of the perfect wine glass are paralleled in typography. There is the long, thin stem that obviates fingerprints on the bowl. Why? Because no cloud must come between your eyes and the fiery heart of the liquid. Are not the margins on book pages similarly meant to obviate the necessity of fingering the type page? Again: the glass is colorless or at the most only faintly tinged in the bowl, because the connoisseur judges wine partly by its color and is impatient of anything that alters it. There are a thousand mannerisms in typography that are as impudent and arbitrary as putting port in tumblers of red or green glass! When a goblet has a base that

12 / 14

All the virtues of the perfect wine glass are paralleled in typography. There is the long, thin stem that obviates fingerprints on the bowl. Why? Because no cloud must come between your eyes and the fiery heart of the liquid. Are not the margins on book pages similarly meant to obviate the necessity of fingering the type page? Again: the glass is colorless or at the most only faintly tinged in the bowl, because the connoisseur judges wine partly by its color and is

14 / 16

All the virtues of the perfect wine glass are paralleled in typography. There is the long, thin stem that obviates fingerprints on the bowl. Why? Because no cloud must come between your eyes and the fiery heart of the liquid. Are not the margins on book pages similarly meant to obviate the necessity of fingering the type page? Again: the glass is colorless or at the most only faintly tinged in the bowl, because the connoisseur judges wine partly by its color and is impatient of anything that alters it. There are a thousand mannerisms in typography that are as impudent and arbitrary as putting port in tumblers of red or green glass! When a goblet has a base that looks too small for security, it does not matter how cleverly it is weighted; you feel nervous lest it sho

18 / 20

All the virtues of the perfect wine glass are paralleled in typography. There is the long, thin stem that obviates fingerprints on the bowl. Why? Because no cloud must come between your eyes and the fiery heart of the liquid. Are not the margins on book pages similarly meant to obviate the necessity of fingering the type page? Again: the glass is colorless or at the most only faintly tinged in the bowl, because the connoisseur judges wine partly by its color and is impatient of a

24 / 25

All the virtues of the perfect wine glass are paralleled in typography. There is the long, thin stem that obviates fingerprints on the bowl. Why? Because no cloud must come between your eyes and the fiery heart of the liquid. Are not the margins on book pages similarly meant to obviate the necessity of fingeri

36 / 36

All the virtues of the perfect wine glass are paralleled in typography. There is the long, thin stem that obviates fingerprints on the bowl. Why?

Berthold Univers 57 Condensed Regular

6 / 8

All the virtues of the perfect wine glass are paralleled in typography. There is the long, thin stem that obviates fingerprints on the bowl. Why? Because no cloud must come between your eyes and the fiery heart of the liquid. Are not the margins on book pages similarly meant to obviate the necessity of fingering the type page? Again: the glass is colorless or at the most only faintly tinged in the bowl, because the connoisseur judges wine partly by its color and is impatient of anything that alters it. There are a thousand mannerisms in typography that are as impudent and arbitrary as putting port in tumblers of red or green glass! When a goblet has a base that looks too small for security, it does not matter how cleverly it is weighted; you feel nervous lest it should tip over. There are ways of setting lines of type which may work well enough, and yet keep the reader subconsciously worried by the fear of "doubling" lines, reading three words as one, and so forth. Now the man who first chose glass instead of clay or metal to hold his wine was a "modernist" in the sense in which I am going to use that term. That is, the first thing he asked of this particular object was not "How should it look?" but "What must it do?" and to that extent all good typography is modernist. Wine is so strange and potent a thing that it has been used in the central ritual of religion in one place and ti

8 / 10

All the virtues of the perfect wine glass are paralleled in typography. There is the long, thin stem that obviates fingerprints on the bowl. Why? Because no cloud must come between your eyes and the fiery heart of the liquid. Are not the margins on book pages similarly meant to obviate the necessity of fingering the type page? Again: the glass is colorless or at the most only faintly tinged in the bowl, because the connoisseur judges wine partly by its color and is impatient of anything that alters it. There are a thousand mannerisms in typography that are as impudent and arbitrary as putting port in tumblers of red or green glass! When a goblet has a base that looks too small for security, it does not matter how cleverly it is weighted; you feel nervous lest it should tip over. There are ways of setting lines of type which may work well

10 / 12

All the virtues of the perfect wine glass are paralleled in typography. There is the long, thin stem that obviates fingerprints on the bowl. Why? Because no cloud must come between your eyes and the fiery heart of the liquid. Are not the margins on book pages similarly meant to obviate the necessity of fingering the type page? Again: the glass is colorless or at the most only faintly tinged in the bowl, because the connoisseur judges wine partly by its color and is impatient of anything that alters it. There are a thousand mannerisms in typography that are as impudent and

12 / 14

All the virtues of the perfect wine glass are paralleled in typography. There is the long, thin stem that obviates fingerprints on the bowl. Why? Because no cloud must come between your eyes and the fiery heart of the liquid. Are not the margins on book pages similarly meant to obviate the necessity of fingering the type page? Again: the glass is colorless or at the most only faintly tinged in the bowl, becau

14 / 16

All the virtues of the perfect wine glass are paralleled in typography. There is the long, thin stem that obviates fingerprints on the bowl. Why? Because no cloud must come between your eyes and the fiery heart of the liquid. Are not the margins on book pages similarly meant to obviate the necessity of fingering the type page? Again: the glass is colorless or at the most only faintly tinged in the bowl, because the connoisseur judges wine partly by its color and is impatient of anything that alters it. There are a thousand mannerisms in typography that are as impudent and arbitrary as putting port in tumblers of red or green glass! When a goblet has a base that looks

18 / 20

All the virtues of the perfect wine glass are paralleled in typography. There is the long, thin stem that obviates fingerprints on the bowl. Why? Because no cloud must come between your eyes and the fiery heart of the liquid. Are not the margins on book pages similarly meant to obviate the necessity of fingering the type page? Again: the glass is colorless or at the most only faintly tinged in the bowl, because the conn

24 / 25

All the virtues of the perfect wine glass are paralleled in typography. There is the long, thin stem that obviates fingerprints on the bowl. Why? Because no cloud must come between your eyes and the fiery heart of the liquid. Are not the margins on book pages similar

36 / 36

All the virtues of the perfect wine glass are paralleled in typography. There is the long, thin stem that obviates fingerprints

Berthold Univers 58 Condensed Italic

6 / 8

All the virtues of the perfect wine glass are paralleled in typography. There is the long, thin stem that obviates fingerprints on the bowl. Why? Because no cloud must come between your eyes and the fiery heart of the liquid. Are not the margins on book pages similarly meant to obviate the necessity of fingering the type page? Again: the glass is colorless or at the most only faintly tinged in the bowl, because the connoisseur judges wine partly by its color and is impatient of anything that alters it. There are a thousand mannerisms in typography that are as impudent and arbitrary as putting port in tumblers of red or green glass! When a goblet has a base that looks too small for security, it does not matter how cleverly it is weighted; you feel nervous lest it should tip over. There are ways of setting lines of type which may work well enough, and yet keep the reader subconsciously worried by the fear of "doubling" lines, reading three words as one, and so forth. Now the man who first chose glass instead of clay or metal to hold his wine was a "modernist" in the sense in which I am going to use that term. That is, the first thing he asked of this particular object was not "How should it look?" but "What must it do?" and to that extent all good typography is modernist. Wine is so strange and potent a thing that it has been used

8 / 10

All the virtues of the perfect wine glass are paralleled in typography. There is the long, thin stem that obviates fingerprints on the bowl. Why? Because no cloud must come between your eyes and the fiery heart of the liquid. Are not the margins on book pages similarly meant to obviate the necessity of fingering the type page? Again: the glass is colorless or at the most only faintly tinged in the bowl, because the connoisseur judges wine partly by its color and is impatient of anything that alters it. There are a thousand mannerisms in typography that are as impudent and arbitrary as putting port in tumblers of red or green glass! When a goblet has a base that looks too small for security, it does not matter how cleverly it is weighted; you feel nervous lest it should tip over. There are ways of

10 / 12

All the virtues of the perfect wine glass are paralleled in typography. There is the long, thin stem that obviates fingerprints on the bowl. Why? Because no cloud must come between your eyes and the fiery heart of the liquid. Are not the margins on book pages similarly meant to obviate the necessity of fingering the type page? Again: the glass is colorless or at the most only faintly tinged in the bowl, because the connoisseur judges wine partly by its color and is impatient of anything that alters it. There are a thousand mannerisms in typography that are

12 / 14

All the virtues of the perfect wine glass are paralleled in typography. There is the long, thin stem that obviates fingerprints on the bowl. Why? Because no cloud must come between your eyes and the fiery heart of the liquid. Are not the margins on book pages similarly meant to obviate the necessity of fingering the type page? Again: the glass is colorless or at the most only faintly tinged in the

14 / 16

All the virtues of the perfect wine glass are paralleled in typography. There is the long, thin stem that obviates fingerprints on the bowl. Why? Because no cloud must come between your eyes and the fiery heart of the liquid. Are not the margins on book pages similarly meant to obviate the necessity of fingering the type page? Again: the glass is colorless or at the most only faintly tinged in the bowl, because the connoisseur judges wine partly by its color and is impatient of anything that alters it. There are a thousand mannerisms in typography that are as impudent and arbitrary as putting port in tumblers of red or green glass! Wh

18 / 20

All the virtues of the perfect wine glass are paralleled in typography. There is the long, thin stem that obviates fingerprints on the bowl. Why? Because no cloud must come between your eyes and the fiery heart of the liquid. Are not the margins on book pages similarly meant to obviate the necessity of fingering the type page? Again: the glass is colorless or at the most only faintly tinged in the bowl,

24 / 25

All the virtues of the perfect wine glass are paralleled in typography. There is the long, thin stem that obviates fingerprints on the bowl. Why? Because no cloud must come between your eyes and the fiery heart of the liquid. Are not the margins on book pages

36 / 36

All the virtues of the perfect wine glass are paralleled in typography. There is the long, thin stem that obviates fingerp

Berthold Univers 67 Condensed Bold

6 / 8

All the virtues of the perfect wine glass are paralleled in typography. There is the long, thin stem that obviates fingerprints on the bowl. Why? Because no cloud must come between your eyes and the fiery heart of the liquid. Are not the margins on book pages similarly meant to obviate the necessity of fingering the type page? Again: the glass is colorless or at the most only faintly tinged in the bowl, because the connoisseur judges wine partly by its color and is impatient of anything that alters it. There are a thousand mannerisms in typography that are as impudent and arbitrary as putting port in tumblers of red or green glass! When a goblet has a base that looks too small for security, it does not matter how cleverly it is weighted; you feel nervous lest it should tip over. There are ways of setting lines of type which may work well enough, and yet keep the reader subconsciously worried by the fear of "doubling" lines, reading three words as one, and so forth. Now the man who first chose glass instead of clay or metal to hold his wine was a "modernist" in the sense in which I am going to use that term. That is, the first thing he asked of this particular object was not "How should it look?" but "What must it do?" and to that extent all good typography is moder

8 / 10

All the virtues of the perfect wine glass are paralleled in typography. There is the long, thin stem that obviates fingerprints on the bowl. Why? Because no cloud must come between your eyes and the fiery heart of the liquid. Are not the margins on book pages similarly meant to obviate the necessity of fingering the type page? Aga in: the glass is colorless or at the most only faintly tinged in the bowl, because the connoisseur judges wine partly by its color and is impatient of anything that alters it. There are a thousand mannerisms in typography th at are as impudent and arbitrary as putting port in tumblers of red or green glass! When a goblet has a base th at looks too small for security, it does not matter how cleverly it is weighted; you feel nervous lest it should ti

10 / 12

All the virtues of the perfect wine glass are paralleled in typography. There is the long, th in stem that obviates fingerprints on the bo wl. Why? Because no cloud must come betw een your eyes and the fiery heart of the liqu id. Are not the margins on book pages similar ly meant to obviate the necessity of fingering the type page? Again: the glass is colorless or at the most only faintly tinged in the bowl, because the connoisseur judges wine partly by its color and is impatient of anything that alters it. There are a thousand mannerisms in

12 / 14

All the virtues of the perfect wine gla ss are paralleled in typography. There is the long, thin stem that obviates fin gerprints on the bowl. Why? Because no cloud must come between your ey es and the fiery heart of the liquid. Are not the margins on book pages simila rly meant to obviate the necessity of fingering the type page? Again: the gl ass is colorless or at the most only fai

14 / 16

All the virtues of the perfect wine glass are paralleled in typography. There is the long, thin stem that obviates fingerprints on the bowl. W hy? Because no cloud must come between your eyes and the fiery he art of the liquid. Are not the margins on book pages similarly meant to obviate the necessity of fingering the type page? Again: the glass is colorless or at the most only faintly tinged in the bowl, because the connoisseur judges wine partly by its color and is impatient of an ything that alters it. There are a thousand mannerisms in typography that are as impudent and arbitrary as putting port in tumblers of red

18 / 20

All the virtues of the perfect wine glass are paralleled in typography. There is the long, thin stem that obviates fingerprints on the bowl. Why? Because no cloud must come between your eyes and the fiery heart of the liqui d. Are not the margins on book pages similarly meant to obviate the necessity of fingering the type page? Ag ain: the glass is colorless or at the most only faintly tin

24 / 25

All the virtues of the perfect wine glass ar e paralleled in typography. There is the lon g, thin stem that obviates fingerprints on the bowl. Why? Because no cloud must c ome between your eyes and the fiery hear t of the liquid. Are not the margins on boo

36 / 36

All the virtues of the perfect wine glass are paralleled in typography. There is the lon g, thin stem that obviates fi

Berthold Univers 68 Condensed Bold Italic

6 / 8

All the virtues of the perfect wine glass are paralleled in typography. There is the long, thin stem that obviates fingerprints on the bowl. Why? Because no cloud must come between your eyes and the fiery heart of the liquid. Are not the margins on book pages similarly meant to obviate the necessity of fingering the type page? Again: the glass is colorless or at the most only faintly tinged in the bowl, because the connoisseur judges wine partly by its color and is impatient of anything that alters it. There are a thousand mannerisms in typography that are as impudent and arbitrary as putting port in tumblers of red or green glass! When a goblet has a base that looks too small for security, it does not matter how cleverly it is weighted; you feel nervous lest it should tip over. There are ways of setting lines of type which may work well enough, and yet keep the reader subconsciously worried by the fear of "doubling" lines, reading three words as one, and so forth. Now the man who first chose glass instead of clay or metal to hold his wine was a "modernist" in the sense in which I am going to use that term. That is, the first thing he asked of this particular object was not "How should it look?" but "What must it do?" and to that extent all good typography is

8 / 10

All the virtues of the perfect wine glass are paralleled in typography. There is the long, thin stem that obviates fingerprints on the bowl. Why? Because no cloud must come between your eyes and the fiery heart of the liquid. Are not the margins on book pages similarly meant to obviate the necessity of fingering the type page? Again: the glass is colorless or at the most only faintly tinged in the bowl, because the connoisseur judges wine partly by its color and is impatient of anything that alters it. There are a thousand mannerisms in typography that are as impudent and arbitrary as putting port in tumblers of red or green glass! When a goblet has a base that looks too small for security, it does not matter how cleverly it is weighted; you feel nervous le

10 / 12

All the virtues of the perfect wine glass are paralleled in typography. There is the long, thin stem that obviates fingerprints on the bowl. Why? Because no cloud must come between your eyes and the fiery heart of the liquid. Are not the margins on book pages similarly meant to obviate the necessity of fingering the type page? Again: the glass is colorless or at the most only faintly tinged in the bowl, because the connoisseur judges wine partly by its color and is impatient of anything that alters it. There are a thousand manneris

12 / 14

All the virtues of the perfect wine glass are paralleled in typography. There is the long, thin stem that obviates fingerprints on the bowl. Why? Because no cloud must come between your eyes and the fiery heart of the liquid. Are not the margins on book pages similarly meant to obviate the necessity of fingering the type page? Again: the glass is colorless or at the most only

14 / 16

All the virtues of the perfect wine glass are paralleled in typography. There is the long, thin stem that obviates fingerprints on the bowl. Why? Because no cloud must come between your eyes and the fiery heart of the liquid. Are not the margins on book pages similarly meant to obviate the necessity of fingering the type page? Again: the glass is colorless or at the most only faintly tinged in the bowl, because the connoisseur judges wine partly by its color and is impatient of anything that alters it. There are a thousand mannerisms in typography that are as impudent and arbitrary as putting port in tumblers of

18 / 20

All the virtues of the perfect wine glass are paralleled in typography. There is the long, thin stem that obviates fingerprints on the bowl. Why? Because no cloud must come between your eyes and the fiery heart of the liquid. Are not the margins on book pages similarly meant to obviate the necessity of fingering the type page? Again: the glass is colorless or at the most only fai

24 / 25

All the virtues of the perfect wine glass are paralleled in typography. There is the long, thin stem that obviates fingerprints on the bowl. Why? Because no cloud must come between your eyes and the fiery heart of the liquid. Are not the margins on

36 / 36

All the virtues of the perfect wine glass are paralleled in typography. There is the long, thin stem that obviates fi

DjRa	Gg	TrPa
1EaQp	GgT	Par
fau	gh	dje
eagMa	5rE2	Akrf
Zak	igD4	Gj
2KOa	rD	T&a.

GRAPHIS DIGITAL FONT ANNUAL 1

Monumental technological changes have forced society to redefine the very nature of communication. How should this process affect the role of Type as an essential vehicle of communication? Contemporary type designers are attempting to find their own answers to question. Graphis Digital Font Annual 1 provides a comprehensive view of some of the best examples of this effort. The work of distinguished type designers from around the world is featured in a format that displays both the typefaces they have created as well as the types' applications. Available direct from Graphis in Spring 1996.

GRAPHIS BOOKS

BOOK ORDER FORM: USA, CANADA, SOUTH AMERICA, ASIA, PACIFIC

BOOKS	ALL REGIONS
☐ GRAPHIS ALTERNATIVE PHOTOGRAPHY 95	US$ 69.00
☐ GRAPHIS PACKAGING 6	US$ 75.00
☐ GRAPHIS DESIGN 95	US$ 69.00
☐ GRAPHIS ADVERTISING 95	US$ 69.00
☐ VIDEOTAPE: TV COMMERCIALS 95	US$ 119.00
☐ GRAPHIS BROCHURES 1	US$ 75.00
☐ GRAPHIS PAPER PROMOTIONS	US$ 69.00
☐ GRAPHIS PRODUCTS BY DESIGN	US$ 69.00
☐ GRAPHIS TYPOGRAPHY 1	US$ 75.00
☐ GRAPHIS TYPE SPECIMEN	US$ 40.00
☐ GRAPHIS PHOTO 94	US$ 69.00
☐ GRAPHIS NUDES	US$ 85.00
☐ GRAPHIS POSTER 95	US$ 69.00
☐ GRAPHIS T-SHIRT 1	US$ 75.00
☐ GRAPHIS CORPORATE IDENTITY 2	US$ 75.00
☐ GRAPHIS LETTERHEAD 2	US$ 69.00
☐ GRAPHIS LOGO 2	US$ 60.00
☐ GRAPHIS EPHEMERA 2	US$ 75.00
☐ GRAPHIS ANNUAL REPORTS 4	US$ 75.00
☐ GRAPHIS PUBLICATION 1 (ENGLISH)	US$ 75.00

NOTE! NY RESIDENTS ADD 8.25% SALES TAX

☐ CHECK ENCLOSED (PAYABLE TO GRAPHIS)
(US$ ONLY, DRAWN ON A BANK IN THE USA)

USE CREDIT CARDS (DEBITED IN US DOLLARS)

☐ AMERICAN EXPRESS   ☐ MASTERCARD   ☐ VISA

CARD NO.   EXP. DATE

CARDHOLDER NAME

SIGNATURE

(PLEASE PRINT)

NAME

TITLE

COMPANY

ADDRESS

CITY

STATE/PROVINCE   ZIP CODE

COUNTRY

SEND ORDER FORM AND MAKE CHECK PAYABLE TO:
GRAPHIS US, INC.,
141 LEXINGTON AVENUE, NEW YORK, NY 10016-8193, USA

BOOK ORDER FORM: EUROPE, AFRICA, MIDDLE EAST

BOOKS	EUROPE/AFRICA MIDDLE EAST	GERMANY	U.K.
☐ ALTERNATIVE PHOTO 95	SFR.123.–	DM 149,–	£ 52.00
☐ GRAPHIS PACKAGING 6	SFR.137.–	DM 162,–	£ 55.00
☐ GRAPHIS DESIGN 95	SFR.123.–	DM 149,–	£ 52.00
☐ GRAPHIS ADVERTISING 95	SFR.123.–	DM 149,–	£ 52.00
☐ TV COMMERCIALS 95	SFR.175.–	DM 208,–	£ 87.50
☐ GRAPHIS BROCHURES 1	SFR.137.–	DM 162,–	£ 55.00
☐ PAPER PROMOTIONS	SFR.123.–	DM 149,–	£ 52.00
☐ PRODUCTS BY DESIGN	SFR.123.–	DM 149,–	£ 52.00
☐ GRAPHIS TYPOGRAPHY 1	SFR.137.–	DM 162,–	£ 55.00
☐ GRAPHIS TYPE SPECIMEN	SFR. 54.–	DM 64,–	£ 27.00
☐ GRAPHIS PHOTO 94	SFR.123.–	DM 149,–	£ 52.00
☐ GRAPHIS NUDES	SFR.168.–	DM 168,–	£ 62.00
☐ GRAPHIS POSTER 95	SFR.123.–	DM 149,–	£ 52.00
☐ GRAPHIS T-SHIRT 1	SFR.137.–	DM 162,–	£ 55.00
☐ CORPORATE IDENTITY 2	SFR.137.–	DM 162,–	£ 55.00
☐ GRAPHIS LETTERHEAD 2	SFR.123.–	DM 149,–	£ 52.00
☐ GRAPHIS LOGO 2	SFR. 98.–	DM 112,–	£ 39.00
☐ GRAPHIS EPHEMERA 2	SFR.137.–	DM 162,–	£ 55.00
☐ ANNUAL REPORTS 4	SFR.137.–	DM 162,–	£ 55.00
☐ GRAPHIS PUBLICATION 1 ☐ ENGLISH ☐ GERMAN	SFR.137.–	DM 162,–	£ 55.00

(FOR ORDERS FROM EC COUNTRIES V.A.T. WILL BE CHARGED IN ADDITION TO ABOVE BOOK PRICES)

FOR CREDIT CARD PAYMENT (DEBITED IN SWISS FRANCS):

☐ AMERICAN EXPRESS   ☐ DINER'S CLUB
☐ VISA/BARCLAYCARD/CARTE BLEUE

CARD NO.   EXP. DATE

CARDHOLDER NAME

SIGNATURE

☐ PLEASE BILL ME (ADDITIONAL MAILING COSTS WILL BE CHARGED)

(PLEASE PRINT)

LAST NAME   FIRST NAME

TITLE

COMPANY

ADDRESS

CITY   POSTAL CODE

COUNTRY

PLEASE SEND ORDER FORM TO:
GRAPHIS PRESS CORP.
DUFOURSTRASSE 107, CH–8008 ZÜRICH, SWITZERLAND

GRAPHIS MAGAZINE

SUBSCRIBE TO GRAPHIS: USA, CANADA, SOUTH AMERICA, ASIA,

MAGAZINE	USA	CANADA	SOUTHAMERICA/ ASIA/PACIFIC
☐ ONE YEAR (6 ISSUES)	US$ 89.00	US$ 99.00	US$ 125.00
☐ TWO YEARS (12 ISSUES)	US$ 159.00	US$ 179.00	US$ 235.00
☐ AIRMAIL SURCHARGE (6 ISSUES)	US$ 59.00	US$ 59.00	US$ 59.00

☐ 25% DISCOUNT FOR STUDENTS WITH COPY OF VALID, DATED STUDENT ID AND PAYMENT WITH ORDER

☐ CHECK ENCLOSED

USE CREDIT CARDS (DEBITED IN US DOLLARS)
☐ AMERICAN EXPRESS
☐ MASTERCARD
☐ VISA

CARD NO.   EXP. DATE

CARDHOLDER NAME

SIGNATURE

☐ PLEASE BILL ME

(PLEASE PRINT)

NAME

TITLE

COMPANY

ADDRESS

CITY

STATE/PROVINCE   ZIP CODE

COUNTRY

SEND ORDER FORM AND MAKE CHECK PAYABLE TO:
GRAPHIS US, INC.,
141 LEXINGTON AVENUE,
NEW YORK, NY 10016-8193, USA

SERVICE BEGINS WITH ISSUE THAT IS CURRENT WHEN ORDER IS PROCESSED. (C9B0A)

SUBSCRIBE TO GRAPHIS: EUROPE, AFRICA, MIDDLE EAST

MAGAZINE	EUROPE/AFRICA MIDDLE EAST	GERMANY	U.K.
☐ ONE YEAR (6 ISSUES)	SFR. 164.–	DM 190,–	£ 68.00
☐ TWO YEARS (12 ISSUES)	SFR. 295.–	DM 342,–	£ 122.00
☐ AIRMAIL SURCHARGES	SFR 65.–	DM 75,–	£ 30.00
☐ REGISTERED MAIL	SFR 20.–	DM 24,–	£ 9.00

☐ CHECK ENCLOSED (PLEASE MAKE SFR.–CHECK PAYABLE TO A SWISS BANK)

☐ STUDENTS MAY REQUEST A 25% DISCOUNT BY SENDING STUDENT ID

FOR CREDIT CARD PAYMENT (ALL CARDS DEBITED IN SWISS FRANCS):
☐ AMERICAN EXPRESS   ☐ DINER'S CLUB
☐ VISA/BARCLAYCARD/CARTE BLEUE

CARD NO.   EXP. DATE

CARDHOLDER NAME

SIGNATURE

☐ PLEASE BILL ME

(PLEASE PRINT)

LAST NAME

FIRST NAME

TITLE

COMPANY

ADDRESS

CITY   POSTAL CODE

COUNTRY

NOTE TO GERMAN SUBSCRIBERS ONLY:
ICH ERKLÄRE MICH EINVERSTANDEN, DASS MEINE NEUE ADRESSE DURCH DIE POST AN DEN VERTRIEB WEITERGELEITET WIRD.
PLEASE SEND ORDER FORM AND MAKE CHECK PAYABLE TO:
GRAPHIS PRESS CORP.
DUFOURSTRASSE 107
CH–8008 ZÜRICH, SWITZERLAND

SERVICE BEGINS WITH ISSUE THAT IS CURRENT WHEN ORDER IS PROCESSED. (C9B0A)